The Official Wilderness
First-Aid Guide

The Official Wilderness First-Aid Guide

by
Wayne Merry
for
St. John Ambulance
Ontario Council

Canadian Cataloguing in Publication Data

Merry, Wayne
    The official wilderness first-aid guide

Includes index.
ISBN 0-7710-8250-9

1. First aid in illness and injury.   2. Outdoor life – Accidents and injuries.   3. Wilderness survival.   4. Medical emergencies.
I. St. John Ambulance. Ontario Council.   II. Title.

RC88.9.095M47 1994   616.02'52   C94-930293-7

The author and St. John Ambulance invite readers to share their experiences of wilderness first aid and to comment on this book's contents. Please write:

Wayne Merry
c/o St. John Ambulance Ontario Council
46 Wellesley Street East
Toronto, Ontario M4Y 1G5

The masculine form is used throughout as a non-specific personal pronoun and is intended to represent both male and female subjects.

Illustrations by Paul McCusker
Printed and bound in Canada

McClelland & Stewart Inc.
The Canadian Publishers
481 University Avenue
Toronto, Ontario
M5G 2E9

1 2 3 4 5 98 97 96 95 94

Contents

Part IV
How to Recognize and Handle Common Illnesses

Appendices

List of Illustrations

Acknowledgements

A successful partnership develops when two organizations are able to collaborate on a project that meets their common goals. The Donner Canadian Foundation, building on its long involvement in the north, funded this project as it fit within their mandate to look at alternative resource management regimes in the Arctic. This includes the meshing of the traditional knowledge and practices of native people with conventional science and technology. The mission of St. John Ambulance is to enable Canadians to improve their health, safety, and quality of life by providing training and community service.

The contribution of the Donner Canadian Foundation, whose financial support made publication of this book possible, is gratefully acknowledged.

Physicians on the St. John Ambulance, Ontario Council Medical Committee, and their colleagues are acknowledged and thanked for their expertise – Robert Salter, Richard Butson, John Frim, Kenneth Hedges, Gordon McCauley, Colin Harwood, and Ronald Groshaw. Thanks also to David Clee of the Program Committee.

The author acknowledges and thanks the following for their help in the developmental stages: Peter Steele, physician, mountaineer, and author; Carol Boyko, Donna Hall, and Louise Dodds, outpost hospital nurses; Robert Dalgliesh, dentist; Bruce Rigby and Lin Maus, educators at Arctic College; Linda Schmidt, consultant; Norm Graham, Discovery Helicopters; Paul Albertson, Yukon EMO Director; Cindy Merry, understanding wife and "editor."

Lastly, special thanks to Leslie Kennedy, Director, Standards and Certification, St. John Ambulance, Ontario Council, for her coordination of the project.

Foreword

by Kenneth H. Hedges, CStJ, MB, ChB, MSc, MFPHM,
MFOM, DTM&H, DIH, MCFP

According to the Royal Geographic Society, one-third of the earth's land mass is still in a state of absolute wilderness with no permanent settlements or construction such as roads, dams, or mines. By this measure, Canada today is 65% wilderness. This book, therefore, will be especially useful for those who live and move across the remote areas of Canada, a country which in area is second only to Russia.

In 1990 the Ontario Council of St. John Ambulance felt a responsibility to develop first-aid training with special reference to the needs of remote communities. With the aid of generous support from the Donner Canadian Foundation, this book is produced as a reference for Wilderness First Aid training.

The consequences of inadequate preparation are compounded in remote locations where prompt professional help may be unobtainable. "Hope for the best – but plan for the worst" will be the motto of the prudent traveller in remote areas where communications are unreliable. It is here that self-help, the "buddy system," and group morale become decisive factors in the outcome of any journey – especially if someone gets hurt. In the wilderness, there will be no conventional Emergency Medical Services, no easy deployment of Advanced Trauma Life Support. In their place, a realistic emphasis must be placed upon planning – anticipating the odds and being prepared for appropriate interventions. I urge all readers, especially those who have not yet taken the St. John Ambulance Wilderness First Aid course, to familiarize themselves with this book's contents, including its glossary and appendices, before they head off into the wilderness, and before they are confronted with illness or injury. Safety is a discipline we must be trained to observe, and first aid remains a skill that you practise before you need it.

However, first aid is not a static body of knowledge. It is subject to modification in the light of new insights into casualty care. First-aid techniques change as anecdotal remedies are reassessed by means of clinical studies and published review. So we no longer offer "hot, sweet tea and a cigarette" to casualties of shock, and we no longer burn gunpowder on venomous snakebites, as was the vogue when Stanley traversed Africa.

Education should be more than just the processing of new information – it should also help us to understand the application of that information. The intent of this book, therefore, is not simply to have the reader better informed about health issues in remote regions, but also to help the first-aider working in a "real" and rigorous situation make careful judgement calls that reach beyond the obligation of conventional first aid.

Bon Courage.

Formerly a Senior Specialist in Public Health Medicine with the Royal Army Medical Corps, Dr. Hedges has extensive experience in wilderness travel in, among other places, Southeast Asia, South Arabia, equatorial Africa, the Sahara, Scandinavia, and Greenland. He was a member of the four-man party that completed the first crossing of the Arctic Ocean, a journey of 476 days by dogsled. As Regimental Medical Officer to the Special Air Service (SAS) he trained and supervised medical self-support for SAS units in remote areas where conventional help was inaccessible. He is a member of the College of Family Physicians of Canada, has served with the Canadian Ski Patrol, and has certified in Advanced Cardiac Life Support (ACLS), Advanced Trauma Life Support (ATLS), and Mine Rescue.

Introduction

The Special Challenges of Wilderness First Aid

Most first-aid courses are designed for people who live in or near cities and close to medical help. The first-aider usually has only a few minutes before an ambulance arrives. During that time, he must protect the casualty, be sure that he can breathe, stop any serious bleeding, and, possibly, splint fractures. When the casualty is transported, the first-aider's job is finished.

How different it is for those who live and travel in the wilderness! There, the first-aider must not only provide immediate care, he must also move the casualty to a safe camp, or make a camp. He must understand the problem well enough to describe it to a doctor or nurse over a radio. He must care for the casualty for long periods under very cold and unsanitary conditions, with very limited supplies. Lacking a large first-aid kit, the first-aider must often create bandages and dressings from what is at hand and make them sterile, or at least very clean. He must make splints from whatever is available. He must watch for infection developing in wounds, and know what to do if it develops. He must give the casualty the proper fluids and food. Often he must transport the casualty for many hours or even days to reach medical care.

Some of the things that a wilderness first-aider might be called upon to do are not really "first aid" as we think of the term. Some practices might be called "second aid" – medical treatment, or field nursing. But when the first-aider does things that are beyond first aid, he must never do them needlessly but only when he absolutely must and when there is no choice. He must do these things with a very clear understanding of what he is doing and what the hazards are. He must never experiment.

For example, most first-aid courses describe cooling, cleaning, and covering serious burns, but prohibit giving burn casualties anything by mouth. There are good reasons for this. It is assumed that the casualty is near medical help, and that intravenous (IV) fluids may be started very soon. It is assumed that the casualty may vomit, and each time he vomits, there is danger he may get vomit into his lungs, which could kill him. There is also the risk of the wrong fluids being given, which could have grave effects on blood chemistry. It is also assumed that the casualty will soon be in the hands of a surgeon and have a general anaesthetic. Anything in his stomach would complicate the physician's job.

However, in the wilderness, many hours or days from help, a burn casualty is not going to get IV fluids, and if the burn is serious, he will almost certainly go into shock and die from loss of fluids through the burn. The only way he can be kept alive is to give with care the proper fluids by mouth, and hope that he can hold them and benefit enough to survive. Many such casualties *can* be saved by simply drinking enough of the right fluids. In a wilderness situation, the first-aider *must* take an informed risk rather than say, "Well, I'm not supposed to give anything by mouth," and thus watch the casualty go into shock and die.

The wilderness traveller must make many tough decisions which he would not be faced with in town. If someone has a "bellyache," the first-aider must decide whether it is serious enough to break camp and make the long trip back to town. If he decides not to move and the illness turns out to be serious, the casualty might die before reaching help. On the other hand, if the first-aider decides to break camp and go home, and the casualty just has the stomach flu, the whole expedition may have been for nothing. If someone freezes a foot, the first-aider must decide whether or not to thaw it. If he does, he must know how to do it correctly and how to treat the injury afterward – for if he tries and does it wrong, he may make things much worse.

First-aid practices that make perfect sense in town could be dangerous in the wilderness. For example, in town it is common practice to cut away clothing and remove footgear to expose a possible fractured leg for assessment and splinting. In the wilderness, if the temperature is subzero and the wind is strong, one simply can't do that without risking exposure (hypothermia) and frostbite. Instead, one must estimate the injury without undressing the casualty and splint him with his clothing on so that he can be moved to a warm camp for better treatment.

Wilderness first aid presents some fearsome challenges and sometimes seems terribly different from town first aid. But the basics are the same. One may simply have to carry them further. In wilderness first aid, it is more important to understand the *why* of first aid, for then one can react more intelligently and improvise ways of dealing with problems.

Part I

Your First Response

1

Some Critical Wilderness Basics

In wilderness first aid, there are certain basic problems one must always consider regardless of what the injury or illness is. Because these are so basic and so important, they should be understood right from the beginning. They are:

- breathing problems
- cold problems
- shock
- dehydration.

Let's consider these one at a time.

Breathing Problems

Many an injured person has died needlessly in the wilderness simply because he was left lying on his back while someone went for help. In most cases, he became unconscious and his relaxed tongue fell back and blocked his air passage. In some cases, he vomited, and because he was on his back and unable to help himself, he got some of the vomit into his lungs. The acid in the vomit caused a fast-acting pneumonia, which killed him quickly. In still other cases, blood from his nose or mouth collected in the airway and he asphyxiated.

If his companion had simply placed him on his side and braced him there before going for help, he might not have died. What a simple thing to make the difference between life and death!

An unconscious person who is placed on his side to protect against fluids in his airway is said to be in the **recovery position**, because in that position he may regain consciousness without danger of suffocation. It is also called the **drainage position** because it allows fluids to drain from the mouth and throat without getting into the airway. Placing an unconscious casualty in this position is one of the most important and basic parts of first aid.

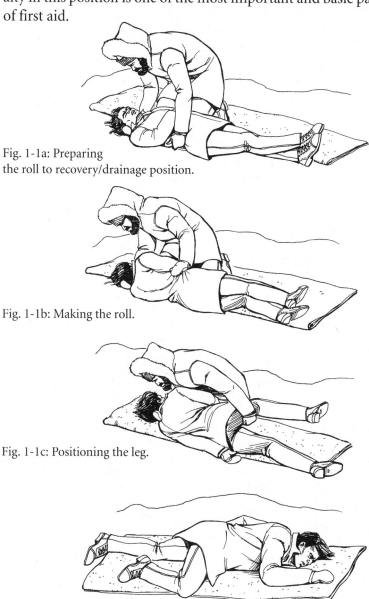

Fig. 1-1a: Preparing
the roll to recovery/drainage position.

Fig. 1-1b: Making the roll.

Fig. 1-1c: Positioning the leg.

Fig. 1-1d: Casualty in final position.

To do this you should:

- cross the casualty's legs at the ankles, far side on top,
- place the near arm along his side, the far arm across his chest (**Fig. 1-1a**),
- support his head with one hand, grip clothing at the waist on the far side,
- roll the person gently toward you, protecting head and neck, and rest him against your knees (**Fig. 1-1b**),
- bend his upper knee toward you to form a support (**Fig. 1-1c**),
- position his head with chin slightly extended to keep his airway open,
- place his upper arm as shown to keep him from rolling on his face,
- place the lower arm along his back so that he cannot roll onto his back. (**Fig. 1-1d**)

If the casualty is on snow, you should place a blanket, sleeping pad, hide, or other protection to keep his face out of the snow and reduce heat loss.

Fig. 1-2: The semi-sitting position makes breathing easier.

Other casualties have died because they could not get enough air. Again, simple body position makes a difference. A person lying down cannot breathe as well as one sitting up. This is because when we lie down, our intestines tend to move up and push against the *diaphragm*, the flat sheetlike muscle that separates our lungs and guts, and helps us to breathe. Lying down keeps the diaphragm from working well, so we get less air into the lungs. That is why people with breathing problems such as chronic obstructive pulmonary disease (COPD), emphysema, or asthma prefer to sit up. That is why we put people in a sitting or semi-sitting position whenever they have trouble getting enough air. (**Fig. 1-2**)

Why is air so important? Air carries oxygen, a colourless gas that our blood must carry to every cell of our body. If our air – which means oxygen – is cut off for as little as four minutes, we may die. If the amount of oxygen we get falls below normal, we may die. This is why:

Breathing problems are always the first thing that we check in first aid.

Cold Problems

Our body needs warmth almost as much as oxygen. Actually, it is the burning of oxygen in our body that produces warmth, so these issues are closely related. If the inside temperature of our body drops only a few degrees, our brain and other organs do not work as well. If our interior (core) temperature drops to the air temperature of a warm summer day, we may die.

Anyone who is sick or injured is much more vulnerable to cold than is a healthy person. He feels the cold more and is less able to produce heat to fight it. Less blood flows to his skin to keep it warm.

Because of this, he may get frostbite or suffer from exposure much more easily than the first-aider.

In warmer climates, maintaining body warmth is considered an important part of first aid. Imagine how much more important it is in the northern wilderness! Even in summer, the north is rarely a truly warm place. In any other season it is often bitterly cold. One of the first things a wilderness first-aider must do is:

Protect the casualty from cold.

This must be done as soon as it is certain that nothing threatens the casualty's life. Usually, it is simply a matter of covering the casualty with an adequate sleeping bag or blankets or extra clothing – but don't forget to put something *underneath*, too. A major part of body heat is lost to the ground or snow beneath – and moisture seeps in from the ground or from snow.

Later on, even after first aid is completed, the casualty will still be very sensitive to cold. It is quite possible for him to get frostbite *inside* a heavy sleeping bag if he is being transported on an open sled or similar vehicle. Always be extremely careful to keep the casualty warm and dry, and watch for the signs of hypothermia (exposure) any time conditions are marginal.

A true story shows the importance of this. Five men on a ski trip in the mountains encountered bad weather. One of them was sick with gastroenteritis (stomach flu), so they decided to make camp. That night it snowed heavily. In the morning, the sick man was still ill and the snow was too deep for him to travel. The other four decided to go back to town for help. They left the sick man wrapped in two down sleeping bags, in a good tent, with a stove and food close by. Two days later a rescue party reached his tent. He had been dead for about a day, from hypothermia. There was nothing else wrong with him but gastroenteritis.

In his weakened condition, his body wasn't able to produce enough heat to balance the heat loss, even in two sleeping bags.

Read the chapter on hypothermia carefully (Chapter 9), and always be ready for it.

Shock

Shock may be present with almost any injury or illness, and is usually present in any serious one. Exactly what is shock?

Shock is what occurs when there is inadequate organ perfusion; that is, decreased oxygen passing through the organs. To understand this, we need to know how the circulatory system works.

The heart is a pump. The veins and arteries work like flexible hoses, carrying blood to and from every part of the body. Near the heart, the arteries, which carry blood *from* the heart, are large. They branch often, and get smaller and smaller. Finally, at the outer ends of the branches, they become so fine that parts of the blood pass *through* their walls. This blood reaches each cell of the body, bringing oxygen and food to it. The food and oxygen are used or "burned" in the cells, keeping the cells healthy and producing the heat needed to live.

When the blood leaves the cells, it carries their waste products back into tiny veins, which pour into larger ones and finally into the largest veins which feed directly into the heart.

Now the blood has almost made a round trip – but there is one more stop before circulating once again. The heart pumps the blood to the lungs and back to the heart. In the lungs, the blood loses the waste gases (mostly carbon dioxide) it has picked up in the cells, and each red blood cell picks up a new load of oxygen. Then it returns to the heart and the heart pumps it again through the arteries to the cells.

The blood also goes through an amazingly effective "filtering system" called the kidneys. The kidneys remove all the liquid wastes which couldn't be taken out by the lungs. They also remove the extra salts and minerals the body doesn't need. These wastes as urine pass down tubes called ureters into the bladder.

The most important point of this whole process is the provision of oxygen and food to the cells. If this is interrupted for only a few minutes, cells start to die. If the cells that die are in the vital organs – especially the brain, heart, or kidneys – the whole body will also quickly die. *When organs are not getting enough oxygen to work properly, the signs of shock start to show.*

But what causes shock?

In order for the blood to get oxygen to the cells, the blood has to be under some pressure. This pressure is provided by the pump – the heart – and maintained by the veins and arteries, which are able to get slightly larger or smaller to control the pressure.

Several things might cause this pressure to drop. If there is a "leak" in the system, from a bad cut, blood flows out and the pressure drops. The body tries to deal with this automatically. How can we tell it is doing this?

- **Because** circulation to the skin is not as important as circulation to vital organs, the body cuts down the size of blood vessels at the surface, so *the skin gets paler and cooler.*

- **Because** there is not enough blood to fill the system, your heart automatically beats faster to get more oxygen to all the cells, so *your pulse rate goes up.*

- **Because** your cells are not getting enough oxygen, *your breathing rate automatically speeds up.*

- **Because** the body is trying to save all the fluid in it, it stops producing saliva and *you feel thirsty.*

- **Because** circulation to the stomach and intestines is less important than that to vital organs, the body cuts down blood flow to the gastrointestinal tract, so absorption of food and water stops and *you may feel nauseated.*

- **Because** the cells of the body need more oxygen, *you feel "hungry" for more air.*

- **Because** the brain is not getting enough oxygen, *you get confused and anxious.*

Now that you know what happens in the body, you can see what causes the signs and symptoms of shock. Again, these are:

- pale, cool, clammy skin
- rapid pulse rate
- rapid breathing

- thirst
- nausea and sometimes vomiting
- air hunger
- anxiety or nervousness
- confusion
- decreased amounts of urine.

Other factors besides blood loss can cause shock. Serious burns almost always do. Clear or pale yellow fluid, which comes directly from the blood, oozes from the burn in large amounts and also goes into the tissues around the burn as *swelling*. Because this fluid comes directly from the blood, the amount left in the system is less, and shock occurs.

Several types of illnesses can bring on shock by causing the large blood vessels in the trunk to loosen and expand. The vessels become bigger and can hold more, but the amount of blood in them remains the same, so the blood pressure drops. Sometimes, a severe emotional shock can cause this to happen. ("Fainting" is not the same as shock but is caused by a shortage of blood to the brain.)

A violent allergic reaction to a drug or insect sting can cause shock. So can injury to the spinal cord.

Once shock starts, it may be difficult to reverse. If it is not stopped or reversed, the casualty will die. So you must always:

**Expect shock in any severe injury or illness,
and work to prevent it.**

How do you prevent shock, or stop it?

Field prevention and treatment of shock are simple. You must:

- ensure a good airway
- control bleeding
- lie the casualty down, feet raised 8 to 12 inches (Do not tilt the entire body if there is difficulty breathing.) (**Fig. 1-3**)
- keep the casualty comfortably warm
- avoid rough handling

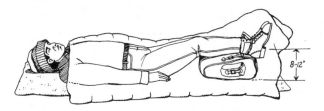

Fig. 1-3: Elevate the legs of a casualty in shock.

- reduce pain as much as possible (for example, by splinting fractures)
- reassure the casualty.

Since the problem is basically one of oxygen shortage to the cells, you must be sure that the casualty is breathing with maximum efficiency. Since low blood pressure is a factor, you must be sure no more blood is lost. Raising the legs increases return of blood to the heart. Keeping the casualty warm is especially critical, because the skin, with a decreased blood supply, is more vulnerable to injury from cold.

Rough handling increases shock. So does pain. And reassurance has been shown to have a positive effect on blood pressure and certainly on the casualty's survival attitude.

The first-aider should not be fooled into thinking there is no shock problem if shock does not appear serious immediately after blood loss. The body compensates in so many ways for the initial blood loss that pressure may be maintained for a time. With continuing loss, however, shock may appear rapidly.

Dehydration

Dehydration is not usually a factor in urban first aid. In the wilderness, however, it often affects us more than we think. Dehydration is what occurs when the body loses more water than it takes in.

Dehydration is usually caused by:

- not drinking enough
- losing too much water through the skin by perspiration
- losing too much water through the lungs by evaporation

- losing water through vomiting or diarrhea
- frequent urination.

Because of the cold, very dry air of the north, especially in winter, evaporation is very rapid, and a person who is working hard outdoors for several days with little opportunity to drink may become severely dehydrated, and may show signs and symptoms similar to shock. But dehydration *by itself* is not usually the main problem, for almost everyone if they can will eventually satisfy his thirst with the needed fluids. The *combination* of dehydration and other conditions may be a real problem.

Suppose, for example, an active hunter has lost 5% of his total blood volume by dehydration. The body will compensate – much as it does in shock – by reducing blood flow to the skin. This makes the skin colder and much more likely to be frostbitten.

Suppose the same hunter is injured and loses blood. Since his blood volume is already decreased, it takes less blood loss to produce shock.

Suppose that same hunter had a chest injury or a respiratory infection. Because the body fluids have become more viscous (thicker and stickier) from dehydration, it is harder for the hunter to cough up the fluids which accumulate in the lungs.

Prevention

To balance normal water loss, simply drink more water during outdoor activity. Try to drink often even if you don't feel thirsty. The traditional tea stop while travelling is very valuable in this and other ways, although tea and coffee are not as good as plain water or the broth from boiled meat, because tea and coffee are diuretics (that is, they make you urinate more). Alcohol should not be drunk, as it *increases* dehydration. (In fact, much of the discomfort of a hangover is due to dehydration brought on by too much alcohol.)

Although you can reduce thirst for a short time by nibbling on snow, remember that melting any amount of snow in your mouth takes an enormous amount of heat from your body and produces little water. Any water you can get, no matter how icy, will use up less body heat and be more thirst-quenching.

Most northerners have heard stories about people who were trapped without water and "survived" by drinking their own urine. If the stories are true, it is likely that they survived *in spite of* drinking urine, not because of it. Neither urine nor seawater should be drunk, even in small quantities, as the salts in them will draw further water from your tissues.

Dehydration in babies is very dangerous, and accounts for many millions of deaths worldwide each year. Most of this dehydration is due to diarrhea or vomiting. A baby cannot tell you if he is thirsty, and it is easy to overlook. It is also easy for seniors to become dehydrated.

Dehydration by normal means is best combatted by plain water or other ordinary drinks. Dehydration due to vomiting or diarrhea should be fought using Gatorade or the salt, soda, and sugar mix described in Chapter 20.

How to Tell

A mildly dehydrated person may show some or all of the following signs:

- thirst
- dry tongue
- discomfort
- tiredness
- nausea
- sleepiness
- pale, cool, clammy skin
- faster pulse
- pinched skin on back of hand slow to flatten out
- little urine, dark in colour.

A person who is getting adequate fluids and is healthy will produce at least 1,000 mL (about four cups) of urine each 24 hours. When a baby cries but produces no tears, look for dehydration.

2

What to Do at the Scene

Our first reaction on seeing a serious injury is often emotional and confusing. To some degree, we tend to panic. Often all the things we have learned about first aid vanish. We have a blind urge to "do something – anything!" to help the casualty, and sometimes it is only after we have done "something" without thinking that we start to calm down and remember what it is we *should* have done.

On the other hand, most of us react well to less serious problems. When a person gets a cut or a scrape or gets a fishhook stuck into him, or even when he falls and breaks an arm, it is easy to see and understand what is wrong and to handle it without great emotion or confusion.

Rescuer panic happens most often when the casualty is unconscious or dazed, or where there is a great deal of blood or serious disfigurement, or when we don't know exactly what is wrong with the casualty but suspect it is quite serious: *This is the kind of problem that we will be addressing.* If you know exactly what the injury is and know that there are no complications, then you can deal immediately with that problem without going through the complete head-to-toe assessment, life-saving precautions, and intense care we are getting into now.

Remembering What to Do

In every first-aid situation, before doing anything else, you must be sure that there is no further hazard threatening you or the casualty. Take care of the hazard first, or get yourself and the

13

casualty away from it. You can be of no help to anyone if you are injured or dead.

Safety first!

Let us imagine a situation that easily might happen to you, and see how you might react to it.

Imagine that you are travelling through a snowstorm, hardly able to see, and one of your companions drives his snowmobile off a cliff as high as a house. You find him unconscious. You must think clearly, for if you act quickly but wrongly you may further injure or even kill him. If you think about it too long before doing anything, he might also die. How do you make yourself think clearly in this moment of crisis? What do you do to prevent quick death?

Good first aid requires a **Priority Action Approach.** This means that you take care of *the most life-threatening things first,* then move to the less critical problems.

It helps to have some method, and one of the most common is to use the first letters of the alphabet – the ABCDEF's – as clues:

- **A** = **Airway and cervical spine**
- **B** = **Breathing**
- **C** = **Circulation – bleeding**
- **D** = **Disability**
- **E** = **Expose and examine**
- **F** = **Freezing (cold injury)**

And to this list, we should always add the "S" for shock, since it may be present in any serious injury or illness.

- **S** = **Shock**

So here you are, standing by the unconscious casualty and you think, "What do I do now? Oh yes – the ABCDEF's!" Priorities first. One step at a time. So you start with A.

A = Check his AIRWAY. Is it open? Is there anything blocking his mouth (packed snow or blood, for example)? Clear it

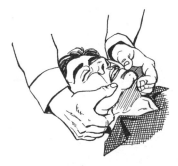

Fig. 2-1: Open the **airway** using jaw thrust without head tilt.

Fig. 2-2: Look, listen, and feel for **breathing**.

away. Is his tongue falling back blocking his throat? To open the airway, move his lower jaw upward without moving his neck. See Chapter 21 for details. (**Fig. 2-1**)

Assessment of the CERVICAL SPINE is important. To determine the possibility of injury note how the injury happened, what the conscious casualty tells you, and carefully feel his back for deformity or tenderness. Immobilize the neck with a cervical collar or improvised collar. (See Chapter 17.)

B = Be sure he is BREATHING. Remember, he may only live four minutes if he is not! Put your ear down next to his lips. Listen for breath, feel it on your ear or cheek, watch his chest rise or fall. (**Fig. 2-2**) If he is not breathing, start rescue breathing immediately. (See the section "Respiration (Breathing)" in Chapter 4 for details on assessment of breathing. Also see Chapter 21.)

C = Check his CIRCULATION. Does he have a pulse? The pulse in the neck (carotid pulse) is easiest to check, because it is strongest and you can usually slip your fingers into the neck area without removing clothing and risking frostbite. (**Fig. 2-3**) (See "How to Read a Pulse" in Chapter 4 for details.) If there is no pulse, and you have cardiopulmonary resuscitation (CPR) training, start CPR. If his heart is beating and he is breathing, then check nail-bed refill (see "Nailbed Refill," Chapter 4) to further assess circulation.

Wearing latex or surgical gloves, check for SEVERE BLEEDING. Slide a hand beneath him, feeling for the wetness of blood. You must be sure that he is not bleeding badly from a point you cannot see. (**Fig. 2-4**) If he is bleeding badly, you must stop it.

D = Check for DISABILITY. Check his level of consciousness or LOC (see Chapter 4 for details). Record your findings on the Consciousness Record, Appendix D. If you suspect neck or head injury, immobilize the neck immediately with a cervical collar. (See Chapter 17 for details.) Feel carefully underneath the casualty for any obvious bumps, irregularities, or tenderness in the spine indicating damage. Shock is a life-threatening disability. If the casualty shows or is likely to show the signs and symptoms of shock, begin treatment immediately. (See "Shock" in Chapter 1 for details.)

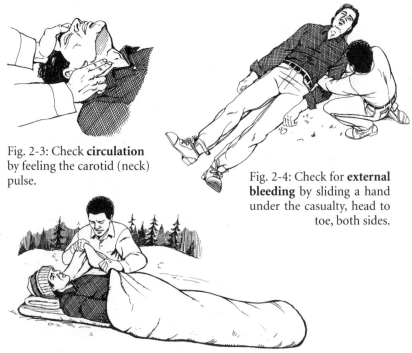

Fig. 2-3: Check **circulation** by feeling the carotid (neck) pulse.

Fig. 2-4: Check for **external bleeding** by sliding a hand under the casualty, head to toe, both sides.

Fig. 2-5: Prevent **freezing** and exposure by keeping the casualty warm.

E = EXPOSE and EXAMINE. If the environment permits, bare as much of the body as possible to look for bleeding and injuries.

F = Prevent FREEZING. Cover him to keep him warm, and get something between him and the snow or the cold ground. Be sure that his hands and feet are protected. Protect him from wind and from moisture as soon as possible. (**Fig. 2-5**)

S = Prevent SHOCK. (See "Shock," Chapter 1.)

This complete check should take only a couple of minutes! Now you have done all you can to prevent quick death, and you have time to think about what to do next.

These steps are fairly simple. They do not even require a first-aid kit. Yet the ABCDEF'S are probably the most important first aid of all. *You are more likely to save a life in the first few minutes!*

If there is any one thing you should memorize in wilderness first aid, it is the ABCDEF'S. If you can remember the Priority Action Approach, you will probably remember how to get started in almost any wilderness first-aid emergency.

Rescuer Safety

Because of the increasing danger of HIV (the AIDS virus), hepatitis B, and other diseases transmitted by blood or other body fluids, first-aiders should wear latex gloves whenever they may come into contact with such fluids. Every first-aid kit should include one or more pairs of gloves, which are quite inexpensive and can usually be obtained at a drug store or at a nursing station in a remote community. Get a large size to fit all.

After use, the contaminated gloves should be carefully removed, so as not to touch the contaminated surface, and burned. Any blood which accidently spatters onto skin must be washed immediately and well with soap and water.

3

How to Move a Casualty to Shelter

Now that you have solved immediate problems, you must examine the casualty more carefully so you will know what to do for him. If it is very cold, you can't do this without getting him – and yourself – into shelter. But he may have broken bones, or other injuries you don't know about, and if you move him improperly, he may suffer great injury. The best thing to do, if you can do it safely, is to:

Do the assessment and give first aid on the spot.

If you can put a shelter over the casualty, do it – or put one up within a few feet to minimize movement. However, this may not be safe or possible. The area may be too exposed to weather, to rockfall or avalanche, to shifting ice, or to any number of other hazards.

Move the casualty to safety if there is danger.

If there is any danger either to rescuers or the casualty, you must make a quick decision. Choose a leader, decide what you will do, then do it carefully and immediately.

If the casualty is unconscious, someone must be assigned to care for and watch him continuously while the rest of the party prepares a move or a camp. Ensuring that the casualty's airway is open is most important.

Do not take chances in the confusion of an emergency.

It is very common for rescuers to get so excited and concerned about the casualty that they forget the most basic precautions for their own safety. Remember that you may not have time later to stop and correct your mistakes. If you take a chance and get wet or soaked with sweat, you may suffer cold injury later. If you rush to lift someone when you are in an awkward position, you may injure your back and become a casualty yourself. If you drive a snowmobile for help at high speed, you may crash. This kind of event happens often in the rush to help another.

**Keep watching
an unconscious casualty.**

If the casualty is conscious, talk to him. Reassure him that he will be taken care of. Put yourself in his position.

How would you feel if you regained consciousness after a crash or fall and your companions were all standing around talking about you? You can hear them but not see them. They are saying things like, "Oh, no – he really looks bad!" "His face is a mess!" "What shall we do?" "Maybe he's going to die!"

Think of the difference if you were to awake and find a friend with his hand on your shoulder, saying that he is taking care of you and not to worry.

An apparently unconscious person can often hear quite well, so reassure him even if his consciousness is in doubt. Don't lie to him, but don't make him feel any worse.

**Reassure the casualty.
Touch him when you talk to him.**

Touch is a very important part of reassurance. Many injured people have said that the attendant's hand on their shoulder was the most important thing in the world, and they felt that without it they would die!

Short Moves and Carries

Almost any wilderness emergency will require helping or carrying a casualty at least a short distance. As often as not, there may be only one or two rescuers.

It is extremely difficult to carry an adult for any distance, even with a strong team, and it is easy to injure him further while carrying. Rarely should you try to lift and carry on snow; it is almost always safer and easier to drag on a tarp or sled. Following are some means of moving casualties short distances.

Drags

A casualty should be dragged only if he must be moved quickly out of danger – and severe cold, strong winds, blowing snow, and water should all be considered serious dangers. It is important to assess the casualty before attempting a drag, because some injuries, if not yet stabilized, may be aggravated by premature movement.

If there is only one rescuer, dragging may be the only means of moving a casualty.

Whenever you drag, observe the following rules:

- **Drag a casualty headfirst.** This allows you to support his head and neck and keep his body straight.

- **Keep the body in line.** The casualty's body must not twist or bend. Avoid major bumps.

- **Support the head and neck.** The neck should not bend sharply, nor should the head fall forward or to the side.

Fig. 3-1: Grip clothing firmly behind armpits to drag carry.

Fig. 3-2: Modified drag carry.

To drag a person, reach under his body and grip his clothing just below shoulder level on either side of centre, so that your forearms support his head and neck. Crouch or kneel as you drag him backwards. Move him only until he is safe. This drag is hard on the rescuer's back, so be careful! **(Fig. 3-1)**

If the casualty's clothing pulls up too much or is not strong, place a spare shirt or jacket over his chest and bring the sleeves under his back to provide a firm grip. **(Fig. 3-2)**

If possible, secure the casualty's hands together before dragging to protect them. You can use his cuff buttons or Velcro, mitten ties, or a piece of cord.

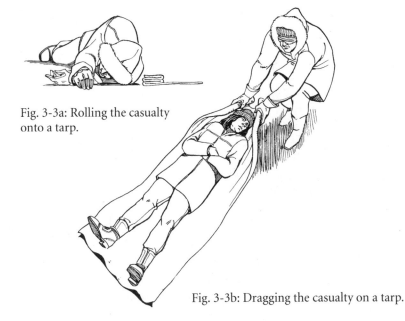

Fig. 3-3a: Rolling the casualty onto a tarp.

Fig. 3-3b: Dragging the casualty on a tarp.

Dragging on a plastic camp tarp is easier on everybody. Use it doubled if it is an old one. A blanket, sail, tent, or large hide may also be used. Fold about one metre (three feet) of it into short accordion folds and place it next to the casualty. Log-roll the casualty toward you and brace him there with your knees while you use one hand to slide the folds close against his back. Roll him gently back onto the folds. Reach under and pull the folds out straight. (**Fig. 3-3a**)

Grip the tarp to hold the casualty's head and shoulders off the ground and in normal position, and drag carefully. (**Fig. 3-3b**)

The tarp-drag is an excellent method on snow, and will greatly reduce friction on bare ground. A single rescuer may make a ramp of snow and slide a casualty onto a sled.

This drag is also a good way to move a casualty onto some sort of insulating material to protect him from cold ground or snow.

You may wish to leave the tarp under the casualty to aid in a later lift. Always put a person into a basket stretcher with a backboard, blanket, or tarp under him, as it is otherwise difficult to remove him without excessive movement.

A travois may be built with the tarp even while a casualty is on it, and will greatly aid one-person transport.

Be careful with a tarp-drag on sloping snow – you may lose control on a downhill slope.

Single-Rescuer Carry

Most single-rescuer carries are necessarily short, and cannot be used to transport people with major injuries, as they cause much movement and bending of the casualty's body. All are extremely strenuous. They are often used to transport casualties with injuries of the lower extremities, but it is easy to bump extremities during these manoeuvres.

Packstrap Carry

This is a quick, easy carry for very short distances, to be used only if injuries permit. The casualty must be able to stand to get into position with his arms across your shoulders like packstraps.

Bring his arms forward across your shoulders, crossing his

Fig. 3-4: Packstrap
carry.

Fig. 3-5: Pick-a-back
carry.

Fig. 3-6: Carrying seat
with wide strap.

wrists in front and holding them there while you bend forward enough to lift the casualty's feet off the ground. Be sure his arms are bent at the elbow, or there will be great leverage on his upper arms and shoulders. (**Fig. 3-4**)

Pick-a-Back Carry

This familiar carry is good for short-distance transport of conscious casualties with minor injuries, and may be used to carry children for fairly long distances. (**Fig. 3-5**)

Carrying Seat

A quick and easy backpack seat to assist the pick-a-back system may be made with a simple loop of wide strap, as shown in the illustration. It may be necessary to adjust the length once or twice for maximum comfort. This seat is best if the casualty is noticeably lighter than the rescuer, otherwise it puts painful pressure on the rescuer's neck and shoulders. (**Fig. 3-6**)

Rope-Coil Carry

This is very good for short-distance transport of a conscious casualty with minor injuries, and can be effective in moderate-distance carries on good footing and with alternating rescuers. Rescuers should take short shifts, "trading off" before they are tired.

Fig. 3-7: Rope-coil carry.

Make a rope coil about two feet long (stretched), fasten it with a tight, secure wrap, and "split" the coil into two equal parts. The casualty places a leg through each half. You then crouch and take the coils over your shoulders from behind like putting on a pack, and rise using your legs to take the strain. It may take two tries to get the coil length just right for comfort. A short strap or cord holding the two coils together across your chest may be desirable. A fairly thick coil is necessary to provide reasonable comfort, but a thinner coil may be used and padded with extra clothing. (**Fig. 3-7**)

Wide straps or strips of canvas may be used in the same way. (**Fig. 3-8**) Two long, narrow holes cut in an animal hide (e.g., caribou) may be used like the holes in the coil, and the surplus hide may be wrapped around the weight-bearing surfaces for padding.

**Both the carrying seat and the rope-coil carry
reduce circulation in the casualty's legs.
In severe cold, rest often to relieve the pressure
and check to avoid frostbite.**

Two-Person Lift and Carry

Lifting is half as strenuous if there are two rescuers, but carrying for any distance is – surprisingly – not much better, because two carriers must often compensate for each other's movements to keep in balance.

The chance of error is multiplied with each added person in a lifting team, and injury to the casualty often occurs if lifts are bungled.

Whenever more than one person lifts, observe the following rules:

- One person must be clearly designated leader and responsible for giving all commands.

- The partner(s) must be told exactly what is to be done and what the commands will be.

- The lift should first be practised without the casualty, or on an uninjured person.

- Rescuers should maintain eye contact while lifting.

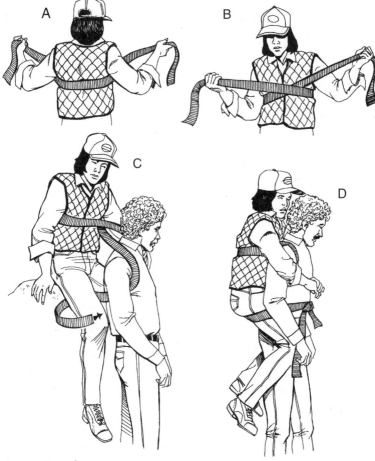

Fig. 3-8: Strap harness.

Fig. 3-9: Fore-and-aft lift and carry.

Fig. 3-10a: Hand grip for the two-hand seat.

Fig. 3-10b: Two-hand seat grip and lift.

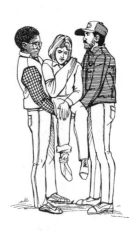

Fig. 3-10c: Two-hand seat and carry.

The best means of assuring good timing in a two-person lift is to look straight into your partner's eyes during the lift. If you do this, it is almost impossible to get your signals mixed.

The Fore-and-Aft Lift and Carry

This should be used only for minor injuries. It may be used for an *unconscious* casualty if his injuries permit. On rough ground, it may be the easiest method of lifting a casualty onto a stretcher or other means of transport. As it produces some pressure against the chest, it will restrict the casualty's air exchange somewhat.

If the casualty is conscious, help him to sit. If the casualty is unconscious, have your partner take the casualty's hands and pull him into the sitting position. Cross the casualty's arms on his chest. Crouch behind him, reach under his arms, and grasp his opposite wrists. Your partner may crouch at the casualty's knees, facing his feet, and take both legs under one arm. At your signal you and your partner both rise, keeping your backs straight. (**Fig. 3-9**) If the move is longer, your partner may wish to bring the casualty's legs to either side of his waist for better balance and comfort.

Two-Hand Seat

This two-person lift and carry is good for casualties who cannot hold onto your shoulders for support, or who are not fully alert.

Rescuers crouch on either side of the casualty. Each slides one hand under his thighs, locking fingers over a pad (**Fig. 3-10a**), or wearing mitts or gloves so that fingernails don't dig in. Reach across his back and grip his belt and pants at the other hip, so that the rescuers' arms are crossed. Rise on command and step off on the inside foot. (**Figs. 3-10b, c**)

This supports the casualty's back well; however, the fingers of the gripping hands will tire quickly. For longer carries, try gripping your partner's wrists rather than his fingers. If you are wearing mitts, gripping the wrist will be more secure than gripping the hand.

If the casualty is unconscious, he may be lifted easily to a sitting position. One rescuer pulls on the casualty's hands while the other lifts and supports his head; then the rescuers move into position while supporting his head and back.

Two-Person Rope-Coil Carry

This carry works well for moderate distances if the casualty is not too heavy, as it allows the rescuers to walk with less twisting and supports the weight on their shoulders rather than hands and arms. The casualty must be conscious and able to support his upper body with at least one arm.

Make a coil as in the rope-coil carry, and split it. Place half of the coil over each rescuer's outside shoulder. The securing wraps form the seat between them. Padding is desirable for the carriers' shoulders and seat, and is essential if the coil is a thin one.

Ask the casualty to sit in the seat with his arms around the rescuers' shoulders, shifting himself with his arms into the most comfortable position before the rescuers rise. Rescuers then rise from a kneeling position on outer legs first.

Your inner hands may be used to support the casualty's back. Outer hands are free. You may wish to have a short walking stick in your outside hand for extra support and better balance on rough ground. (**Fig. 3-11**)

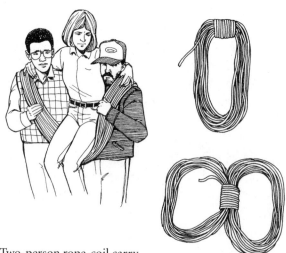

Fig. 3-11: Two-person rope-coil carry.

Two-Person Horizontal Lift

When a casualty has injuries that prohibit bending of the body, "arms-only" lifts become extremely difficult with two rescuers, and are more frequently bungled than not. Often footing is insecure, the ground irregular, help not available, and the casualty too heavy. In most cases the best method is to log-roll the casualty onto a rigid board (for example, plywood, cabin door, boat floorboards, flat toboggan) and lift it as a stretcher.

If no board is available, log-roll the casualty onto a tarp or blanket, roll sturdy poles into its sides to make a litter (see Appendix A), and lift from the sides to reduce litter flexing. (**Figs. 3-12a,b**)

With all such improvised litters, it is extremely important to tie the casualty firmly in place so that he cannot fall from the litter or board.

Two rescuers can also drag a casualty on a tarp over pre-smoothed ground or snow with less danger of body flexing than by attempting a lift.

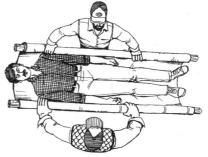

Fig. 3-12a: Rolling poles into tarp before a lift.

Fig. 3-12b: Lifting from sides to reduce pole flexing.

Multi-Person Lift

Three or more persons can usually lift a fourth with minimal body flexing if they are extremely careful and their timing is good. Six rescuers are best, with one at the head, four along one side of the body, and one to move the board or stretcher under the casualty.

Because the numbers and terrain will vary and several of the group may never have done such lifts, you should concentrate on basic principles rather than on trying to memorize precise techniques in an ideal setting.

- Appoint a single leader, and follow his commands precisely.

- Practise on an uninjured person of about the same size before lifting the casualty. There is no shame in having to practise – but there is shame in making a bad lift and hurting the casualty. Practise every time, and include lowering too.

- The leader should stabilize the head. He should grip the shoulders at the base of the neck and support the head with his forearms.

- The casualty should be supported evenly so that the most and strongest hands are slid fully under the heaviest parts of the body. The strongest rescuers should be at the chest and hips, which are heaviest.

- When ready to lift, maintain eye contact with the leader and exactly follow his commands.

If these rules are followed, even inexperienced rescuers should be able to perform a multi-person lift reasonably well. *The importance of one or more practice lifts cannot be overemphasized.*

Rigging Temporary Stretchers

Stretchers can be improvised from a variety of wilderness equipment and clothing, and even from natural materials such as light poles lashed close together across two larger poles. (**Fig. 3-13**) Most stretchers improvised from clothing tend to sag and be uneven, and their strength depends upon the buttons, zippers, or other fastenings.

Good stretchers may be improvised from blankets (**Fig. 3-14**), but blankets are not commonly available when travelling.

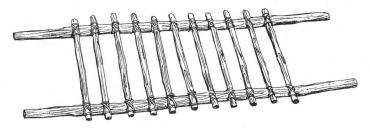

Fig. 3-13: Pole stretcher. A good pad must be used for comfort.

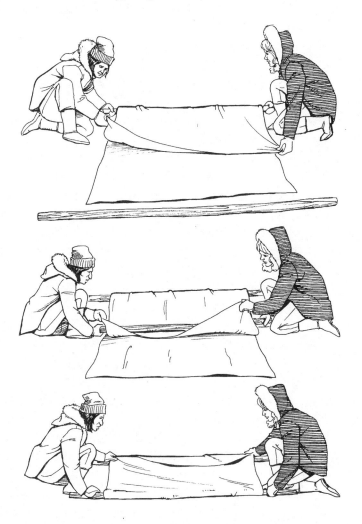

Fig. 3-14: Improvised blanket stretcher.

A good stretcher can be made from a heavy-duty rectangular sleeping bag with poles pushed through it, provided that the zipper side is reinforced with several cord ties so that the zipper will not unzip or fail catastrophically. (**Fig. 3-15**) The casualty must be placed on top of this stretcher, and not in the bag itself. It provides excellent insulation beneath, unlike most stretchers; however, it leaves one member without a sleeping bag during its use.

The most commonly available stretcher material is the ever-present reinforced plastic tarp, or less commonly these days, the canvas tarp. These may be utilized just as the blanket stretcher above.

First, fold the tarp so that it will be about 6 inches longer than the casualty at either end.

Proceed as with the blanket stretcher. There is one important difference: *the plastic tarp is slick and an extra complete wrap around the poles is required to keep it from slipping.* (**Fig. 3-16**)

Once the tarp is in place, lash a crosspiece just above and below the carrying surface, stretching the tarp as tightly as possible. This will reduce sagging. Trim the crosspieces as close to the main poles as possible to reduce snagging on brush.

The most common error is in using poles that are too flexible. Use poles that are at least 2 inches in diameter at the small end. As northern trees often have a rapid taper, this means they may be quite thick at the other end. Trim them down with a knife or axe for less weight and more comfortable grips. Use the heavier, less flexible ends at the head end of the stretcher.

In the far north where spruce are very small, two may be lashed together with the butts at opposite ends to make a single sturdy pole. Be sure that the poles extend about 1½ feet beyond the tarp at either end, so that bearers can easily get between them.

Spruce makes good poles, being very tough but somewhat springy. Standing dead spruce will be stiffer than green spruce, and much lighter. Pine is good if well seasoned, but not as strong as spruce. Willow, aspen, and cottonwood are poorer, being heavy and flexible when green, and weak when dead. Alder is good. Test poles carefully before making the stretcher.

Fig. 3-15: Improvised sleeping bag stretcher.
Note cord ties to reinforce zipper side.

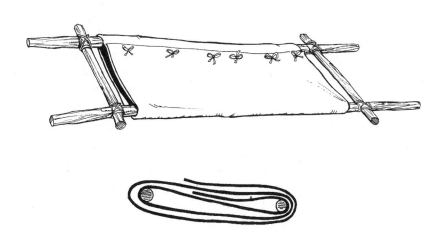

Fig. 3-16: Plastic tarp and pole stretcher.
Note extra complete wrap to prevent slipping.

4

How to Tell What Is Wrong

Now that you have the casualty in a safe, warm place, it is time to determine exactly what is wrong with him.

If the casualty has simply sprained his ankle or cut his hand with a knife, it won't be necessary to do a complete examination. But if the casualty has been unconscious, is dazed, had a violent crash or fall, or you aren't sure exactly what is wrong, do a complete exam (called a secondary survey) even if he makes no complaint. One pain may "mask" another. Such a casualty may have serious injuries and not even suspect it. Also, if you determine right now exactly what the casualty's condition is by taking his vital signs (pulse, breathing rate, level of consciousness, temperature, etc.), you will be establishing a baseline and will be able to tell later if he is getting better or worse. This will help you to understand what is wrong and to decide what you must do. It will tell you whether you must break camp and evacuate the casualty or stay where you are. When and if you contact medical advice on a radio, the doctor will need to know these details to make a diagnosis.

A careful examination will also help to reassure the casualty and set his mind at ease.

Every question has a purpose. You may use the same examination whether the casualty is sick or injured. It is better to ask too many questions than not enough.

Watch the casualty's face carefully, whether you are asking questions or checking for injury – often his reactions will give you a clue you might miss otherwise.

If a casualty is unconscious, you have to forgo the questions and see what you can discover from the full-body examination. When he regains consciousness, you can complete the questioning.

The Assessment Checklists

In the appendices of this book you will find checklists to help you assess injury or illness. *Make several copies to include in your first-aid kit.* The checklists will remind you of what to look for and how to look for it, and provide a written record to help you keep track of the casualty's condition. If he is evacuated to medical help, send completed checklists with him.

The Secondary Survey

The first part of the survey is called the **history**. Ask the casualty the following questions, but don't restrict his answers. Let him tell you how he feels.

- **What are his name and address?** You can skip this if you know it and the casualty is alert, but don't fail to ask if he is disoriented or has been unconscious. If he is confused, this indicates a lower level of consciousness. If he goes by more than one name, find out which one is used on his hospital records.

- **Who is his physician or nurse?** If he has a medical problem, radio contact with his own physician will be much more effective than with any other physician or nurse.

- **What happened?** Find out exactly what he thinks happened, and what it did to him. You may get valuable clues to his problem.

- **What is his primary complaint?** This means simply what is bothering him the most.

- Ask **the casualty** to **describe the pain.** Is it sharp, dull, shooting, aching, throbbing, or burning?

- On a scale of 1 to 10, **how bad is the pain?**

- **What is its timing?** Is it constant, or does it come and go? When? How often?

- **Does the pain stay in one place or does it move elsewhere?**

- **When did it start?** Was the start related to something he was doing?

- **Has it happened before?** Ask this question if you are investigating a medical complaint.

- **What makes it worse, or better?**

- **Does the casualty have any other problems?**

- **What is the casualty's medical history?** This includes operations, hospital admissions, diabetes, asthma, etc.

- **Is the casualty currently under medical care?** For what?

- **Is the casualty taking any medications?** This includes over-the-counter medications like Aspirin or acetaminophen (Tylenol), vitamins, seasickness pills, birth control pills, insulin, etc.

- **Does the casualty have any allergies?** Many people are seriously allergic to medicines – especially penicillin and other antibiotics, and over-the-counter medications – and it is critical that you know this.

This completes the **history**. If the problem is a medical one – that is, caused by sickness rather than by injury – you should have some valuable clues by now. With the help of this book you may be able to form a good idea of what is wrong. However, never fail to get medical advice, if it is available, before acting on your own.

The Head-to-Toe Exam

You are now ready to start the **head-to-toe exam.** You are looking for clues to tell you what is wrong. Do an exam if there is any doubt about the illness or extent of injury.

**If the casualty has any major injury,
immobilize his head and neck before beginning.**

Tell him what you are going to do. Be discreet and considerate, but thorough. You need not check genital areas unless you have reason to believe something is wrong there. If possible, have someone of the casualty's sex do this part.

If you can remove the casualty's clothing, do so to see clearly, otherwise it is easy to miss signs of injury such as large bruises which may signal major blood loss.

Warm your hands before starting, or you won't know if the casualty is flinching from pain or your cold hands. Be gentle, but firm enough to detect injuries. Before starting, ask the casualty if he has any numbness or tingling anywhere. This may indicate reduced blood flow or nerve damage.

With the casualty lying on his back, start your examination at the top of his head and work to the bottom of his feet. You may do the arms and hands on the way down, or come back and do them after the feet. Develop a system and do it the same way every time. Watch his face whenever you are probing for injury; sometimes a dazed person will wince but not say anything.

**To determine whether a part is swollen or deformed,
compare it with the same body part on the other side.**

This list looks long and complex, but you should be able to do it in about 3 minutes after a little practice!

- **Head and face:** Look for cuts and bruises, feel gently for swellings or dips which indicate injury. Don't miss the back of the head.

- **Eyes:** Are the pupils of equal size? When you shine a light into them, do they close down equally? If not, this may indicate serious head injury. Are they very tiny? This may indicate drug use. Is there any injury to the eyes? Does the casualty see normally? If not, how?

- **Ears:** Is there any injury to them? Is there any blood or clear fluid in them? These suggest skull fracture. Can the casualty hear normally?

- **Nose:** Is there any blood or clear fluid? These could mean skull injury. Is there injury to the nose? Can he breathe through it?

- **Mouth:** Is there any injury, obstruction to breathing, or dentures that might fall out? Is there any smell to breath? Can the casualty open and close, and bite hard?

- **Face:** Is the face red, hot, pale, cool and clammy, or bluish, especially around lips?

- **Neck:** Are there injuries? (Check the spine again as you did with the ABCDEF's; see Chapter 2.) Does the casualty wear a Medic Alert necklace? Is there a stoma (artificial opening to breathe through)? If so, keep it clear. Are lymph glands swollen? These indicate infection. Are there enlarged neck veins, or is the windpipe out of line? These are clues to respiratory injury.

- **Arms:** Are shoulders normal shape? Difference could mean fracture or dislocation. Are there injuries? Ask the casualty to move his joints. Do his joints work normally? Ask the casualty to squeeze your hands. Is his grip strength equal on both sides? Does he have equal feeling in both arms? If not, it could mean nerve injury, arm injury, or reduced circulation. What is the colour of his nail beds? Blueness means lack of oxygen. What is the nailbed refill time? (See "Nailbed Refill" later this chapter.) If hands are warm, over 2 seconds could mean shock or dehydration. Is there a Medic Alert bracelet?

- **Trunk:** Are collar bones normally shaped and unbroken? Are ribs fractured? Look, feel, but don't push. (You may not feel fractures from this gentle touch, but the casualty will feel pain if there are breaks.) Does the chest inflate equally on both sides? Watch very carefully – if not, a lung may be collapsed.

Are there any rattling or wet breathing sounds? It could mean respiratory problems or infection. Is there any bruising? It could indicate broken ribs or internal bleeding. Is there pain anywhere? It may mean injury beneath.

- **Belly (abdomen):** Feel the abdomen very gently. Are muscles rigid or soft? Can they be relaxed on command? Is there pain at touch? Rigidity, inability to relax abdominal muscles, or pain could mean serious internal injury or infection. Look for bruises. They could indicate injury beneath. Is the belly swollen, indicating a possible problem with intestines?

- **Hips and genital area:** Is there any obvious bleeding or injury, or signs of hernia? (See the section on hernia in Chapter 22.) Are bones evenly positioned on both sides? Press gently on prominent front pelvic points; pain indicates pelvic fracture. Has the casualty lost bladder or bowel control? Your nose will tell you. Is there bleeding from the meatus (opening for urine)? It may mean pelvic, bladder, or urethra injury. Discharge here indicates infection.

- **Legs:** Is there any obvious injury? Are the legs equal length when the body is straight? Is either foot flopped outward abnormally? Differences could indicate fracture or dislocation.

- **Feet:** Is foot-push against your hand of equal strength on both sides, and is sensation equal? A difference could mean nerve damage or circulation problems. Are both feet the same temperature? Are pulses in the feet equal? If not, there may be possible circulation problems.

- **Spine:** Feel carefully underneath the casualty for any obvious bumps, irregularities, or tenderness in the spine indicating damage.

By the end of this exam, you should have discovered any injuries which were overlooked until now, and have a much better idea of what is wrong. The next step is to take the vital signs.

Vital Signs

You could have taken the vital signs earlier, but the casualty might have still been excited or fearful, which would make the readings untrue. The examination has given him time to calm down so that vitals will be more nearly true.

Be sure that you keep a record of the vitals. Note them in one of the checklists found in the appendices. That way you can see how the casualty's condition is changing.

You should check vital signs at least every 15 minutes if you suspect a serious illness or injury. When the signs are returning to normal, you can decrease this to every 30 minutes, then to once every few hours when all signs are nearly normal.

The vital signs you can check in the field, without any equipment other than a watch, are:

- **pulse**
- **respiration (breathing)**
- **nailbed refill**
- **temperature**
- **level of consciousness**
- **reaction of the pupils.**

Blood pressure is an important vital sign, but you can't read it without an instrument. You can estimate if it is high or low by watching other signs.

Pulses

Pulses are caused by heartbeats. Each beat pumps a "squirt" of blood under pressure through the arteries. It is these pressure waves you feel as pulses when your fingers are above an artery. A pulse can tell you the following things:

- **Heart rate.** The speed of the pulse tells you how fast the heart is beating. The average rate in a healthy, calm person is somewhere between 60 and 100 beats per minute, with the average for adults about 72. An infant's heart rate is very rapid, close to 100 beats per minute. A child's rate is a bit slower than an infant's but faster than an adult's. An athlete may have a pulse of 50 beats per minute or even less.

Fear or excitement will make the pulse faster; rest will make it slower. Blood loss will make it faster, as the heart tries to make less blood take the same amount of oxygen to all the tissues. If fear is the cause, the pulse will slow again. If blood loss is the cause, the pulse rate will stay high, and will rise if loss continues.

Be especially alert for changes in the pulse rate. The first reading tells you something too, but compare it with later readings for the truest picture. (If you have no watch, try to compare the casualty's pulse with others in the party. Is it much faster and increasing?)

- **Blood pressure.** If much blood has been lost, the pulse will feel weak or "thready" because there is less blood for the heart to pump and the arteries are not as full.

- **Heart rhythm.** A normal heart beats regularly. Some illnesses or injuries cause the heart to beat irregularly, with "skips" or "extra beats" that are detectable in the pulse. Record these and report them to medical help.

How to Read a Pulse

You should learn to take pulses in two places – the wrist (called a radial pulse), and the neck (called a carotid pulse). The wrist

is easy to reach, but in very cold weather it may be easier to slip your hand into the casualty's parka opening and take the pulse in his neck so you don't have to remove his mitts. An injured person's hands freeze easily.

The radial (wrist) pulse is located on the thumb

Fig. 4-1: Taking a radial pulse.

side, between the tendons

and the bone. Press gently with two fingers (not your thumb). If you don't find it, move around a little, press harder or less hard. Experiment with this until you get it every time. (**Fig. 4-1**)

Count the number of beats in one minute, or take the number in 15 seconds and multiply by 4. This gives you the rate. Note if the pulse is strong or weak, and if it is regular or irregular. Write your findings down each time.

The carotid (neck) pulse is stronger; if you can't find a pulse in the wrist, try the neck pulse. It lies between the Adam's apple and the large muscle at the side of the neck. Place two fingers on the Adam's apple and slide them toward you into the hollow. (**See Fig. 2-3, p. 16**) Press very gently. If you don't feel the pulse, slide your fingers upward a little and press a little harder.

Don't reach across the throat, and don't try to feel both sides at once, as this may cause problems. Count just as with the wrist pulse.

The casualty will appreciate it if the neck pulse is taken with warm hands!

Respiration (Breathing)

Breathing can tell you things about the condition of the lungs, breathing passages, and the amount of oxygen being delivered to the tissues. You look for three things – the **rate**, **depth**, and **character**.

- **Breathing rate.** The respiratory rate (breathing speed) usually rises and falls with the pulse rate, and for much the same reasons – fear, excitement, and blood loss all make it faster. The normal speed in adults who are completely at rest is between 10 and 18 breaths per minute, although in very fit people it is often lower. (A complete inhale-exhale cycle counts as one.) Children's rates are faster, normally up to 25 or 30 breaths per minute, and infants' rates may be up to 55 breaths per minute.

  To take a breathing rate, hold the casualty's hand on his chest or belly while you take his pulse, and after the pulse is counted, leave the hand there to feel the rise and fall of his chest. Don't let the casualty know you are watching his breathing, for he may unconsciously change the rate. It is best to time it for a full minute, but you may also count for 30 seconds and multiply by 2.

- **Breathing depth.** The casualty may breathe deeply, completely filling his lungs, or shallowly, with less air exchange each time.

- **Breathing character.** Breathing may be even and effortless, which is normal, or it may be *laboured, uneven, loud, snoring, gasping, rattling, wheezing*; there are medical terms for each, but use any words that describe the character to you.

Nailbed Refill

Blood pressure cannot be estimated easily, but you can determine if a person's blood pressure is low by checking his nailbed refill. Squeeze the casualty's fingertip and nail between your own thumb and forefinger, release suddenly, and time how long it takes the nail to turn from white to its normal pink colour. If it takes longer than about two seconds (count "one-one thousand, two-one thousand" or use your watch), it indicates that blood pressure is low. If hands are severely chilled, this may not be accurate.

Temperature

Temperature (by mouth) is normally 37.5°C or 98.6°F, although it may vary one or two degrees. Without a thermometer, you can't tell exact temperature, but you can estimate if it is higher or lower than normal. A warmer than normal feel most often indicates a fever, especially if the casualty feels ill and his pulse rate is up 10 counts per minute or more. If there is a fever, look for an infection.

Chills are often related to fever. The casualty may feel much colder than the surroundings should make him, with chattering teeth and shivering that are followed by a rapidly rising temperature.

Cool, clammy skin may indicate shock. Very cool skin may indicate hypothermia. By itself, relative temperature tells you little, but combined with other signs it may tell you a lot.

To estimate temperature, place the back of your fingers against an unclothed part of the person's body, and compare the warmth with your own – but be sure that your hand is itself near a normal temperature.

Level of Consciousness

Level of consciousness (LOC) describes how alert the casualty is and how he responds to his surroundings. A variety of things can affect the LOC; head injury is an obvious one. Shock, high temperature, low temperature, nervous disorders, and low oxygen levels in the blood all influence consciousness. LOC may be an important indication of the casualty's condition by itself or when interpreted with other signs. Three types of responses are used to assess LOC – those of the eyes, the voice, and the muscles. When assessing these, note that each has three levels. Observe them and *write them down,* so you can tell later if the casualty has improved or become worse. Don't count on your memory.

Eye opening response:
- Eyes open normally and the casualty watches what is going on.
- Eyes open only when the casualty is spoken to or when pain is felt.
- Eyes do not open for any reason.

These levels are easy to identify. If the casualty watches you as you approach and work on him, he is at the first level. If he does not, speak to him. If his eyes don't open, pinch the skin on the inside of his arm or the tip of his earlobe. If they open, he is second level. If they don't, he is third level.

Verbal response:
- Alert, knows who and where he is and what happened.
- Confused, does not speak clearly, uncertain.
- Does not speak.

You should be able to determine the casualty's verbal response level by getting his history. If he knew where he was, what happened, and could answer your questions without problem, he is alert and oriented. If he was uncertain about things he should know, or didn't make sense, he is in the second category. If he did not answer at all, he is at the third level.

Motor (muscular) response (again, there are three levels):
• Obeys commands.
• Reacts to pain.
• Has no response.

When you were doing your head-to-toe exam, you asked the casualty to push his feet against your hands, or to move his arms and legs. If he did these things, he is in the first category. If he did not, but moved when you pinched him, he's in the second. If he did not move when you pinched him, he is at the third level.

By repeating these tests at intervals, you can tell whether the casualty's LOC is getting better or worse. This is important information to pass along to his physician. Remember that injury can affect any of these things, and allow for that.

Pupils

The pupils (black centres) of the eyes can indicate such things as severe brain injury, drug use, serious blood loss, even death. To check pupils, simply note whether they are equal in size. Unequal pupils indicate a severe brain injury – but some people are born with unequal pupils, so if you see a difference, ask the casualty about it.

Note if the casualty's pupils react to light. Shine a flashlight into his eyes, or shade his eyes from bright sun and watch their reaction when you pull your hand away. If they do not react or do not react equally, there may be brain injury or drug influence.

Very tiny (pinpoint) pupils may indicate drug abuse. Pupils that are dilated (very large) and will not react to light may be a sign of death, if no other vital signs are evident. To show that pupils are normal, write PERL on your checklist, which means "pupils equal and reactive to light."

A Provisional Diagnosis

When you have completed the examination, you should have a good idea of what is wrong, and you can make a "provisional diagnosis." If no medical advice is available, you can start your first aid knowing that you have discovered all you can. But you are not a doctor, and it is terribly easy to make mistakes, which can have serious consequences.

**Always get medical advice
if you possibly can!**

At the very least, you now have a good description of the casualty's signs and symptoms that you can radio to a doctor so that he can make the diagnosis and tell you what to do. And you have a record that will enable you to tell how the casualty is doing as time goes by.

How to Get Medical Advice by Radio

After you have made your secondary survey – noted the casualty's history, completed the head-to-toe exam, and recorded the vital signs – radio for medical advice and a possible air medevac. Arrange to talk directly to a doctor or nurse – don't count on a third party to relay what you have learned, for he may get it wrong. When you are talking to the doctor, don't give the casualty's name unless the doctor definitely asks for it, because the casualty may not want his name and condition announced over the air, and because listening friends and relatives may become needlessly worried. Just give the casualty's sex and age, and then read from the checklists whatever you have discovered. Do not mention your diagnosis.

Describe your situation: where you are, what kind of shelter the casualty has, what means you have to transport the casualty, and transportation time. Tell him if you have any antibiotics or other medicines. Tell him if there is an airstrip near, its condition, and the local weather. Advise if there is water that would take a floatplane. Very often you will be unable to get through next time you use the radio, or they won't be able to reach you, so give – and get – all the information you can while it is working well. Doctors may not understand this communication problem and are interested only in the casualty information, so tell him that you may not be able to talk with him again.

The doctor will tell you what to do. *Write it down!* Ask him to repeat it if there is any doubt in your mind. If you still aren't sure, read back to him what you think he said, and see if it is right. If the casualty is seriously injured or ill, you can't afford to make a mistake.

In the next chapter, you will learn how to monitor a casualty's condition so that you will know what to do and what to expect.

Death

In spite of your best efforts, you may witness an unavoidable death.

Because only a physician can legally pronounce death, and because it may be difficult for you to identify it, you must continue to do your best for a casualty and not assume that he is dead until certain unmistakable signs become evident. No harm can be done in trying to resuscitate someone whose vital functions have truly ceased, and there are numerous stories of success. However, you must be absolutely certain that there is no heartbeat or respiration, especially in a hypothermic person, before trying resuscitation.

When you are far from medical help, the chance of resuscitating someone whose vital functions have ceased as a result of trauma are slim. However, there is a reasonable chance of saving a seemingly dead casualty of drowning, electric shock (as in lightning strike), or choking.

How to Tell

The most common definition of death is permanent cessation of heartbeat and breathing. In a casualty who has suffered profound hypothermia or a near drowning in cold water, both heartbeat and breathing may be so faint and slow that they are undetectable by a layman. In these cases, *death cannot be assumed until the casualty is completely warmed and still has no vital signs.*

Some other problems may mimic death, especially coma from drug intoxication, diabetic reaction, or paralysis due to disease or drugs. If any of these are suspected, you must continue first aid and not assume death until it becomes obvious.

With the exception of the examples above, you may reasonably suspect death if:

- there is not the slightest movement or response to any sight, sound, or painful stimulus
- you are unable to detect breathing by sight, sound, or touch
- you are unable to detect heartbeat by radial (wrist) or carotid (neck) pulses or by placing an ear to the bared chest
- the casualty's pupils are mid-sized or large, and do not change size when exposed to bright light or alternating light and dark
- the casualty does not blink when the surface of his eye is touched with a piece of tissue
- there is no gag reflex when the back of the throat is stroked.

In time, three other signs become apparent. While you may still not legally pronounce death, these signs, in addition to the previous ones, leave no doubt:

- the body will cool, starting with the extremities, even in a comfortable environment
- the body will stiffen (*rigor mortis*) several hours after death
- 15 to 30 minutes after death, blood will sink to the lowest parts of the body and pool there, giving a bruised, mottled appearance (*dependent lividity*) except on pressure points.

What to Do

Your job as a first-aider and as a caring human being does not cease with a casualty's death. You must make every effort to record the circumstances, treat the deceased with dignity, and comfort friends and relatives who may be present.

If the circumstances of death are unknown or homicide is possible, *don't disturb anything* any more than is necessary to confirm death. You should:

- leave the body as you found it
- rope off the area for a hundred feet around the body and allow no disturbance by human or animal
- notify the police authorities
- record what you have seen and done in as much detail as possible
- keep watch on the body until the authorities have arrived, and advise them of all that has taken place.

If the death has occured from observed trauma or illness, you should stay in control and:

- treat the body and all observers with sympathy and dignity
- record your observations, including the time you made them
- close the eyelids and straighten the body for transportation before it stiffens
- cover the body and protect it from insect and animal disturbance
- notify medical or police authorities, if possible
- identify (tag) the body with name, next of kin, and the time and date you first examined it.

In no case should the name of the deceased be mentioned on the radio. Simply advise authorities that there is a deceased person present, and let them ask the questions.

People in the wilderness usually do what they have to do, and most emotional problems occur after the need for action is over. Consult your physician, nurse, or spiritual counselor for guidance in dealing with any strong emotional reaction. Sharing your feelings with others who have been involved in the event is often healing.

Part II

How to Care for a Casualty in the Wilderness

5

How to Keep a Casualty Warm

The Vulnerability of the Sick and Injured

People who need help in the northern wilderness are almost always in some danger from heat loss. Controlling heat loss is considered a high priority, following the ABCDEF's. It is easy to forget that the casualty is far more vulnerable to cold than the rescuer, even if he is warmly dressed. He is vulnerable for many reasons.

- Anyone whose blood pressure is lower than normal will have less circulation to the skin. Lower blood pressure may be caused by shock, medications, prolonged rest, or a variety of illnesses.

- Ill persons often burn food and eliminate wastes less efficiently, and so produce less heat.

- An ill person may be unable to eat, so his body will not have the fuel to burn.

- Ill persons often become dehydrated. (See Chapter 1.) Dehydration makes the blood thicker and slows circulation in the fine blood vessels, reducing warmth to that area.

- Ill persons who are not completely alert may be unable to feel or to tell you that they are losing heat. You must then think for them to prevent heat loss.

Because of this vulnerability and the environment, hypothermia is a threat to almost every casualty, and must be watched for and prevented. Frostbite, too, can occur quickly, even with sleeping bags or clothing that would keep a healthy person adequately warm.

**Never assume that because you are warm,
a casualty is also warm.**

How to Reduce Heat Loss

The sick and injured lose heat the same ways healthy people do, but they lose it more quickly. The remedies are the same too, but when a single sleeping bag is enough to keep you warm, an injured person may require *twice* the thickness to keep him warm. *If you err, err on the side of warmth.* It is easy to cool someone quickly, but it is difficult to warm him up after heat has been lost.

Here are some basic rules for maintaining body heat in casualties:

- **Remove damp or wet clothing as quickly as possible**, and replace it with dry clothing. Water carries heat away many times faster than air, so wet clothing must be removed.

- **Protect the casualty as soon as possible**, using less compressible material beneath. Heat loss to the ground or snow is great. The weight of the body compresses clothing or insulation below it and reduces its warmth.

- **Do not leave a casualty covered with waterproof materials such as plastic or coated nylon.** The water vapour from his body will condense (turn to water droplets) when it touches the cold material, and will make the insulation wet. EXCEPTIONS: warming a hypothermic casualty, preventing heat loss in high winds, and covering casualties against rain. Wherever possible, leave space between a waterproof cover and the insulating material to reduce condensation.

- **Provide extra padding for the head and neck.** These areas lose heat faster than others. A person in a sleeping bag loses a great deal of heat from his neck. Use an extra piece of dry clothing as a neck drape, but be sure that there is no danger of strangulation.

- **Provide extra padding to pressure points.** Wherever the casualty pushes tightly against his sleeping bag, the bag becomes thinner and should be padded with extra clothing. These points are commonly over the knees, under the hips, under the heels, and over the toes. Heavy socks should provide well for the feet. If the casualty is lying on his side, the pressure points will be shoulder, hip, knee, and foot. If a double bag is used, there may be no need for extra point insulation.

- **Protect the casualty from wind chill.** Check the casualty often if the wind is blowing, as it will greatly speed his heat loss.

- **In severe cold, provide a parka tunnel for the casualty.** A good parka hood with fur ruff drawn into a tunnel will provide a pocket of prewarmed, humidified (moistened) air around his face, which will reduce heat loss from the neck and face, reduce dehydration, and reduce the risk of facial frostbite. If it is not practical for the casualty to wear a parka, a partial hood may be improvised.

Heating Aids for Casualties

In severe cold it may be necessary to provide the casualty with something that will produce heat. A variety of heating aids may be improvised. They all have a common danger.

Casualties who have reduced circulation to their skin, or who are not fully alert, are easily burned by temperatures that would not injure a normal person.

When skin circulation is low, the blood does not carry off excess heat as fast, and heat may build up in the skin tissues. At the same time, the skin is less sensitive to pain, and the casualty may not feel a developing burn.

This means that any hot-water bottle or substitute must be very carefully wrapped in thick cloth so that it cannot work loose, and must then be tested and found to be only comfortably warm by the first-aider.

Another danger is leaking. Never use a container that will leak even slightly. Heat it fully, then seal it, shake it, turn it upside down, and squeeze it as hard as you can to test for leakage.

Placing Body Heaters

Cold feet are a common complaint, and a single device at the feet will prevent this. A casualty with a leg fracture may have impaired circulation to that foot, and the foot, even inside a bag, may be in danger of cold injury. *It is important that the heater does not provide direct heat to the fracture site, as that will promote swelling.*

Remember that a heater at the feet will cool off faster than one against the body.

Cold hands are also common. A (not too heavy!) heater placed on the casualty's belly will allow him to fold his hands on it, and it will also provide heat to his body in general.

General coldness is best fought by placing heaters over the major arteries of the groin, against the chest wall under the arms, or against the neck. Any of these may warm the casualty quickly, so watch him and do not allow him to overheat.

Casualties who can move around in their bags and can curl up may find that curling around a device will make it last longer and provide excellent general warming, as almost all of the heat is absorbed by the surrounding body. (This is also a survival trick well worth remembering!)

Improvising Hot-Water Bottles or Body Heaters

Commercial heating pads and hot-water bottles are of course ideal, but rarely found on a wilderness trip. Chemical pads are convenient, but if they are frozen when you need them they are worthless. They must be at room temperature to be activated and to perform as advertised.

Excellent body heaters can be improvised, with caution. *The larger and heavier an object, the more heat it will store.* Heaters about 1 quart or litre in size are practical, and can usually be insulated well with several layers of extra socks, or with extra kamiks or mukluks.

Glass bottles and jars full of hot water are excellent if leakproof. Water stores a great deal of heat. In subzero weather, the water won't freeze, so is available later for drinking or first-aid use. The bottle or jar when empty may then be pressed into use as a (male) urinal within the sleeping bag, and when tightly resealed, may then be pushed down to provide minor warmth to the feet. *Danger! Be sure a bottle used as a urinal is warm. If it is very cold, the warm urine may cause it to shatter.*

Plastic bottles and jars are also excellent, but may deform somewhat with very hot water, so test them carefully for leakage.

Hot rocks are good *if not heated too much.* An excessively hot rock will burn the wrapping and probably the casualty. It is best to heat these *beside* the fire over a longer time, rather than *in* it. *Beware of cracked or porous rocks which may contain water and explode violently when heated!* Best are solid, rounded rocks of granite which are found well away from water.

In some cases, you can maintain a continuous supply of hot rocks by wiring a couple of properly shaped rocks against the exhaust pipe in the engine compartment of a snowmobile. However, there is then the risk of a rock becoming loose in the engine compartment.

Sealed tin cans containing liquids (best) or foods (not as good) are easy to use, although the smaller ones cool quickly. *Never heat a closed can over direct heat,* as it will explode violently when steam is generated. Almost all commercial canning is done at boiling temperature, so you may cover cans with water in a pot and bring them just to a boil. Watch them constantly, and if the lids start to swell, remove them from heat immediately. Canned food used for body heating will remain unfrozen in a sleeping bag, and may later be used for a pre-warmed meal on the trail when it has served its purpose.

Oil bottles and cans, litre or quart size, containing snowmobile, outboard, or chain-saw oil, make excellent body heaters if they are leakproof. They are a convenient size, are comfortable to handle, and their oil will store much heat. They may be used with the oil in them, heated in hot water like the cans. Watch them carefully during heating, and remove if they begin to deform or swell. Again, these will pour easily after they cool, which makes later use for their intended purpose much easier if weather is 30° or 40° below zero.

Hot sandbags make good heaters. Sand or salt (not sugar, which will melt) may be heated in a pan, then poured into a bag or closely woven sock.

Metal objects are poor heaters, because they transmit their heat very quickly and tend to burn insulating fabrics. They may be heated by direct heat or in boiling water, which is safer.

In an emergency on the trail, rescuers may urinate into a leakproof bottle and use the bottle to warm a casualty's feet or hands threatened by frostbite. The heat is minor, but may be adequate to stave off cold injury.

A warm body may also be used to warm a cold casualty, as in emergency hypothermia treatment. If no other source is convenient and the casualty is seriously cold, this must be considered. Skin-to-skin contact is quickest, as it takes a long time for heat to pass through winter clothing. In severe cases, "sandwiching" a casualty between two rescuers may be required. It may also be necessary to "relay" a series of bodies, and this provides the warming rescuer an opportunity to rest.

This idea is usually greeted with much good-natured laughter, but it does work. Be assured, however, that warming a seriously hypothermic casualty, no matter how attractive, is about as much fun as cuddling up to a side of meat from a refrigerator!

Heat from Inside

In the north, our most dependable heat is that which we generate ourselves, through the burning of food in our bodies.

**In every case where cold is a problem and a casualty
can take food without danger, keeping the casualty
well-nourished is a high priority.**

CAUTION: Food should not be given to casualties who are or
may become nauseated, because vomiting creates a risk of
choking, robs the body of fluids, and drains energy. Ordinarily,
injured persons are most likely to be nauseated shortly after the
injury, and may improve after a time.

What to Feed Casualties for Heat Production

When we eat, our digestion transforms food – especially
starches and sugars – into blood sugar (glucose) and other solutions, which enter our blood stream. Blood sugar is quickly con-
verted to energy fuel for the body to use.

For quick heat, starchy or sugary foods are ideal.

Liquid foods are most easily tolerated by casualties, and
provide much-needed fluids too, so sweet drinks are high on
the list. Coffee and tea, however, also encourage urination and
may promote dehydration, so other sweet drinks are preferred.

Fats and proteins produce the most heat over a longer period,
but are slower to digest and may be more likely to cause nausea.

Feeding "Heat Foods" – Some Basic Rules:

- Do not feed anyone who is nauseated, in shock, has internal or
  head injury or a severe stomach ailment, or is not fully alert.

- Feed only non-fatty liquids at first. Warm, sweet liquids will
  produce body heat fastest. Soups and salty liquids will help
  to restore blood components if blood or fluids have been
  lost. Avoid coffee at first. Tea should be weak. Avoid alcohol
  completely.

- Starches and sugars will produce heat rapidly. Candy, sugar,
  dried fruit, breads, and jams are all good and are common
  camp foods.

- Feed small amounts often, rather than lots at once.

- Fats and meats should be held until the casualty is sure he can hold them down, then fed in small amounts.

External Heat Sources

A camp that feels comfortably warm to a healthy person may feel cold to an ill or injured person. When a casualty is moved to a warm camp for assessment and first aid, be certain that the air is as warm as possible before your remove his clothing.

Campfires are poor heat sources unless the casualty is between the fire and some reflecting surface. Reflection may be greatly improved by using an aluminized rescue blanket or strips of aluminum foil.

When there is no snow on the ground, the earth may be warmed by a campfire which is then thoroughly scraped away to provide a warm sleeping surface. It must be well covered with boughs or other insulation, so that the casualty is not burned or overheated. This heat will last for many hours.

Kerosene heaters and naphtha appliances are commonly used to heat tents. In the rush to heat an emergency treatment tent, several may be used at once, but the risk of carbon monoxide (CO) poisoning is greatly increased. (See Chapter 24 for more about CO poisoning.) Remember that the casualty may be much more vulnerable to carbon monoxide than a healthy person.

If a cold casualty is brought into a warm tent or cabin, remember that it will take a long time for warmth to penetrate a sleeping bag. It may be necessary to open the bag so that the warmer air can more readily get to the casualty. Feel inside the bag to determine if it is warmer or cooler than the surrounding air.

External Heat Sources Versus Shivering

Shivering is the body's natural defence mechanism against heat loss. The peak of shivering intensity occurs at a deep body temperature of about 35°C (approx. 95°F), which represents the transition from mild to moderate hypothermia. A casualty who is not shivering from exposure is either adequately warm or so hypothermic that body function has been severely impaired.

As a severely hypothermic (non-shivering) casualty is being rewarmed, shivering will again set in and increase in intensity as the body approaches 35°C (95°F). Shivering is an excellent source of internal heat production, and it will warm the body more rapidly than most field rewarming techniques. When you consider using external heat, keep in mind that its use may blunt the natural shivering response and consequently slow the rewarming process.

6

How to Give "Second Aid"

In a wilderness situation, there may be long delays in getting to medical help. Casualties may need care for many hours or even days, often in primitive conditions, usually with few medical supplies or medications. The first-aider must then become a "second-aider." Don't underestimate the importance of this expanded role – your aid may make a critical difference to the casualty.

Fortunately, if the human body is well nourished and allowed to rest, it will often begin to heal without medical help. Even if it is not healing, good care will buy time until help can be reached. In this chapter, you will learn how to care for a sick or injured companion while awaiting the chance to move him to medical care.

The main concerns in wilderness care are breathing care, warmth, position, morale, rest, fluids, diet (food), care of body functions (bowel care and urination), and observing and recording (monitoring).

Breathing Care

When a person is inactive for long periods, his lungs do not expand fully. Fluids and mucus may build up, which may encourage bacterial growth and pneumonia, especially if he has a chest injury.

Encourage the patient to take deep breaths and cough often, *even if it is painful.* If injuries permit, raise him to a sitting position and have him hold his sides and cough deeply.

A patient should not smoke, especially if he has chest or lung problems. Smoking reduces the amount of oxygen delivered to the tissues. Explain this to him. And if *he* can't smoke, don't *you* smoke where he can smell it.

Warmth

See Chapter 5, "How to Keep a Casualty Warm."

Position

Body position may have a profound effect on the patient. Often, he may want to get into a position other than lying on his back (supine). If he can do this without injury, let him try it. You rarely go wrong if you allow a resting patient to get into his own "position of comfort."

Certain positions will produce specific results, as follows:

- **The recovery position**, also called a drainage position, is used (if injuries permit) when the patient is unconscious, not fully alert, or is nauseated and may vomit. It is useful if drainage or bleeding into the mouth interferes with breathing. (**See again Fig. 1-1d, p. 3**) If the patient is fully alert, he may prefer to sit in order to vomit or clear breathing passages.

- **The sitting or the semi-sitting** position makes breathing easier, as it reduces the pressure of the abdominal organs on the diaphragm. It is valuable in most cases where there are breathing problems – chronic obstructive pulmonary disease (COPD), asthma, pneumonia, chronic bronchitis, emphysema, heart attack, lung injury. Such a patient may insist on sitting up. Let him!

  Sitting may also improve morale, so allow a patient to sit if he wishes and his injuries permit. If he is ill enough that sitting has a bad effect, he will automatically want to lie flat again. You must, however, use good judgement if there is a possible spine injury.

  If you can raise the foot of the stretcher slightly when you

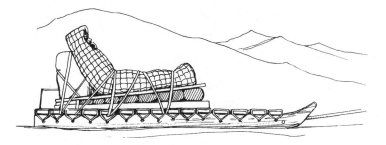

Fig. 6-1: Transport sitting casualties with feet slightly raised to prevent sliding down.

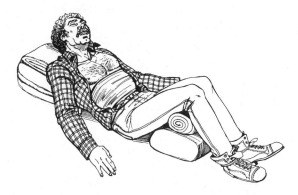

Fig. 6-2: Bent knees provide more comfort for casualties with injury to belly.

prop him up, the patient will tend not to slide down so much and will be more comfortable. **(Fig. 6-1)** If he is sitting in a moving sled or boat, raising the foot of the stretcher is essential – otherwise he will slide down.

- **The knees-raised position** reduces tension on the front of the chest and abdomen, and is more comfortable when there is an injury or ailment in the chest or abdominal area. Provide a cushion for support under the knees. Sometimes it will help to raise the head and chest slightly too. **(Fig. 6-2)**

- **Shock position**, on his back (supine) with legs slightly raised, or with the foot of the stretcher slightly raised, is valuable for shock or faintness. If the patient is in shock but also has trouble breathing, do not raise the foot of the stretcher; raise his legs only so that the intestines don't push up against the diaphragm. **(See again Fig. 1-3, p. 10)**

- **Elevation of injured arms or legs** will help to reduce swelling from most causes, and will also reduce bleeding there. Raising the legs will increase the flow of the blood returning to the heart.

Position Changes

If a patient must remain lying down for long periods, his position, for comfort, should be changed frequently. Moving also helps to prevent pressure sores (bedsores). These are not usually a problem unless the patient is unmoving for several days, but can occur in a few hours if a patient is strapped to an unpadded board. Try to move an immobile patient slightly every two hours or so.

Whenever a patient is transported for hours on a backboard, the board *must* be well padded.

If sores develop, clean and manage them as you would an infected wound, and *avoid any further pressure on them.*

Morale (Patient Attitude)

Reassurance continues to be important during every moment of care. A patient may fear for his life. He may fear unavoidable pain. He may fear becoming permanently handicapped or disfigured. A strong person may hate to be weak or dependent. Everyone hates to lose dignity.

His feelings will have an effect on his physical condition, so it is up to you to continue to reassure him as part of your care. Here are some ways you can maintain his spirits:

- **Keep your own attitude cheerful and optimistic**, even if you do not feel that way. If you look or act worried, he will worry too.

- **Reassure the patient often.** Explain what you are doing to care for him. Do not present him with obvious lies (don't tell him "You're going to be just fine" if he won't be) but be as upbeat as possible.

- **Touch the patient often** in a comforting, companionable way. Warm human contact is a major part of reassurance.

- **Don't discuss the patient's condition in his hearing**, unless you can be very optimistic.

- **Involve him in his own care.** Encourage him to do whatever he reasonably can. Have him hold things while you change dressings, let him wash himself, feed himself, take care of bathroom calls. The less helpless he is and the more he can retain his dignity, the better his morale will be.

- **Keep him informed of your plans.** If you plan to move him by sled as soon as the weather improves, tell him. If you have sent someone for help, if you expect an air medevac, tell him. Uncertainty is a powerful enemy of optimism. If you are pinned down by bad weather, you have to admit it – but tell him what you will do the moment the weather breaks.

Rest

Rest promotes healing, reduces tendencies to bleed or swell, and often reduces pain and stress. Sometimes, pain will prevent adequate rest. If pain medicines are available and used as prescribed, they will help.

Fluids

Maintaining a proper fluid intake is one of the most important things you can do for a sick person who is far from help.

When you see a very sick person under medical care, he will usually be getting intravenous (IV) fluids. There is nothing magic about such fluids. They are mostly water, with a little sugar and/or salt and a few other minor items added. In the wilderness, you can do almost as much good with oral fluids, if the patient can take them.

To give or not to give fluids by mouth is one of the most vexing problems for the rescuer. Fluids should *not* be given to patients with certain internal injuries and ailments, or when they cause vomiting. Unfortunately, the rescuer is not always able to identify these cases. And unfortunately, dehydration over a day or two may cause more damage than small amounts of fluid, even when they are not recommended in normal first-aid practice.

Here are some rules of thumb to help guide you:

- **Attempt to get medical advice if in doubt.**

- **Give no fluids if the patient is unconscious, nauseated or vomiting, or has abdominal injuries.**

- **Give only small amounts at first** until you determine that the patient will not vomit. Always be ready for vomiting.

- **Give small amounts often** rather than lots at once. If he can barely swallow, give him sips every 5 or 10 minutes.

- **Give nutritious fluids.** Soups and fruit juices are excellent. The liquid from boiled meat is wonderful, and makes a good substitute for coffee and tea if the patient is accustomed to them. Avoid all alcohol – also coffee, tea, and hot chocolate, as these diuretics cause more frequent urination and increase dehydration.

- **Give water or rehydration solution** to any shock, burn, or dehydration patient who can tolerate it.

- **Maintain liquid intake of at least 5 to 6 litres or quarts per day.** If severe illness or injury are factors, requirements may be increased. Measure how much he takes, and write it down. The patient should urinate 3 or 4 times each day. If he shows signs of dehydration, encourage him to drink more.

Remember that these are very general rules. Certain conditions will call for more or less fluid, and these are explained later in the text.

Diet (Food)

If the patient feels like eating, let him, unless he has certain abdominal problems. In general, avoid giving food if you think shock may occur. If a patient is already "shocky" he will probably not want to eat anyway. If you do feed a patient who is in shock, he will not be able to digest the food and it will make him vomit.

No food should be given to patients with acute abdomen (see Chapter 22), appendicitis, or a penetrating injury of the abdomen.

Feed the patient energy foods such as porridges of cereal, rice, or potato. You may add a little vegetable oil or margarine and some sugar to the porridge for added energy. Breads are also suitable. Bannock is good if the patient can tolerate the large amount of fat in it. Fruit juices are good food as well as drink, as is liquid Jello.

Give body-building foods such as meat, milk, cheese, eggs, fish, fruit, and vegetables – especially during recovery. If the patient is weak and cannot eat easily, make these into soups. The liquid from boiled game meat is one of the best possible foods and fluids.

If the patient can eat only a little at a time, feed him small amounts several times a day.

Some problems, such as diabetes, gallbladder attacks, ulcers, and "heartburn" require special diets.

Bowel Care

Patients who eat little, move little, don't drink enough, and resist the urge to defecate may easily get constipated and become unable to have a bowel movement. Patients who are receiving codeine are especially vulnerable.

Be sure that patients are kept well hydrated and move whenever possible. If they can walk a little without difficulty, encourage them to do so. Tell them not to put off bowel movements or be embarrassed by them.

Urination

If a patient can't get up, give him a urinal or bedpan, which can be improvised from a jar or cooking pan. Record how often he urinates and about how much. Check his urine for blood and for dark colour or strong odour, both signs of dehydration. A healthy individual will urinate at least 1,000 mL (about 4 cups) every 24 hours. If he voids less, suspect dehydration or shock.

Observing and Recording (Monitoring)

In order to tell if your patient is improving or getting worse, you must check his condition frequently. *Always write down your observations on your checklists* (see Appendix D), and record the time and date, as these are easy to forget.

When the patient is sent to medical help, send the records with him. Give them to an attendant or tuck them into his clothing against his skin where they will be found even if he is unconscious. The information may be vital to the doctor or nurse.

Use the chart on your checklists to record vital signs, or make your own chart, showing date, time, pulse, breathing, nailbed refill, temperature, level of consciousness, and reaction of the pupils. The level of consciousness (LOC) and the reaction of the pupils are especially important if the patient has a head injury, but need not be taken if the patient is alert and seems to be recovering. Pulse, breathing, and temperature should be watched carefully at all times.

Watch for changes! Increasing pulse and breathing may indicate continued bleeding or increasing shock. Slower nailbed refill and other shock signs and symptoms confirm this. Rising temperature with rising pulse and breathing may indicate infection. Decreasing alertness accompanies brain injury, increasing shock, hypothermia, severe infection, and some other disorders such as diabetes. Reading the first-aid treatment for individual injuries and ailments will give you other clues.

Take the vital signs every 15 minutes if the patient is in critical condition. As he improves, you may reduce this from every 30 minutes to once every few hours when all signs are nearly normal.

7

How to Move a Casualty to Help

Every person with a major illness or injury should be taken to medical help. After the first aid – and maybe the second aid – has been given, you must ask yourself, "Is it *safe* to move this person? If so, *how* should we move him?" The answers could be a matter of life or death.

If you are in contact with medical authorities, you should leave the decision to them. Give them all the facts and let them decide. Here is where your examination and recording will be of tremendous value. In most cases, authorities will try to arrange an air medevac if it is needed. This is the best possible method; it is fastest and is easiest on the casualty. In critical cases, advanced life support can be brought to the casualty. In some cases, military Search and Rescue Technicians have been parachuted into rough country to help people in difficulty.

If you cannot contact medical advice, you must make the decision. If you are in doubt, transport the casualty.

**For anything you think is serious,
first try for an air medevac.**

If you must move the casualty yourself, first answer some important questions.

- **Has the casualty "stabilized"?**
- **Is there a suitable means of transport?**
- **Will the move be hard on the casualty?**
- **Is there a time problem?**

- **Are there dangers on the route?**
- **Can the casualty be cared for during the journey?**

Has the casualty "stabilized"?

Right after an injury, a casualty's condition may be changing rapidly. Bleeding may not have stopped. Vital signs may be changing rapidly as his system attempts to compensate. He may be frightened. Swelling may be increasing. He may not yet have developed all the signs which will tell you what is wrong. *Do not rush into a long transport!*

Wait for the casualty to "stabilize," and give yourself time to discover the full extent of injury or illness, and to give the best possible first aid.

If an injury is critical and the casualty is failing rapidly, it will probably do no good to rush into a rough journey of many hours or days. Hard travel may kill him. However, this may be a difficult call if help is only a few hours away.

Is there a suitable means of transport?

If there is any question about being able to make the trip safely, without breakdown or delay, or without danger to the casualty, you should balance your options carefully.

Will the move be hard on the casualty?

Certain injuries, such as major fractures of the upper leg or pelvis, may be so painful on movement that the roughness of land transport would be unbearable, and possibly increase shock or do more damage. The movement of travel may cause some soft tissue and internal injuries to bleed. Persons who are suffering from severe infections may be unable to stand the difficulties of travel.

Your observations and your knowledge of the transport methods at hand should tell you if you should try a move.

Is there a time problem?

You may know that a storm is due in a day or so, and that you will be pinned down for some time, or that the ice is becoming dangerous for travel, or that tides will not be suitable.

Are there dangers on the route?

If there are, will you be able to keep the casualty safe and cared for all the way? Will you be taking a serious risk yourself? Might you get stranded without good shelter?

Can the casualty be cared for during the journey?

Consider what sort of care he will need. Are there enough hands to provide this and keep the party safe? If the casualty is unconscious, is there someone who can monitor him constantly? Will you be able to provide fluids and food, manage bowel and bladder functions, change dressings if needed, adjust splints or bandages, check circulation, or whatever is required, without exposing the casualty to severe cold or yourself to danger of any sort?

Packaging for Transport

Transport over northern land or by small boat can be quite rough. The casualty may bounce around or vibrate. Bandages and splints tend to loosen and the movement will hasten the process. Wind chill generated by movement alone may be severe, so the casualty must be covered for warmth.

At the same time, the attendant will need access to check injuries and help with the casualty's bowel and bladder functions.

This demands careful "packaging" of the casualty, so that your first aid is not undone. Here are some rules for packaging:

- **Be sure that all splints are held firmly.** Add extra bandages if necessary to ensure that splints do not loosen. A full wrap (except over the wound) with gauze or crêpe bandage will help.

- **Be sure nothing is too tight.** Anything which is even slightly uncomfortable before starting will become painful later. Swelling may cut off circulation.

- **Splint the joints around a major cut**, so that movement will not open it.

If the casualty is on a backboard and will be transported by land or boat:

- Be sure the board is well padded. Use padding equal to 1 or 2 inches of soft foam. If using closed-cell foam pad, you can use 2 or 3 thicknesses. (*Do not* use 3-inch or 4-inch foamies on a board for back injuries, because they allow too much movement.)

- Be sure body hollows are padded at neck, back, and knees.

- Fill the spaces beside the body with rolled blankets or other pads to keep the casualty from shifting. (**Fig. 7-1**)

- Place board on two 3-inch or 4-inch foam pads, and fasten them securely. These will act as shock absorbers.

- Secure board to a sled with quick-release knots or straps so that board and casualty can be tipped together quickly if he vomits. Do *not* tie a backboard or stretcher into a boat.

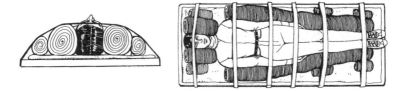

Fig. 7-1: Casualty secured with blanket rolls to prevent shifting.

If the casualty is splinted, but not on a board:

- Place the casualty on a foamie+board+foamie sandwich to provide good padding and shock absorption with some stiffness.

- Pad a splinted arm or leg into a comfortable, slightly raised position so that it cannot move.

- Place the casualty in his position of comfort.

If body movement will not hurt the casualty:

- Place him on two pads, as above, without the board.

- Pad him if he wishes, with head and legs slightly raised so that he won't slide down and so that he can see. (**See again Fig. 6-1, p. 63**) This will help his morale. As his face will be exposed to wind, provide a scarf or facemask for cold.

For all casualties:

- Provide sunglasses, a cap, insect repellant for his face, and a handkerchief if conditions warrant. Remember that anything you need, he will also need.

- Provide a sealable urine container for a male casualty if he can help himself. For a woman, carry an improvised bedpan inside the bag in cold weather to keep it warm. (*Remember not to use a very cold glass container for a urinal, as it may shatter from the quick temperature change when warm urine hits it!*)

- Provide "diaper" or soaker pads if the casualty is unable to help himself. Place a sheet of plastic beneath these to keep the sleeping bag dry.

- Provide snack foods and liquids inside the sleeping bag if the casualty is able to tolerate them. Be sure to do this if weather is below freezing.

- Put some extra clothing inside the bag so the casualty can pad cold or hard spots as they develop.

- Pack first-aid supplies where you can reach them quickly for dressing changes or retying splints.

- Place an attendant where he can observe the casualty's face constantly. This is *critical* if the casualty is unconscious or has breathing problems. It is less important if his airway is not threatened and he is fully alert.

- Cover the casualty with a windproof tarp to protect him from wind, snow, and rain. If available, use a canvas tarp rather than plastic to prevent condensation. If it is raining, use plastic for protection. (In a strong wind, condensation will be less.)

- Secure the casualty so that his injury can be reached with minimum "unpacking."

Transport Methods

The most common overland transport methods for casualties in the north are hand-carried stretchers, various sleds and toboggans, riding directly on snowmobiles and all-terrain vehicles (ATV's), or in ATV trailers. Water transport is usually by canoe or open boat, cabin cruiser or fishing boat.

Hand-Carried Stretchers

Stretchers are rarely used for long evacuations because of the slow pace, enormous effort, and large number of carriers they require.

All stretchers should be well padded for warmth, and the casualty well secured so that he will not shift when tipped. Rolls of blanket or fabric along either side of his body will help greatly. (See again Fig. 7-1)

Three stretcher types are common: improvised, flat canvas, and basket.

Improvised stretchers are rarely comfortable, rigid, or easily carried, and long carries should be avoided. Buttons or zippers used to fasten them often fail suddenly, so backup ties are required.

Improvised backboards from cabin doors, boat floorboards, etc., are often heavy, difficult to handle, and hard to secure a casualty to, and may be too big to fit into a small aircraft for medevac. If possible, boards should be no wider than the casualty's shoulders and may be slightly less.

Flat canvas stretchers are fairly common, and are often military surplus. They should be tested carefully before use, as the canvas may be rotten. Casualties must be well secured, and this may be difficult.

Basket stretchers are generally the best, especially in rough country. They provide good casualty protection (unless leg splints protrude), and are rigid. If lined with a plastic tarp, they provide dry transport even in poor conditions. Older models are usually made of metal rod and chicken wire. They are good for carrying as the top bar can be gripped almost anywhere along its length; however, they will not slide well on snow and the casualty must be well protected from cold, wet, and snow beneath.

Newer models are often bright orange plastic. They have a large and comfortable top bar for gripping, but the number of possible hand positions is often limited by the construction, and the hand cutouts are often too small to accept heavy mitts. For this reason, if such a stretcher is available, slightly enlarge the hand cutouts using a sabre saw.

Plastic stretchers can easily be slid on snow or ice and provide good casualty protection, *but must be used with caution.* They are usually advertised as being good in any temperature, but the head end has been known to break when slid on snow in cold weather.

Carrying Stretchers

Stretcher carries of more than a few miles should not be considered unless there is no other way and many helpers are available. A good number for a journey of several miles is 15 to 20, rotating often.

Ideally, six persons should carry the stretcher at once unless the casualty is very small. Even if one or two slip, the others will usually be able to hold the stretcher. Bearers should change position often, about every five minutes. Do not wait to move until your hand is very tired, as it will take much longer to recover. A regular rotation should be arranged. One system that works well is shown in **Fig. 7-2.** Everybody moves forward in pairs with each change, and the pair in front moves to the rear.

If the casualty can see what is happening, carry him feet first. Carry him head first going uphill and feet first going down,

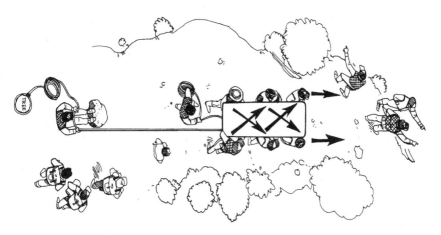

Fig. 7-2: Typical stretcher team rotation.

unless he is in shock and it will help to have his head lower.

Use whatever straps are available and make shoulder loops to take the weight off your hands. Remove the shoulder loops on very rough ground or while carrying on sidehills, so that you can keep the stretcher level.

On steep ground, one or two ropes may be attached to the head of the stretcher and used to secure descents. This will add safety and give support and steadiness to the bearers. On continuous steep ground, the two belayers may "leapfrog" each other, so that one is ready to take the belay as soon as the rope runs out.

Belaying is best done by passing the rope around a tree or rock, as the added friction will allow one man to better support the weight. (**Fig. 7-3a**) If neither a tree nor a rock is available, the belayer may sit in a well-braced position and let the rope pass around his waist, so that he can give some support without being pulled out of position. (**Fig. 7-3b**)

Safety note: On steep ground, the persons above the stretcher must always take care not to kick loose any rocks onto those below. It is best not to follow directly behind the stretcher in this case. If there is the potential for rockfall, try to protect the helpless casualty by putting a hard hat on him or by building up

Fig. 7-3a: Protect the stretcher and bearers on steep ground with a belay around a tree or rock.

ATTACHED TO STRETCHER

Fig. 7-3b: Protect stretcher and bearers with a sitting hip belay if no tree or other solid anchor is available.

padding around his head and shoulders with, for example, extra sleeping bags.

Transport by Sled

All types of sled transport can be very rough. The faster the sled, the colder the ride.

The casualty must be extremely well padded against bumps and cold. Komatiks and western dogsleds with flat bottoms are especially cold underneath. If a sled with high sides is available, it should be used, as the possibility of roll-over is always present. **(Fig. 7-4)**

In areas where komatiks are used, build up other luggage at the casualty's head and feet, so that he is protected in case of roll-over.

Almost all sleds are built with tied joints so they will flex but not break. This means that the "bed" of the sled will usually twist slightly as it moves over rough snow. If the casualty has a major fracture, he should have a rigid board between him and the sled bottom.

The casualty must be well tied down so that bouncing does not move him.

The rear of any sled gives the smoothest ride, so, if possible, place the casualty there. He will prefer to ride facing forward, but if the injury is a bad leg fracture, you may want to place him with his injury at the very rear to reduce pounding.

The driver should be able to observe the casualty at all times.

Dogsleds

Dog transport is less predictable than snowmobile/sled transport. *Never* leave a casualty unattended with the team hitched up, as he will be helpless if the team moves unexpectedly.

If snow is deep and soft, it may be desirable to have another team go ahead to break trail. If trees are present, the lead team can drag a small spruce or fir, butt first, to plough a trail. This not only makes the pulling easier for the following sled but will reveal hidden bumps. If the trailbreakers are a half-hour or so ahead, the snow will have time to recrystallize and create a firmer and faster surface.

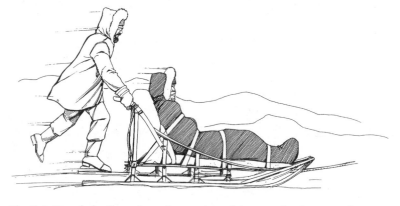

Fig. 7-4: Dogsleds allow close observation of the casualty, but are often too small to allow casualty to lie down.

Snowmobile Sleds

Sleds pulled by snowmobiles are faster and more predictable than dogsleds, but are noisy, and the added speed may make them rougher to ride.

Four types of sleds are in common use – the freight toboggan, the western dogsled in various forms, the komatik, and the "skimmer" or akio. If the sled is on a short rigid hitch, the casualty will be in the exhaust fumes unless there is a good cross wind. If the injury or illness has produced shock or shortness of breath, this should be considered before starting the move, as the carbon monoxide in the exhaust may slightly reduce the casualty's ability to absorb oxygen. A rescuer should take a short experimental ride on the sled before determining the extent of the problem. He cannot smell carbon monoxide, but he can smell the exhaust fumes.

A further hazard is snow and slush thrown up by the track. The casualty must be well covered and protected. If the machine runs through overflow on lake or river ice, the sled may be plastered with frozen slush and water. If this is expected, a good tarp cover is essential and the casualty's face should be shielded.

Freight Toboggans. Long, narrow toboggans are often used to haul freight. Some are quite narrow, so that a casualty's shoulders will not fit across; these are unsuitable for transport unless the casualty is protected by something like a basket stretcher. All such toboggans are quite flexible, so a rigid backboard must be used to transport casualties with fractures. Some have vertical "handlebar" attachments for a rider, which will allow an attendant to ride while observing the casualty.

Western-Type Dogsleds. A variety of dogsled types are pulled by snowmobiles. These tend to be small, flexible, and more "tippy" than others, but generally have a place for someone to ride standing on the runners. This allows an attendant to watch the casualty continuously while being alert to protect against tipping.

Komatiks. The komatik-type sleds are sturdy and stable, but are especially rough riding behind snowmobiles, particularly on bumpy sea ice, and may be poor for transporting major fractures. The very long, loose rope hitches often used on them are extremely unsafe if there is a casualty on board, so if possible a rigid hitch should be used.

Komatiks are big enough that an attendant can easily ride with the casualty. (**Fig. 7-5**) Komatiks with built-up passenger boxes provide good protection from wind and weather. Be sure that the casualty is loaded toward the rear of a komatik.

Fig. 7-5: Komatiks provide room for both casualty and attendant, but require good padding to reduce pounding.

Fig. 7-6: Skimmers provide good protection but ride close to the snowmobile exhaust and make observation of the casualty difficult.

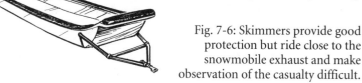

"Skimmers" or Akios. The small, boat-shaped skimmers, usually made of aluminum or fibreglass, look like an oversized basket stretcher and generally have a rigid hitch. (**Fig. 7-6**) The high sides provide excellent protection for the casualty, and make it easy to rig a good cover. They are quite rigid and flex very little, so they are good for casualties with fractures. However, they may be short for a full femur splint. In addition, they are usually quite small, and do not allow for an attendant to ride along. Thus, the driver has to turn often to monitor the casualty. They also tend to ride close to the machine, so they receive a good deal of exhaust.

With a good hitch skimmers are fairly stable, but there is little protection for the casualty in the event of a roll-over.

Hand-Pulled Toboggans

Most hand-pulled toboggans are extremely narrow, designed to ride within the width of a snowshoe track, and so are too narrow for moving a casualty except for short distances in an emergency. (**Fig. 7-7**) They are also extremely flexible. If snow is deep, it may be necessary to pack a wide trail with snowshoes so that a casualty's shoulders do not drag. If a basket stretcher is available, it will reduce the problems of shoulder protection and flexibility. Hand-pulled toboggans are easy to load – even for a single rescuer – and may be the only possible transport.

Fig. 7-7: Hand-pulled toboggans are too narrow and flexible for good casualty transport, but may be the only thing available in an emergency.

Transport on Snowmobiles or All Terrain Vehicles (ATV's)

Direct transport on these vehicles is suitable only when the casualty is able to sit, hold on, absorb bouncing and vibration, and balance himself without difficulty. He must also be strong enough to brace and hold himself against the sometimes quick takeoff, which will leave a weak person on his back in the snow. ATV travel in summer is especially rough.

Transport by Small Motor Boat (Freight Canoe, Open Outboard Boat)

Boats provide good space, rigidity, and ride if the water is smooth. Under good conditions they may be excellent for transporting casualties with most illnesses and injuries. However, they are almost always quite cold, often wet, and can be very rough riding if travel in choppy water is necessary. A casualty riding in the bottom of a boat is easily splashed by spray, bilge water, and sometimes spilled outboard gasoline and oil. The combination of immobility, supine position, gas fumes, and rough water can easily result in seasickness, with all the problems of vomiting.

As with sleds, the smoothest ride is usually in the stern. However, with most manually operated outboard motors, this will place the casualty under the feet of the operator and often next to the fuel tanks and in the area where water accumulates. It may also result in the bow riding excessively high. In rough water, it is better to add rocks or other ballast to hold the bow down than to place the casualty far forward. In calm water this is not a factor.

Protect the casualty from bilge water by wrapping his sleeping bag in waterproof tarps, and by supporting his stretcher off the boat bottom with branches or other improvised floor boards. Rig a spray shield over him. Be sure he is as well protected as if you were travelling in winter, as the wind and dampness will chill him quickly.

Use extra equipment, fuel cans, etc., to hold the stretcher in position so that it will not shift. Allow room for an attendant near the casualty's head.

If the casualty can wear a life jacket, put it on him. Otherwise tie some sort of flotation device to the stretcher so that the casualty would float face up. *Do not tie the casualty to the boat*, as this would make rescuing him very difficult if the boat capsized or sank.

Transport by Cabin Cruiser

A cabin boat is similar to an open boat, but with the advantage of weather protection. As the cabin is always far forward, it may be necessary to balance the need for weather protection against the need for a smoother ride in the stern.

Transport by Canoe

The instability of canoes makes them a poor choice for transport of a helpless casualty; however, there may be no alternative. They do have some advantages:

- a very smooth ride
- good casualty support
- easy fore-and-aft trim for casualty position
- easy to observe the casualty if loaded head to stern
- equipment and supplies may also be carried.

Their disadvantages are:

- capsize easily
- can be very wet
- difficult to work on casualty without going ashore
- difficult to load casualty (depending on thwart arrangement)
- may be quite cold.

A light canoe makes a good substitute for a basket stretcher for short carries, and with enough manpower, can be carried or skidded across portages. In winter, it also makes a good improvised sled to be hauled by people on foot or snowshoe.

Some rules of thumb for transporting casualties in canoes are:

- Do not use to transport helpless casualties unless there is no option.

- Do not use unless the paddlers are expert.
- Travel, if possible, with another canoe or boat.
- Tie two canoes together side by side for stability if conditions permit.
- Load the casualty with the canoe on shore, then slide it into the water.
- Load the casualty with his head toward the stern, leaving room for the stern paddler to change position and to bail if needed.
- Load all materials needed for attending the casualty within reach of the stern paddler.
- Place poles, etc., on the bottom to support the casualty out of bilge water.
- Provide the casualty with a flotation device, and keep his arms free so that he can help himself in case of capsize.
- Do not tie the casualty to the canoe, nor tie a cover over him.
- Wrap the casualty's sleeping bag in waterproof tarps.
- When dragging the canoe over beaver dams, keep one attendant on either side for stability.
- Land parallel to the bank, get out, and haul the canoe up on the bank. (Don't beach the canoe bow first, as it will become very unstable.)

Transport by Aircraft

Aircraft transport is preferred for any serious illness or injury. Details are found in the next chapter.

8

How to Arrange for Air Medevac

Air transport, or air medevac, is the best way to evacuate seriously ill or injured casualties, and it is commonly used throughout the north. Unfortunately, it is also a service often taken for granted and sometimes used when not strictly necessary. Because rescue costs are usually paid by a government agency, we tend to think of them as free. Actually, a rescue may cost thousands of dollars. More important than the expense, though, is the fact that pilots often go to great lengths to help people in trouble. They sometimes take unusual chances, feeling that "you do what you have to do" to help someone in trouble. They may fly in bad weather, and land and take off in places they would not otherwise consider. Pilots have died attempting air rescues, and sometimes the person they were attempting to rescue was not really in trouble. Clearly a first-aider must use judgement when considering whether to order air transport.

Call for an air medevac only if you honestly feel that the casualty's health and safety depend on it.

About Personal Locator Beacons (PLB's)

Radios are more and more common in the north, and are valuable in an emergency because they allow two-way discussion while deciding on the proper action. However, a new device is being marketed in the north – the Personal Locator Beacon. This is a small transmitter which sends a signal through a satellite to one of the rescue centres, which can locate the source of the signal within about a hundred metres or yards and alert local rescue authorities. The signal does not indicate what is wrong, only that someone is calling for help.

The danger in the use of PLB's is that they may become a substitute for good sense. When people know that they can call for help any time, they tend to go less prepared, take more chances, and call for help before it is really needed. The number of incidents and costs and risks to rescuers are likely to increase dramatically.

**Never let the fact that you are carrying a PLB
reduce your preparation or encourage you
to take chances or call for unneeded help.**

You should *never* assume that simply because you have called for help it will automatically come, or will come in time.

Calling for Air Medevacs

When you or a medical authority calls for an air medevac, there are certain things the pilot will need to know. *It is best to give this information during your first radio contact, because you might lose radio contact later.* Tell your radio contact the following:

- **Your exact location.** If you know how to use map coordinates correctly, give the coordinates using either latitude and longitude or the UTM (Universal Transverse Mercator) grid. Be sure to give the names and distances of *several* known local landmarks.

- **The number of passengers to go.**

- **The total weight to be transported.**

- **The extent of illness or injury.**

- **The details of the landing site.**

- **The cloud ceiling and visibility.** The *ceiling* means how far above you (in feet or metres) the clouds are. You can estimate their level on nearby hills. The *visibility* means how far you can see clearly on the level. Both measurements may change rapidly, and the pilot may ask for later updates if weather is poor.

- **The wind direction and speed.** Give the direction the wind is coming from – not the direction it is blowing. Also tell him how fast you think it is, and if it is steady or gusting.

The more accurate your reporting, the safer the flight will be.

Sometimes it will be necessary to move the casualty some distance to a landing site. If you must do this, allow plenty of time to get there and be prepared to stay there for a while. The pilot could easily be delayed.

Transport by Fixed-Wing Aircraft

Aircraft other than helicopters are called fixed-wing. Those used for bush work are usually small, although Otters, Twin Otters, and some other twin-engine models are also used and can take stretchers and several passengers without problems.

On the Ground

Hang a long, bright strip of cloth by one end near the airstrip where it will blow out in the wind, or build a smoky fire near – not on – the strip to show the pilot the local wind direction. Or use a smoke flare as he approaches.

When "packaging" a casualty for air transport, remember that he is even more likely to vomit in an aircraft than during ground transport. He should be packaged so that he can be turned immediately to avoid choking on vomit. If he is on a backboard, he must be so securely fastened that the entire board can be tipped without any body movement. This will also be important while loading, as it is often necessary to tip and turn a stretcher to get it into a small plane.

Because space in smaller aircraft is a real problem, be sure that whatever you use for a backboard or stretcher is no larger than the casualty.

When the aircraft lands, do not rush up to it. Watch the pilot and obey his signals. If he shuts down the engine, wait until the propeller stops turning entirely before getting near it. Even a slow-moving propeller can kill.

In the Plane

Don't slam the doors; pull them gently shut or let the pilot do it.

If you are the casualty's attendant, tell the pilot that you must be positioned close to his head. Use a safety belt if one is provided.

If the casualty is in shock or has heart or breathing problems or chest injury, ask the pilot to fly as low as is safe, because the amount of oxygen in the air drops quickly as you rise. If possible, the plane should not gain 5,000 feet above the landing site, nor rise to a level above 10,000 feet.

If the casualty is wearing an air splint – a plastic splint that inflates – it will expand as you rise and may cut off circulation. Watch it carefully: let off pressure as you go up, and re-inflate the splint as you come down.

Transport by Helicopter

Helicopters are often the best possible answer to difficult air medevacs, because they can land and take off smoothly without an airstrip. In addition, they are easier to fly at low altitudes than other aircraft, and may be able to "sneak in" under a low ceiling where fixed-wing planes cannot. However, the smaller ones are often very cramped, and may not allow room for the casualty to lie down. Some have stretcher kits, which means they have been rigged to carry a stretcher built for the aircraft, and some have doorposts that may be removed to allow stretcher-loading, but even then there will be very little working room for the attendant. Because the aluminum stretchers with the kits are very narrow, it is often necessary to "repackage" the casualty before he can be loaded.

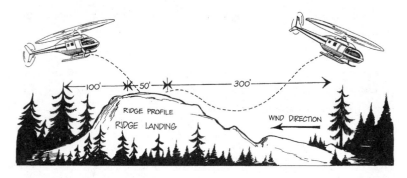

Fig. 8-1: A good helicopter landing spot with clear ground dropping away to windward.

On the Ground

- **Clear away any loose objects or brush** from the landing area.

- **The landing area should be firm.** It should allow the helicopter to move forward into the wind, rather than straight up, when taking off. A flat site with the ground sloping away to the windward side is best. (**Fig. 8-1**) Do not be surprised if the pilot decides to land somewhere else – he knows what he needs.

- **Hang a wind indicator** or build a small smoky fire to show wind direction. Build it at least 50 metres or yards away from the site, not on it!

- **Stay well away from the site** while the helicopter lands. Sand, snow, or anything loose will be blown toward you by the rotor draft, so keep your back turned. If the helicopter should crash while landing, the blades may fly a long distance with enough force to cut you in two.

To prepare a landing pad on the snow:

- Tramp snow level with snowshoes, skis, or feet. If a snowmobile is available, pack the snow first with the machine, then with your feet, then again with the machine. Do this at least half an hour before arrival so that the snow hardens again.

Fig. 8-2: A helicopter landing-mat on deep snow.

- Make a mat of spruce boughs 3m (10 feet) square and 15 cm (six inches) thick.

- Lay five or six strong, trimmed logs each 2.5 to 3m (8 to 10 feet) long on the mat, at half-metre (2-foot) intervals and at right angles to the approach. (**Fig. 8-2**) Be sure they won't roll.

If you are on soft, swampy ground, you must make the same sort of mat and log arrangement.

The pilot may leave the engine running and the rotor turning while loading. Watch him for signals.

- **Keep everyone away** unless they are absolutely needed.

- **Do not approach unless the pilot signals you to do so**, and then approach only from the front or side – *never from the rear!* The small tail rotor is often overlooked, sometimes with fatal results.

- **Always approach from the downhill side, never the uphill side.** The rotor is closer to the ground on the uphill side. (**Fig. 8-3**)

- **Keep low as you approach**, because the rotor tends to drop lower as it slows. (**Fig. 8-4**)

- **Hold onto everything loose** – including your hat – when under moving rotors, since the draft may blow something up into them and cause serious damage.

- **In severe cold, keep yourself and the casualty well covered** while in the draft from the rotor, or you will get instant frostbite.

If the ground is rough and requires that you load while the pilot is holding the machine under power with only one skid on the ground, place weight on the machine gradually, rather than suddenly.

Fig. 8-3: Leave or approach a helicopter from the downhill side, because doing so from the uphill side may take you into the rotor.

Fig. 8-4: Approach a helicopter only on the pilot's signal, and from forward of centre. Never approach from the rear!

In the Helicopter

- Be sure that all seat belt ends are inside before closing the door. Do not slam it; pull it shut gently or let the pilot close it.

- Wear your seat belt.

- Have everything you need for the casualty within reach (airsick bags, blanket, etc.). Ask the pilot if there is room to turn the casualty if he gets airsick.

- Wear the headset, and be sure to ask the pilot how to use it before you start; otherwise you may not be able to hear each other to communicate. (Don't forget to remove it when you get out!)

- Provide ear protection for the casualty if it is available.

- Tell the pilot immediately if you have any problems with the casualty which might require that you land to provide room to work.

- Observe the casualty constantly for any signs of breathing problems.

When you land, wait for the pilot's directions before getting out.

Part III

How to Care for Common Wilderness Injuries

9

Cold Exposure (Hypothermia)

Anywhere in the world where there are cool or cold temperatures, people die from cold exposure, or *hypothermia*. Exposure can kill at temperatures well *above* freezing. Older people who cannot help themselves have died of cold lying in bed in cool rooms of about 16°C (about 65°F). Strong men, hiking in wind and rain at around 5-7°C (about 41-45°F), have died from exposure. Even people who are shipwrecked in relatively warm seas at around 20°C (about 68°F) – which is almost room temperature – can live only about 12 hours before they lose too much heat and die.

Cold exposure is one of the most common problems in northern first aid. It may complicate almost any first-aid situation. Watch for it and prevent it just as carefully as you watch for shock.

What Is Exposure?

Your body produces heat, much as a stove does. The "fuel" is the food you eat. It is changed by digestion into a variety of things like sugars that are "burned" (metabolized) by your body to produce the energy you need to live. Much of that energy is heat and most of that heat is produced in the liver and in the large muscles.

Your body depends on that heat for survival, just as does any other animal's body. The important organs deep inside – especially the heart, lungs, liver, and brain – must be kept at a temperature very close to 36°C or 37°C (about 98°F) to work well. These organs are called the **core**. If your core cools only slightly to about 34°C or 35°C (about 95°F) (which is the temperature of a *very* hot day!), you will shiver, get clumsy, be unable to speak clearly, and your ability to reason will deteriorate. *At this point you are suffering from exposure, but you may not recognize it because your cooled brain is not working well.*

When your core body temperature drops to 32°C (90°F), you will feel lethargic (limited in movement), your breathing and pulse will slow, you will be unable to think clearly, and you may stop shivering. *You are now very close to death, but you may not be able to understand this.*

When your core temperature approaches 30°C (86°F), you will slip into unconsciousness, and when it reaches about 25°C (77°F) – the temperature of a warm summer day – your heart will stop.

Remember that exposure is the cooling of the body core. Hands and feet may get very cold – and may even freeze solid – without threatening life. But if the core cools even slightly, life is in danger.

How We Lose Heat

Before we discuss exposure any further, we should know some things about heat so that we will know how to slow heat loss.

Our bodies lose heat in four main ways: **radiation, convection, conduction,** and **evaporation.** You probably remember from your own experience the feeling of each.

Radiation is the kind of heat you feel from the sun, or when you hold your hand beside a wood stove or near a lightbulb. Our bodies lose heat constantly this way except when they are receiving more from an outside source (stove, sun, fire) than they are putting out. We probably lose more heat this way than any other.

We can reduce this kind of heat loss by wearing warm clothing, but we can't stop it entirely, because we radiate heat into the clothing, and the warmed clothing then radiates that same heat out into the cold.

Convection is another name for air movement. Your skin warms a very thin layer of the air which lies against it, so body heat is lost to that air. When air is warmed, it gets lighter and rises away from your body. Cool air flows in to replace it, it is warmed, rises, and the cycle continues. The colder the air, the faster the convection.

Wind also moves the warmed air away, cooling you very much faster. This is called **wind chill**. The chart shows the cooling effect of wind chill. (**Fig. 9-1**)

We can reduce this sort of heat loss simply by wearing wind-proof clothing, tightening all openings in clothing, and covering any exposed skin, or by getting out of the wind. In high winds

Fig. 9-1: Equivalent Wind-Chill Temperature (°C)

Temperature in Still Air

Wind Speed (km/h)	0	–5	–10	–15	–20	–25	–30	–35	–40
10	–2	–7	–12	–17	–22	–27	–32	–38	–45
15	–5	–10	–16	–22	–28	–33	–39	–45	–51
20	–7	–13	–19	–25	–31	–37	–43	–50	–57
25	–10	–16	–23	–29	–36	–42	–49	–55	–62
30	–11	–17	–24	–31	–37	–44	–50	–57	–65
35	–12	–19	–26	–33	–40	–47	–54	–61	–68
40	–13	–20	–27	–34	–41	–48	–55	–62	–70
45	–14	–22	–29	–36	–44	–51	–57	–65	–73
50	–15	–22	–30	–37	–44	–52	–59	–66	–74
55	–16	–23	–31	–38	–46	–53	–60	–68	–75
60	–16	–24	–31	–39	–46	–54	–61	–69	–77

Minimal Danger

Dangerous
Exposed flesh may freeze within one minute

Very Dangerous
Exposed flesh may freeze within 30 seconds

Courtesy Environment Canada

or in an emergency, wrapping in a tarp or large plastic bags cuts out most wind chill.

Conduction is the movement of heat directly from one object to another. For example, the cold you feel when you hold a snowball in your bare hand is the rapid movement of heat by *conduction* from your hand into the snowball. When you feel cold spots beneath your sleeping bag, it shows that the padding below you has become packed and thin and you are losing heat by *conduction* to the surface below.

Water and other fluids conduct heat away from your body many times faster than dry air, which is why wet clothes are so much colder than dry ones.

Some fluids, such as gasoline, kerosene, and alcohol do not freeze when water does, and so may get extremely cold. There is danger of instant frostbite if any such "supercooled" fluids touch the skin. Sea water also freezes at a lower temperature.

Evaporation is the changing of water into vapour. When sweat evaporates or dries on your skin, it cools you. Every northerner knows how rapidly you cool if your clothes get wet with sweat. There is always *some* sweat on your skin keeping it moist, even though it may be too light to see. It evaporates and cools you constantly. Less recognized is the cooling effect of evaporation when you breathe. This sort of heat loss is reduced by the fur-trimmed "tunnel" hood of a parka. In the tunnel, warm, moist air from around your body and from exhaled breath mixes with the cold, dry air you inhale. This slows the speed of evaporation.

Breathing through a scarf, woollen face mask, or toque also adds some moisture and warmth, although the fabric will ice up eventually. Pulling your head inside your sleeping bag will save heat, but is unwise because the moisture in your breath will pass into the sleeping bag and condense (turn back to water) at the rate of 250 to 500 mL (one or two cups) per night. Each night, your bag will be heavier and colder. Some of this occurs anyway just from the invisible vapour from your body, so it is important to dry sleeping bags in sun and wind whenever possible.

Now let's look at how your body reacts to heat loss.

How Your Body Fights Exposure

Unlike the body core, the skin, fingers, and toes can be cooled almost to freezing without damage, and they often are. This presents a problem. If blood flowed at its usual rate through these cold tissues it would also be cooled. When it flowed back into the core it would cool the core. Because that would present a danger to life, your body automatically reduces blood flow to cold parts by shutting down the blood vessels there. Sometimes, blood flow is reduced as much as 99%.

As a result, the skin becomes pale, cold, and numb. Unfortunately, this makes frostbite much more likely – but it helps save the core temperature.

If your whole body is cooled quickly, as might happen if you were immersed in cold water, the blood vessels in all of your skin and the fatty tissues beneath will close down the same way. With little blood flow to the outside surfaces, you now have a cool, insulating "shell" of skin and fatty tissue which will slow heat loss from the core. It certainly won't stop heat loss, only slow it.

Shivering, a rapid, uncontrollable muscle movement, is an automatic method of heat creation. The muscles at work cause blood sugar to be "burned" to produce heat. A shivering muscle will produce many times as much heat as the same muscle at rest, so the body temperature goes up and the core is made warmer.

Unfortunately, shivering uses up your stores of "fuel," just as any other work does, so it is better to use your limited blood sugar to work toward getting into shelter, rather than counting on shivering to warm you.

When the body's core temperature has dropped to about 32°C (about 90°F), shivering will stop and heat loss becomes more rapid.

Who Is in Danger of Exposure

Anyone, no matter how big, strong, or experienced, can suffer from exposure, but some people get cold faster than others and should always be watched carefully in cold conditions, as they may not realize what is happening to them.

- **Smaller people** – babies, children, small adults – get cold more quickly because small bodies chill faster. Very thin people also cool quickly.

- **Elderly people** cool more quickly.

- **Sick or injured people** are in great danger in cold surroundings.

- **Teenagers** are among the most common exposure fatalities in the north, because they often go snowmobiling, boating, or on ATV's without good preparation. Boys, especially, like to appear "tough" and wear much less clothing than should be worn.

Prevention

To prevent exposure:

- **Prepare for the worst conditions** and take extra clothing.

- **Avoid overheating and sweating.** Wear loose, layered clothing that "breathes." Cotton (as tee-shirts and jeans) wets easily and dries slowly; wool is warm even when wet; and modern "transport" fabrics such as polypropylene and polyester are superior next to the skin. The traditional skin clothing of the north is best of all if worn in a traditional manner but is increasingly hard to get.

- **Avoid long-term cooling.** Take tea breaks often when travelling to allow some exercise and a chance to get out of the wind. Do not continue if you are getting seriously cold. If you try to tough it out, your judgement may fade before you realize it, and you may make other mistakes.

- **Eat often** to provide "fuel" for your "furnace." Sugars and starches work most quickly.

- **Drink lots.** (Avoid alcohol, as it may *speed* cooling.)

Dehydration is a factor in most cases of exposure. Hot sweet drinks are best, but cold water is fine if nothing hot is available. Do not eat snow if you are cold.

- **Keep your big muscles moving** to create heat. If your fingers or toes are cold, wiggling them won't make them warm but exercising the large muscles of your arms and legs will. Swing your arms vigorously to warm your hands or put your hands in your armpits.

- **Check your partners often**. If they get clumsy, shiver, slur their speech, or act strangely, suspect exposure. Remember, they may not realize what is happening.

How to Recognize and Treat Exposure

Exposure has been divided into three levels – **mild**, **moderate**, and **severe**. It is hard to tell where one level starts and the next stops without a special low-reading thermometer, which is rarely found in conventional first-aid kits.

How to Tell – Mild Exposure

In mild exposure, the casualty:

- is awake
- can answer questions intelligently
- complains of being cold
- is probably shivering
- may slur his words
- has probably lost interest in what he is doing.

What to Do

If mild exposure is affecting a companion, you should:

- stop travelling
- prevent any further loss of body heat
- get him into shelter

- replace any wet clothing
- allow shivering to continue as it is the most efficient way for the body to restore its temperature
- give him food and/or sweet hot drinks.

First-aiders should be aware that active rewarming will probably turn off the shivering mechanism. Resist the pressure to use external heat sources. If the casualty is so cold that shivering has stopped, active rewarming is essential.

In the field, heat loss may be temporarily slowed by wrapping the casualty in plastic bags or tarps as well as sleeping bags or clothing. These stop wind chill and some evaporative loss. A reflective "rescue blanket" is even better, as it reduces radiant heat loss as well.

Warmth may be provided by almost any means to correct mild hypothermia. Skin-to-skin contact, while not very effective, may be the only choice when there is little other warmth to be found. The casualty and rescuer (or rescuers) strip to their underclothes and huddle together in a sleeping bag until the casualty is warmed. If the casualty is very cold and the rescuer begins to get cold himself, it is best for him to change with a fresh rescuer so that he does not himself become chilled.

If you use hot-water bottles or heat packs, **use them with great caution**. They must be wrapped in several layers of cloth to prevent burning the casualty.

How to Tell – Moderate Exposure

In moderate exposure, the casualty:

- is confused and illogical
- doesn't want to move much, may be sleepy
- may leave clothes open, take them off, or let fires go out
- is clumsy and stumbles
- stops shivering
- shows signs of muscle stiffness
- has slow breath and pulse rates
- may have a fruity odour to breath

- may have dilated pupils
- may urinate in clothing.

This casualty is in great danger. He is very close to severe hypothermia, unconsciousness, and death.

What to Do

Treat the casualty as for mild exposure, except:

- Avoid rough handling and do not let him walk.
- Do not give him fluids to drink until he is wide awake and understands what is going on. Because he is uncoordinated, he may choke on fluids.

Never handle anyone in moderate or severe exposure roughly, or allow him to move much, because his heart will be very sensitive and may start fibrillating with fatal results.

How to Tell – Severe Exposure

Moderate exposure quickly shades into severe exposure. At this point, the casualty is in a coma and very close to death. *The slightest rough handling may cause his heart to fail.* Even with careful handling, there is less than a 50-50 chance he will survive.

Severe exposure may be brought on slowly by prolonged cold or very quickly if the casualty falls into cold water. In ice water, it may take as little as 20 minutes to reach this point. In severe exposure, the casualty:

- is barely conscious or is unconscious
- has slow, shallow breathing and a weak, slow, irregular or absent pulse
- has pale, very cold, perhaps bluish skin.

In the last stages, the casualty may appear dead. However, there may be a very slow, faint heartbeat and respiration. Some casualties who were thought to be dead have been left in a warm place and later recovered.

> **Never assume an exposure casualty is dead
> until his body is warm again and
> there are still no signs of life.**

Put another way, an exposure casualty should not be considered dead until he is warm and dead.

What to Do

If there is any breathing or a carotid (neck) pulse, you should:

- handle the casualty very gently
- prevent further heat loss
- move him gently to medical care if it is within a few hours; if not call an urgent air medevac.

If air medevac is not available and you are far from help, you should:

- immediately and gently move him into a warm shelter
- apply *heavily wrapped* warm water bottles to sides of his chest, neck, and groin (nowhere else!)
- keep him warm and let him recover very slowly without moving him.

It is critical that these wrapped bottles be only *slightly warm* to the touch, because too much heat may damage his flesh. Continue warming until he starts to recover. *Never rub or warm his hands, feet, arms, or legs, or move them needlessly,* as the blood in the skin, arms, and legs, which has become very cold and acidic, may be circulated back to the irritable heart and cause fibrillation. *Let them stay cool* but do not let them freeze. If there is frostbite, there is no rush; deal with this after he recovers from exposure.

When he starts to recover, his hearing will often return first, then his sight. As he recovers, he may lose control of his bowels. Do not move him to clean up until he has recovered to the mild exposure level.

As he becomes aware of his body again, he may ask to have his hands and feet warmed. *Do not do this.* Let them warm naturally as his trunk warms.

When he has recovered to the mild exposure stage, you may rewarm him as though he were in that stage. Do not give anything by mouth until he understands what is happening.

When all signs of exposure have disappeared, give as many warm sweet drinks as he wants and let him eat, preferably sugars and starches at first. Keep him at rest overnight. He should recover completely by then, though he may be weak.

If the casualty is going to die, it will probably be during rewarming. If you save an unconscious exposure victim, you have beaten the odds!

If there is no apparent breathing or pulse, double-check carefully, feeling for the carotid (neck) pulse for at least 1 to 2 minutes with fingers in different positions, and watch for chest movement with your ear next to the casualty's nose and mouth, feeling and listening for signs of breathing. You may also use the old trick of placing a cold glass surface next to his mouth to see if it fogs up. If there is no trace of pulse or breathing:

- **start rescue breathing (artificial respiration),** and continue it until the casualty breathes by himself or until he is rewarmed and still shows no signs of life

- **prevent further heat loss** by removing wet clothes and providing under-body insulation and dry blankets

- **handle the casualty very gently**

- **move him quickly and gently to medical care if it is available within a few hours; if it is not, call an urgent air medevac.**

There is no clear agreement in medical circles whether or not it is better to use cardiopulmonary resuscitation (CPR) in such a case. In wilderness first aid situations, do not start CPR unless it can be continued and the casualty can be delivered to a hospital within 1 hour. However, rescue breathing will not do harm if done gently, and may provide a little warmth to the core organs.

If no air medevac is available, treat the casualty as though he were an unconscious exposure victim, and hope that he shows signs of life as he slowly warms. Remember that you must not assume he is dead until he is warm and dead.

Cold Water Exposure (Immersion Hypothermia)

Even with care, boats sometimes swamp, and people sometimes fall unexpectedly through thin ice. Northern rivers and oceans are so cold that even a short time in the water produces some degree of exposure and is often fatal.

A person who is suddenly plunged into icy water is so shocked by the cold that he cannot breathe properly. His muscles tighten and reduce coordination. Swimming is thus very difficult. Within a few minutes, fingers and hands become numb and completely useless. In rare cases, his heart will fail and he will sink immediately.

If the casualty is not wearing a flotation device (life jacket), drowning will be very quick.

Always wear a life jacket while boating.

Anyone who finds himself in very cold water has only minutes before his hands are useless and his strength and reasoning ability start to fail, so he must do whatever he has to do *immediately.* This may include taking off snowshoes or skis, removing a backpack, untying cargo to lighten the boat, tying himself to the top of an overturned boat, firing a flare gun, gathering flotation material, or whatever is required to extend survival. Difficult as it may be, he has to think ahead at this point and do it quickly, because there will be no second chance either to act or to think.

How to Live Longer in Cold Water

In cold water, the body quickly reduces circulation to the skin

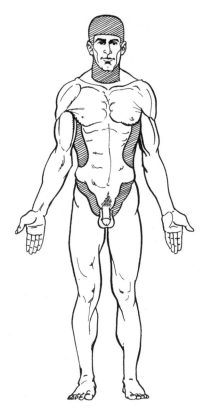

Fig. 9-2: Body heat escapes very rapidly from areas shown in black. Heat is applied to the same areas for most effective rewarming.

and fatty tissues beneath the skin, and to the arms, legs, hands, and feet. (This is why they become numb and useless.) With little blood flowing through them, these outer layers become a sort of insulating shell which slows heat loss from the core.

Unfortunately, there are several areas of the body that are only thinly protected. These are the groin, the sides of the chest just below the armpits, the neck and the head. Major blood vessels or organs lie near the surface in these areas, and lose heat very quickly. (**Fig. 9-2**)

These areas must be protected in cold water. The best way to do this is to take the precaution of having a jacket which is designed both to protect these areas from cold and to keep you afloat. They are made with closed-cell rubber foam padding with a "beavertail" which can be brought up between the legs and fastened in front, thus protecting the groin. Such a jacket will prolong survival several hours depending on the temperature.

Full suits are also available and will extend survival several hours longer than the jacket. Jackets and suits are expensive but double as warm, waterproof clothing, and are used constantly by professionals who spend much time on the water.

Experienced boaters carry a knife and waterproof matches or a lighter in their clothing to build a fire after reaching shore.

Swimming or treading water may make you feel warmer briefly, but will speed heat loss dramatically because muscle movement causes blood flow to the surface tissues.

Here are some basic rules for cold-water survival.

If you swamp a boat and it still floats:

- **Get into or on top of the boat, keeping out of the water as much as possible.** If the boat is overturned and cannot be righted, try to attach yourself to it to keep from sliding off.

- **Bail or splash water out of the boat to increase freeboard.** Throw heavy objects overboard. Canoeists should learn how to "shake" the water out and get back aboard.

- **Put on all clothing and fasten it tightly.** Cover your head and neck. Do this immediately before your hands become numb.

If you can paddle the boat to shore, do so, and immediately build a fire, trying to warm neck, face, chest, and groin first. If you must wait for rescue or for the boat to drift ashore, then:

- **Huddle to preserve heat.** Keep your arms pressed against chest sides and keep legs bent to protect the groin.

- **Get behind a windbreak.** Use whatever material is available – tarp, plastic bags, sail, floorboards, etc.

- **Eat whatever is available.** Keep nibbling whenever you can to keep your blood sugar "fuel" at a high level.

- **Do not try to swim to shore** unless the water is not excessively cold, you have something to keep you afloat, and the distance is less than half a mile with no adverse currents. *Swimming speeds heat loss enormously, and many swimmers never make it.*

Face facts. Unless you have a survival suit or jacket, you will not survive long in most northern waters if the shore is distant and no help is at hand. But you should never give up.

If you cannot get out of the water:

- **Close and tighten all clothing immediately.** Cover your head and neck.

- **Use floating material to keep you high in the water.**

- **Float in a knees-up, arms-in, chin-down position. (Fig. 9-3a)** This will slow heat loss from the groin, ribs, and neck.

- **Use heat-escape lessening postures.** Keep arms pressed against chest sides, keep legs bent to protect groin, or huddle with others to press these areas together to share heat. **(Fig. 9-3b)**

- **Eat** if there is any food in your pockets. Your hands may be useless; just eat candy bars paper and all.

If the shore is close enough, try to swim on your back with your face out of the water, using as little energy as possible. Once ashore, build a fire immediately and try to warm your neck, face, and the front of your trunk first.

Even if you get out of the water, you may still die from exposure if you do not have help or means to build a fire immediately, or if the weather is bad and there is no shelter. **Always carry waterproof matches.**

If You Go Through the Ice

In ice water, you have perhaps 3 to 5 minutes before your hands are useless. You will be helpless in perhaps 15 or 20 minutes, and unconscious shortly afterward. What you should do depends on the ice.

You should immediately remove any snowshoes, skis, pack, rifle, or anything else that will hold you down. If the ice is hard and you have fallen through a thin spot, break quickly toward thicker ice, place snowshoes or skis on the edge to help distribute weight, and try to lift yourself out. Do it immediately, as the strength will soon leave your arms.

If the ice is hard, you may be able to drive in a sharp instrument and pull yourself toward it.

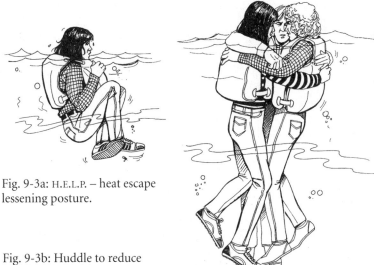

Fig. 9-3a: H.E.L.P. – heat escape lessening posture.

Fig. 9-3b: Huddle to reduce heat loss in cold water.

If the ice is "candled" spring ice (made up of long, vertical crystals), you will probably be unable to get back on top, unless you are near a packed trail under which the ice may be more solid. In this case, try to crush a path toward shore with your arm and elbow. Drag your pack along with you on the ice surface; you will need its contents. You may get very weak and want just to let go and get it over with, but *do not give up.*

If your companion goes through, do not approach him (unless you know the ice is good) but try to help from a distance with a long pole or rope loop. You will probably have to hook or snare him, since shortly he will not be able to grip anything.

What to Do

Once the casualty is out of the water, strip off his wet clothes, place him immediately in a dry sleeping bag, and warm him with skin-to-skin contact. First aid for cold-water immersion is the same as for other exposure, and the levels of hypothermia are also the same.

10

Frostbite

Almost everyone in the north has seen frostbite, and most have had mild frostbite.

**Frostbite is the freezing of body tissues
with formation of ice crystals.**

Frostbite is usually limited to the hands, feet, and face, and occurs when blood flow is reduced.

Surface frostbite (also called superficial frostbite or frostnip) affects only the skin and does not do much damage. It may, however, progress to deeper frostbite.

Deep frostbite may cause loss of tissue and permanent damage, including the loss of parts or all of the hands and feet. It is a serious medical emergency, but proper field care can often make the difference between temporary disability and permanent crippling injuries.

Prevention

Surface frostbite is common on the face and is often associated with wind, from the weather, or from a moving vehicle. A good parka tunnel will usually prevent frostbite because it holds a pocket of warmer air next to the face. In strong winds, cover nose and cheeks with a facemask, scarf, or any piece of warm fabric. Since frostbite is often not felt, the first warning may come from a companion who notices a white spot on your face. Surface frostbite on the fingers often occurs when hands are bared to do work in cold weather, especially when they are touching cold metal or exposed to wind. Any time the temperature is below freezing, frostbite is possible.

Deep frostbite most often happens in an emergency, when hands or feet are exposed to severe cold for long periods with no chance to warm up, or when hands or feet accidentally become wet and freeze quickly. On long trips, it is important to *eat often* to maintain body warmth, *drink often* to prevent dehydration, and *rest often enough* to avoid tiredness and restore circulation. Warm painful or numb feet. Sick, injured, or very tired people are in the greatest danger, even when they are warmly dressed.

Smokers are more likely to be frostbitten than nonsmokers, because the nicotine from one cigarette reduces blood flow to the skin, fingers, and toes to 10% of normal for up to 4 hours. People who abuse alcohol are at great risk, and many amputations (and deaths) have resulted from people passing out in the cold.

Inuit and some others who have lived long in the north have adapted to cold and are at lesser risk. Frostbite risk, however, is always present.

Some folk remedies for frostbite are still in use, but they often cause far worse injuries than would result from correct treatment. Submerging the affected part in fuel or seawater, thawing it in front of a fire or stove, or rubbing the area can be disastrous. An enormous amount of research was done on deep frostbite during the Korean War, and resulted in the first aid described below.

Surface Frostbite

How to Tell

- skin turns white and numb
- tissues beneath are still soft
- casualty may not feel it
- partner may notice white spot

What to Do

- **Fingers**: place the affected parts inside your parka, in your own armpits, or against the skin; leave them there until they are warm again.

- **Toes**: place your bared feet under your partner's parka against his bare skin until thawed, or go inside to warm up. (If you are alone, it may be necessary to stop and take shelter to get the feet warm again.)

- **Cheeks, nose, ears, chin**: thaw them with a warm hand or other warm (not hot) object, or pull the parka hood snugly around your face until the affected area is warm and pink.

- **Protect** the frozen area from further exposure because it will freeze again more easily than other skin.

Deep Frostbite

Deep frostbite is a major injury, even though there is no pain at first. You must treat it with great care to reduce loss of tissue. NOTE: Once a deeply frozen part has thawed, it must not be used, nor should it be allowed to refreeze! The slightest pressure will cause pain, further damage, and tissue loss.

If in an emergency it is necessary to use a frozen foot to walk to safety, it will cause less damage to leave the foot frozen. Frostbite is not likely to creep above the ankle so long as the casualty is active, because circulation, large heat-producing muscles, and clothing protection are greater above the ankle. You must remember that the more a frozen part is used and the longer it is frozen, the more damage there may be.

How to Tell

- Parts affected are usually fingers or toes, heels, entire hands or feet, and rarely parts of the face or ears.

- There may be pain at early stages, followed by numbness. (Check painful or numb feet right away.)

- The part is as cold, white (sometimes purple), and hard as a piece of frozen meat – which it is. There is no pain or feeling at this stage.

- If the affected part has frozen and thawed by itself, there will be pain, swelling, discolouration, and large blisters.

What to Do

If you are away from safety and must continue to travel, do not thaw the affected part. Try to keep the rest of your body warm, well fed, and well watered. To repeat: Use the part as little as possible, but if you must use it to return to safety *leave it frozen*.

When Back in Camp

If a quick air medevac can be called, evacuate the casualty without thawing affected parts.

If evacuation will be long, or no evacuation is possible, then:

- establish a warm, comfortable camp

- give the casualty warmth, food, and plenty of liquids

- make a thawing container big enough to submerge the frozen part without its touching the sides (see Appendix A for improvised containers)

- heat enough clean water, pleasantly warm to the elbow (*no hotter!*), to fill the container (if a thermometer is available, it should be 40-42°C or 104-108°F), and keep more heating

- give the casualty 2 Aspirin tablets before starting

- remove jewellery from the affected part because the part will swell

- submerge frozen part in water and keep it moving slightly

- keep checking water temperature (as it will cool quickly) and try to keep the temperature even

- remove the frozen part from water without touching it and

add very hot water until the temperature is back to starting level (*do not* try to pour hot water next to the part!)

- keep the part thawing for 20-40 minutes, until it is pink or until no further improvement is seen

- put small sterile pads between toes or fingers and cover the injury *very loosely* with sterile dressings

- elevate the affected part and keep it warm; there must be *no* pressure (even bedclothes) on the part.

There may be severe pain during thawing, but this will go away.

The casualty must not smoke or chew any nicotine. Give him 2 Aspirin tablets with plenty of water every 6 hours (unless it causes him stomach upset) until rescue. (Aspirin relieves pain and is felt by some physicians to improve circulation in frostbitten tissues.) Evacuate by air if possible, keeping any pressure off the affected part. It may be necessary to put a frame inside the foot of his sleeping bag to keep the pressure off, or to pad the part gently with a pillow splint.

Blisters will be huge and ugly. Do not break them. If infection starts, begin antibiotics as prescribed by local health authorities, change dressings, and clean the part gently as described in Chapter 11, "Cuts, bleeding, and Infection."

CAUTION: **the affected part will freeze again very easily, so it should not be allowed to get cold during evacuation.** *It must not be allowed to refreeze.*

The casualty may be fearful that he will lose his hands or feet. Even terrible-looking limbs often recover if treated well, so reassure him of this.

In some emergency situations, there may be no choice but to walk on a thawed foot in order to reach safety. In this case, blisters will break, and there will be pain and great tissue damage.

There are times that simple survival is the best you can do.

11

Cuts, Bleeding, and Infection

Cuts are one of the most common wilderness injuries, and most are preventable. How many times have you used a knife or axe incorrectly, knowing perfectly well you were taking a chance – and then cut yourself?

A small scar may be the reminder of a cut from a pocket-knife. The penalty for carelessness with an axe or chainsaw can be very great.

Wilderness people who grow old, live that long because they don't take chances, especially when they are far from help.

Dangers of Cuts

There are two primary dangers arising from cuts and bleeding. They are:

- blood loss leading to shock
- infection.

These can usually be controlled by a first-aider except in severe cases. *(You have read about shock and its causes in Chapter 1. If necessary, read that section again, noting that bleeding is the most common cause of shock.)*

Always expect shock if there is significant blood loss, and start treatment for shock immediately.

What is "significant" blood loss? An adult has in his body a total of 4 to 5 L (about 10 pints) of blood. The loss of 500 to 750 mL (1 to 1½ pints) will usually cause the first stage of shock. However, if the casualty is already dehydrated, in severe pain or emotional distress, or has other injuries, shock could occur with less bleeding, or without any blood being seen. **Be ready for shock in every case.**

It is easy to overestimate the amount of blood lost if it is on a hard surface, such as a floor or the inside of a boat. Unless you have experience, 125mL (½ cup) will look like a large blood loss.

On the other hand, it is dangerously easy to underestimate blood loss if the blood soaks into snow, sand, or dirt. Most hunters have seen the blood from a shot animal melt a little hole through the snow and disappear; the small red hole in the snow may have swallowed up several litres (or quarts) of blood. If you are in doubt, always assume there has been *greater* blood loss rather than less.

How to Tell

When estimating blood loss, you should:

- look for visible blood
- estimate the amount of blood that soaked into clothing, snow, or soil
- watch for signs of shock.

How to Control Bleeding

There are three basic ways to control bleeding. To remember them think of RED, the colour of blood:

- **Rest**
- **Elevation**
- **Direct Pressure.**

Rest does several important things. When the casualty is at rest, his pulse usually slows, and *the pump (his heart) works more slowly* so there is less blood lost. Lying down also ensures a good flow of blood to the brain and other vital organs, and works to prevent shock. (**Fig. 11-1**)

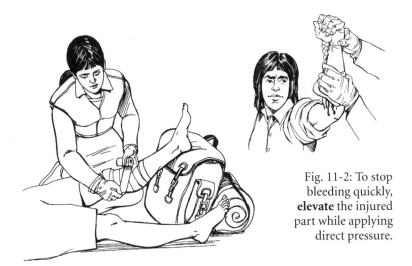

Fig. 11-2: To stop bleeding quickly, **elevate** the injured part while applying direct pressure.

Fig. 11-1: Put the casualty at **rest** to reduce pulse rate and help prevent shock.

Have casualties with relatively small cuts lie down, because some people – even strong men – faint when they see their own blood, and may be injured by a fall.

Elevation has one major effect; it *reduces the blood flow to the cut.* Less blood flow means less bleeding. Remember, the heart is a pump which works well pushing fluids level or downhill, but it delivers less flow uphill. Raising the part has another beneficial effect – it reduces the amount of swelling around an injury. (**Fig. 11-2**)

If the cut is on the body rather than on an arm or a leg, it is obvious that you cannot elevate the body easily. But keeping the injury *above the heart* will still help.

Direct pressure is usually applied with a dressing, a sterile piece of cloth placed directly on a wound. It is held tightly in place with a bandage, which is any piece of cloth used to hold a dressing or splint in place. The pressure of the dressing and bandage does two things; *it squeezes the blood vessels partly shut,* reducing the blood flow, and *blocks the opening* through which blood is escaping. After about five minutes, the blood around the cut will normally start to clot, or thicken and form a plug, which is the body's own way to stop bleeding. Hold the pressure longer than you think is needed.

When bleeding is severe, there may not be time to get a sterile dressing, and some faster means of applying pressure may be needed – even a bare hand. It is good to prevent bacteria from entering a wound, but if a person is bleeding badly, it is *far more important to stop the bleeding quickly to prevent shock*; worry about infection later. Serious bleeding from an artery can cause fatal shock in just a couple of minutes, so use your bare hand or any reasonably clean material to apply pressure.

Most bleeding can be stopped by these three methods – rest, elevation, direct pressure. If it is extremely cold, *watch the injured area – and especially the part beyond it – for cold injury*. The very things that slow blood loss also reduce warmth to the area. Beware of frostbite and hypothermia. Open wounds which are wet with body fluids freeze easily, and must be well protected. They must never be allowed to freeze, as this will increase the likelihood of infection and will slow healing and increase scarring.

Tourniquets

A tourniquet is any band applied around an arm or a leg so tightly that all blood flow beyond it is cut off.

A tourniquet is a last resort, used only if nothing else will stop bleeding and the casualty otherwise is sure to die.

The **arteries**, which carry the blood from the heart to the body, are under much more pressure than the **veins**, which carry the blood from the body back to the heart. Large arteries tend to be deeply situated, often running on the inner side of the large bones. If a major artery is cut, the blood will spurt out with each heartbeat. If this sort of bleeding cannot be controlled with rest, elevation, and direct pressure, a tourniquet may be lifesaving. However, *tissues beyond the tourniquet may die and have to be amputated*. In extreme cold, even if the part does not die from lack of oxygen, it will probably freeze quickly.

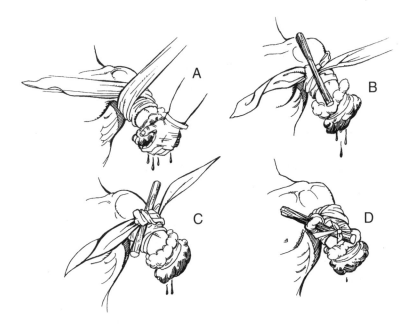

Fig. 11-3: Steps in applying a tourniquet.

Tourniquets should be wide and flat, to prevent crushing tissue. You will need a firm bandage at least 8 cm (3 inches) wide made of cloth that will not stretch. A soft strap or belt, strip of hide, or rolled-up piece of plastic garbage bag will work if you can keep the knot from slipping. (**Fig. 11-3**)

When applying a tourniquet:

• place it as close above the wound as possible.

Since anything below the tourniquet may have to be amputated, place the tourniquet as close to the wound as possible.

• Wrap the tourniquet around twice, tie a half-knot, place a stick, tie another half-knot.

Have ready tape or another bandage to secure the stick, and:

• twist to tighten only until bleeding stops, then tie the stick in place.

Further tightening will damage tissue. When a tourniquet has been applied:

- mark the casualty with "TK" where it cannot be missed, and note the time the tourniquet was put on. Use a large tag, tape, or mark on the casualty's forehead with a pen.

It is *critical* that medical authorities know about the tourniquet the moment the casualty arrives. Be sure the tourniquet and tag or mark are not covered and invisible. You should:

- leave the tourniquet in place if medical help is less than one hour away.

- If you are more than an hour from medical attention, loosen the tourniquet very slowly for 5 minutes at the end of each 45 minutes, maintaining direct pressure on the wound. If bleeding is again heavy, tighten the tourniquet immediately. If bleeding is now manageable, leave the tourniquet in place but do not tighten it again unless severe bleeding starts.

**Any casualty with a tourniquet
must be taken to medical aid.**

Any casualty requiring a tourniquet will almost certainly be in shock, and will be at great risk of hypothermia, as well as frostbite to the injured part. Remember this when preparing to transport.

External Bleeding from Body Injuries

Wounds with external bleeding are usually caused by knives, tools, chainsaws, falling on sharp objects, or animal attacks. Most are preventable. Body cuts are rarer when heavy winter clothing is worn, which is fortunate, since clothing may have to be removed despite the cold to control bleeding.

Rest, elevation, and direct pressure are used to stop external body bleeding, just as they are used for bleeding on arms and legs. However, it is more difficult to apply pressure with bandages, and raising the part is not as effective. Fortunately, large arteries are rarely cut on the surface of the body, and bleeding tends to be more easily stopped.

Direct pressure with a hand over a dressing may have to be applied until the bleeding is controlled. Then the wound can be dressed and bandaged normally.

Wounds Through the Abdominal Wall (Intestines Exposed)

If abdominal organs are exposed, there are three major dangers, aside from bleeding:

- twisting or kinking of the gut
- drying of the exposed gut
- infection.

Any twisting or kinking of intestines may reduce blood flow and cause that section of gut to die. Twisting may also cause intestinal blockage, which is fatal if not corrected. If the gut dries out, the dry part will die. In any opening of the body cavity, infection will occur rapidly and be extremely serious.

For any wound through the abdominal wall, take the following steps:

- Raise the head and shoulders; raise and support the knees.

Fig. 11-4: Raise knees and head to make the casualty with abdominal wounds more comfortable.

(Fig. 11-4) This will keep the wound from gaping and will feel more comfortable.

- Stop bleeding with gentle pressure over a sterile dressing.

If internal organs are NOT protruding through the wound:

- apply a thick sterile dressing to the wound and hold it firmly in place with wide bandages.

If internal organs ARE protruding through the wound:

- do not try to push intestines back into the body
- immediately cover the wound with a sterile dressing, covered in turn by aluminum foil.

Do this to protect the wound from cold and reduce drying while you are getting the casualty sheltered. If you have no aluminum foil, use a waterproof material such as plastic. Keep the casualty and the injury warm.

Once the casualty is sheltered, you should:

- pad around the organs to prevent pressure or further injury
- hold padding and dressings in place with firm (not tight) bandages
- not attempt to clean the area or change dressings
- call in air medevac urgently.

If the air temperature is warm, or if you have the casualty in a warm place and he will not get cold again, you should moisten the dressing with sterile saline or clean water. This will prevent the gut from drying out. *Be sure that the fluid has cooled to body temperature* before trickling it onto the dressing, which must stay in place.

NOTE: Once the dressing is wet, it will be difficult to keep the casualty warm, so *do not moisten it* unless there is no danger of the casualty getting cold.

Give the casualty nothing by mouth except perhaps small ice chips, tiny sips, or a moistened cloth to keep his mouth damp. Keep him in the position of most comfort during transport.

Amputated (Severed) Parts

The tissue of an amputated part will remain "alive" for only 6 hours at room temperature, but up to 18 hours if cooled. The amputated part should be cleansed of obvious dirt, wrapped in a sterile towel moistened with sterile saline, placed in a sterile plastic bag, and stored in an insulated cooling chest filled with crushed ice and water, making sure that the part accompanies the casualty. The amputated part should not be allowed to freeze. The three important points are:

- keeping the part clean
- keeping the part cool (NOT freezing)
- sending the part with the casualty.

Soft Tissue Injuries to Face and Head

Because facial cuts left untreated for a couple of days may result in bad scars, extra care should be taken to get the casualty to early medical help. If this is not possible, clean the cut thoroughly and draw the edges together with tape.

The tongue bleeds heavily and cannot be bandaged. If the tongue is badly bitten, bleeding may be controlled by squeezing the cut firmly between two or more gauze pads until bleeding stops. The casualty should sit leaning forward so that blood and saliva run out of the mouth. He will be unable to swallow if you are gripping his tongue, and the fluids will cause breathing problems.

Nosebleeds are common in the dry air of the north. They may appear as signs of serious head or facial injury.

Most simple bleedings occur near the nostrils, but sometimes they occur higher up in the nose.

Most nosebleeds are not dangerous, but severe ones may produce shock. Rarely, deaths have resulted.

To treat a nosebleed:

- Have the casualty sit leaning slightly forward so that blood will not run down his throat.

- Have him pinch the soft part of the nostrils between his fingers, holding firmly until bleeding has stopped. This usually takes only 4 to 5 minutes, but could take up to 20.
- Apply cold packs to the nose, forehead, and face.

If you suspect skull fracture, do not allow him to blow his nose.

If the bleeding is high up in the nose and shows no signs of slowing or stopping after half an hour of treatment, cut a large gauze pad or a soft cotton cloth into a thin *continuous* strip, and *very gently* pack it up the nostril, using forceps (tweezers). Do not push hard, and be very careful not to injure the inside of the nose. Be sure that the material is in a strong continuous strip, so that when removed, it all comes out in one piece.

Leave the pack there for 24 to 48 hours, then gently remove it. If bleeding starts again, repack the nostril.

If enough blood has been lost to cause signs of shock, and if the casualty is not nauseated, give him lots of fluids in sips, preferably the salt-soda-sugar mixture used in the treatment of burns **(see Fig. 20-2, p. 223)**, or one of the other rehydration solutions (see Chapter 20).

Wound Care and Infection

If wounds will be seen by a nurse or doctor within a few hours, simply stop the bleeding and dress and bandage the wounds.

As it may be some time before a wounded person in the wilderness is seen by a doctor or nurse, good wound care is important to prevent infection and to reduce scarring. If you are far from help, care for wounds as follows.

Cleanly cut wounds, such as those made by knives, sharp tools, or broken glass, will usually bleed freely, which helps to wash out dirt and bacteria, and reduces chances of infection.

If bleeding is serious, it should be stopped using RED: rest, elevation, and direct pressure. If bleeding is *not* serious, allow bleeding to clean the wound.

For clean, freely bleeding wounds:

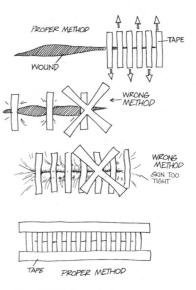

- wash the wound well with soap and water
- cover it with a sterile dressing, bandage firmly, and leave in place for about 48 hours.

Forty-eight hours will allow time for bleeding to stop completely and the wound to start to heal so that it will not bleed more. After 48 hours, examine the wound for signs of infection. If it is infection-free, redress it, and examine again in

Fig. 11-5: Wound closure.

another 48 hours if medical help has not been reached.

CLOSE the wound before dressing it:

- if it is a clean wound on a clean area (face, scalp, arm, upper leg)
- if the edges are clean and will come together well.

To close a wound, you should:

- be sure the area around the wound is clean and dry so tape will stick
- if tincture of benzoin is in the first-aid kit, paint it around the edges to help the tape stick
- start taping past the end of the cut
- stick one side first, draw the edges together, stick the other side as shown in drawing (**Fig. 11-5**)
- leave an open space, then start the next tape from the other side.

Continue alternating strips until the wound is closed. Do not draw the edges together too closely because the skin will wrinkle.

Then:

- anchor all tapes with a strip across their ends
- apply a sterile dressing, and bandage it in place
- change the dressing (NOT the tape) daily, watching for infection
- leave tape on 5 days for wounds on the face, 10 days for wounds on the trunk, and 15 days for wounds on extremities
- if infection occurs, remove the tape, and allow the wound to open for cleaning and drainage.

If you have done a good job and there is no infection, the wound should heal well and leave little scar tissue. However, if the wound becomes infected, you have new and serious problems.

Many wounds are contaminated (dirty) with dirt or bacteria from the skin or from the instrument that caused the wound. These wounds will often become infected if they are not carefully cleaned before dressing. Also, any wound on the hands, feet, lower legs, genitalia, or armpits is likely to be contaminated with bacteria. Any animal bite will be badly contaminated, and the human bite is considered the worst of all. Any wound that is ragged, such as a deep scrape from a fall, a chainsaw cut, a semi-crushing injury, or a forceful tear of the skin, is likely to become infected.

Dealing with a contaminated wound in the field is a difficult, often painful process, and if you can get the casualty to medical care, you should do so. However, if it will be a day or more to medical care, you must do your best to clean the wound. Prepare carefully, and be sure everything is ready before starting.

To care for a contaminated wound, follow these steps:

- **Get the casualty into a warm, comfortable shelter.**

- **Prepare a clean "table" or work surface** to keep your materials from becoming contaminated. The flat cover of a (Coleman type) camp stove is one possibility. Wipe it with alcohol if available, or scrub it with soap and water, or singe a clean cloth over a flame and use that to put equipment on.

- **Prepare a second clean area** to rest the injured part on while treating it.

- **Prepare some clean water or sterile salt solution (normal saline)** to wash the wound.

  1. Boil 2 or more litres (or quarts) of clean water for 10 minutes in a clean pot. Add 2 rounded teaspoons of salt (about 10 mL) for each litre while it is boiling. Allow to cool to about body temperature before using; OR

  2. Fill 1 or 2 plastic bags with a litre (or quart) of water and 2 rounded teaspoons of salt (10 mL) in each and tie them shut. Place them in a pot of water, and boil for 10 minutes. Allow to cool as above.

- When ready to begin, **scrub your hands very thoroughly, including the nails.** Use soap and water. Use water with a few drops of household bleach if it is available.

- **Scrub with soap and water around the wound with a sterile sponge or clean cloth.** Scrub *away* from the edges. Be careful not to breathe or cough on the wound.

- Use sterilized forceps (tweezers), or if none are available, a needle or the tip of a sterilized knife, to **remove any large bits of dirt in the wound.** Sterilize the forceps by washing them with alcohol, or passing them quickly through a flame. An instrument can also be sterilized by boiling it with a piece of thread tied to it to help lift it out. Boiling is preferable to sterilizing by alcohol or flame.

- **Irrigate (wash out) the wound** using a strong, thin stream of sterile saline or clean water. Use at least a litre (or quart). You can pour it into the wound, use a syringe, or make a stream by carefully puncturing a boiled plastic-bagful. **(Fig. 11-6)** You can get more pressure by squeezing the bag slightly. If you are unable to make a saline solution to irrigate a dirty wound, use plain, clean water.

Fig. 11-6: A stream of water from a plastic bag or water carrier may be used to irrigate contaminated wounds.

- **Scrub (debride) the wound vigorously to** remove all dirt, bits of clothing, dead tissue, etc., which may cause infection. Use sterile sponges, sterile dressings, or sterile pieces of cotton cloth. Scrub quickly and firmly; it will be painful and the casualty will not be able to stand it for long. It will bleed vigorously, but it is most important that the wound be completely clean. *It is more important to clean the wound well than it is to close it!*

- **Irrigate again** to flush out loosened dirt.

- **Stop bleeding** with pressure on a sterile dressing.

- **Close the wound, OR put a dressing on the open wound.**

  Leave the wound *open* if:

  - it is very deep
  - it is on a hand, foot, lower leg, the genitals, an armpit, or the groin
  - it is on an area that is stretched often (e.g., the outside of a joint)
  - it is an animal or human bite
  - it is contaminated (dirty).

- Use a sterile dressing, and bandage well.

- If there are antibiotics for wound infection in your first-aid kit, start them as prescribed.

- Change the dressing daily. Watch carefully for infection.

If the casualty is nervous or doesn't feel well, suggest that he not watch what you are doing. If possible, keep the casualty lying down during the procedure; he will feel better and cannot hurt himself if he faints.

Infections

The germs which cause infection live almost everywhere – on our skin, in the soil, on animals, in our mouths, and in our guts.

They can be carried into a wound by almost anything, including our breath. A few germs in a wound can usually be destroyed by the body's natural defences, but when there are very many, as in a very dirty wound, or when the body's defences are weak, the germs quickly multiply and become destructive. The signs we see – redness, warmth, pus – are signs that the body is fighting the infection.

**An infection is the invasion of part of the body
by harmful germs.**

At all levels of infection, it is important that a casualty have good rest, nutrition, and plenty of liquids.

Wound Infection (Localized) – How to Tell

A wound infection will usually show:

- pain and tenderness to touch
- swelling
- redness and warmth
- pus production
- swollen lymph nodes (glands) in the armpits, groin, or under the jaw (sometimes)
- fever (sometimes).

Any wound will cause some pain and redness, and it is not necessarily infection. But if a wound has a warm, reddish swelling that extends more than ¼ inch from the edge, it is probably infected.

What to Do

If a wound becomes infected, you should:

- **Give antibiotics prescribed for infections.** Remember that each antibiotic works best on only a few different germs, and if the infection is not caused by that germ, the medication will not help. Antibiotics are not magic! They are also not always essential. Don't give up on infection if you do not have antibiotics.

- **Allow the wound to drain.** Remove any tape closing the infected area and allow the wound to open naturally. If necessary for full drainage, gently open the edges.

- **Wash the wound 2 or 3 times each day.** Use soap and water and clean dressings or sponges. Get out all the pus. Irrigation (see above) may be less painful than scrubbing, but do what you must to clean the wound.

- **Apply warm saline compresses for 5 to 10 minutes several times a day.** The warmth will increase blood flow to the area, help the body fight the infection, and loosen clots, scabs, and pus.

- **Dress the wound with thick, absorbent sterile dressings.**

- **Elevate the part.** This will reduce swelling and pain.

- **If there is a fever, give Aspirin or Tylenol (acetaminophen) as directed.**

Whole Body (Systemic) Infection – How to Tell

Sometimes an infection will grow and invade the entire body through the blood and lymph systems. This is a very serious, potentially fatal condition. The casualty may have:

- fever and chills
- warm, pink skin
- red lines spreading from wound
- general malaise (all-over discomfort, weakness, sick feeling)
- headache
- increase in swollen nodes
- skin eruptions – pimples, boils (sometimes)
- nausea, diarrhea.

What to Do

Continue the treatment described above and evacuate urgently! This is a very serious condition which may be fatal without hospital treatment.

Gas gangrene is another serious infection, showing most of the signs of systemic (whole body) infection, with a thin, watery, often foul-smelling drainage, crackly tissues around the wound caused by gas in the tissues, and extreme illness. This advances rapidly and may be fatal in as little as 30 hours. *Immediate medical care is needed.*

Abscesses are infections under the skin, most often on the neck, armpits, chest, face, buttocks, or around the rectum. They start out as painful, hard, red swellings, and come to a soft yellow "head," which is pus showing through the skin.

Take the casualty to medical help if it is available for surgical drainage of the abscess. If medical help is not available, then:

- use hot compresses or hot soaks several times each day to bring the swelling to a head

- wash the skin over and around the abscess

- apply ice or snow for 5 minutes to deaden the area (if it is very cold, beware of frostbite!)

- open the yellowish head with a sterilized razor blade or very sharp knife tip to allow drainage, making the cut all the way across the yellowish area to provide good drainage

- flush out the pus with clean, warm water (the irrigation technique with a plastic bag works well)

- pack the remaining cavity with a strip of clean, sterile gauze or sterilized light cotton cloth leaving the end out

- dress the wound

- remove the packing daily (quickly, to minimize pain), irrigate, and repack.

Continue this until the cavity has become too small to pack.

12

Animal Bites and Stings

People living close to the land are more likely to be injured by animals than those living in cities. Black, grizzly, and polar bears can inflict severe and sometimes fatal wounds. Dogs, singly or in teams, frequently bite and sometimes kill humans. Rabid foxes, coyotes, and skunks are common. Trappers are sometimes bitten or clawed by their quarry. Rattlesnakes are found in southern Canada. Perhaps the worst bite of all in terms of infection is the human bite.

Unless the wound itself is immediately life-threatening, *the greatest danger from bites (or claw injuries) is infection.* Rabies and tetanus are also commonly contracted from animal bites.

There are some basic first-aid rules for animal bites and claw wounds:

- treat every bite as a badly contaminated wound

- clean all bites immediately and completely within 3 hours

- get rapid medical care for any bite which breaks the skin even slightly, even though it appears to be minor.

And, if possible, expose bites to direct sunlight after cleaning, as ultraviolet light kills some viruses.

See Chapter 11 for a complete description of the first aid for contaminated wounds.

Bear Safety and Maulings

While the majority of bears flee when encountering a human, every species of North American bear has been known to attack.

Incidents are most common where bears have become used to the presence of humans and learned to steal garbage for food. Areas near dumps are especially dangerous.

Following are some basic safety rules to prevent bear attacks:

- Never camp near a dump, or where bears often feed.

- Butcher game meat far from camp if possible.

- Hang game meat away from camp, and always approach the area cautiously.

- Do not allow children to play alone near a dump site, animal carcass, or gut pile.

- In camp, keep food out of sleeping tents.

- Burn camp garbage immediately, at least 100 metres (or yards) downwind from camp. Use the hottest possible fire so that nothing remains. Do not burn fat in a campfire, as the smell of burning fat will travel many miles downwind and attract bears. If on the seashore, dispose of fat, waste meat or bones, or unburnable waste food below the tide line, where the various scavengers will come to your aid. If inland, bury this waste some distance downwind from camp.

- Hang a shirt, rich with human scent, over meat that must be left for a time, or mark around the carcass with human urine. This may discourage some bears, but don't count on it.

Polar bears, especially younger ones, are often totally fearless and will come right into an occupied camp after anything that smells good. The smell of seal fat is especially attractive to them, so seals, hides, and meat taken in hunts should be kept far from camp, or where dogs will be able to spot an approaching bear and give warning. If a separate cook tent is used for a large camp, it should be away from the sleeping tents, and located where it can easily be seen. Some experienced Arctic campers place sleeping tents in a line rather than a circle so there is less chance of hitting another tent if shooting must be done in the dark.

Grizzly Bear–Human Meetings

It is extremely rare for a grizzly to enter camp and attack a human with the intent of eating him. Most injuries are due to surprise encounters at close range. If this happens and the bear does not flee, keep facing the bear but avoid direct eye contact, which for bears is aggressive behaviour. Look submissive and retreat slowly – don't run. If you can get about 15 feet up a tree in a hurry you are probably safe, but remember that a grizzly can probably run 50 yards while you are climbing 10 feet.

A grizzly has a variety of methods of driving you out of its space. It may simply turn sideways to show you how big it is. It may make a bluffing charge, or several of them. When making a bluffing charge, it may quarter in to get downwind as it comes, with head up, perhaps running a bit sideways as dogs sometimes do. It may come very close. It may growl, pop its jaws loudly, and cuff the dirt. It is warning you off – and you will have no doubt of that!

If it makes a serious charge it will come straight in, very fast. Toss your pack toward it on the chance that it will stop and maul it while you escape. If it gets you, it will usually knock you down and bite at your head. The only thing you can do if you are unarmed is to roll quickly onto your face, with your hands clasped around the back of your neck, and play dead. It is a gamble. Grizzlies will often take a few punishing bites and depart, and you can only hope that they will not be big bites. They often are not. Wait a *long* time to be sure it is gone before you get up, because it may stay and observe you for a while.

People who have been badly mauled often say that in their shock they were aware of great pressure but not so much of specific pain. It *is* possible to play dead!

Black Bear–Human Meetings

Black bears are more easily frightened away than grizzlies and less likely to attack in a surprise meeting, but if they *do* attack, it may be with the idea of making a meal. They are more likely to attack a person alone, especially a smaller person or a woman. They will often show "stalking" behaviour, following and circling the casualty before charging. When they do charge they will knock the casualty down and start to eat whatever part appeals to them. In a recent case in the Yukon, a black bear ate part of the buttocks and upper leg of one casualty. In Alaska, a bear ate most of both arms of another casualty. Both casualties survived, but were badly maimed.

Black bears will also make bluffing charges to drive you away from food they want. They will stare right at you and advance slowly, sometimes swinging the head, sometimes making a short, pouncing movement. If you are unarmed and have food or a pack, toss it toward the bear, and try to leave the area, but do not run.

If a black bear shows stalking behaviour or if you cannot afford to lose your pack, you are better off being aggressive. According to bear researchers, black bears can often be intimidated. Making loud noises, adopting an aggressive posture, throwing rocks (large ones!) will all help. Show no fear. If it still attacks, fight back! Gouge at its eyes and strike at its nose with your fist or a rock. Don't play dead or it may simply begin to eat.

Polar Bear–Human Meetings

Polar bears have no natural enemies and are often extremely aggressive. Their main prey is seals, but they have been known to stalk, kill, and eat humans. They may walk into a camp at any time, or stalk a human on sea ice or on land. They are so large and strong that without a powerful weapon a human has no chance. It is extremely foolhardy to venture into polar bear country unarmed. A good dog is an excellent alarm, and will keep a bear busy while you escape or get your gun.

Polar bears are known to enter tents and sometimes igloos, often through the walls. As many northern hunters leave their guns outside to prevent condensation of moisture on the cold metal, they are sometimes caught inside without defence. Some hunters have struck an intruding nose with a snow knife or other hard object to drive bears away.

If a polar bear catches you, don't play dead. Fight as hard as you can. Go for its eyes.

Do everything you can to avoid attracting polar bears into camp. It is a great shame to have to shoot these magnificent animals.

Twelve-gauge shotgun shells firing plastic bullets are sometimes available. These sting bears without causing serious injury and may drive them away. They have been shown to be effective on polar bears and will probably discourage most black bears, but would probably only antagonize grizzlies. They should not be used unless they are backed up by adequate firepower. Experienced people often load one or two plastic bullets, filling the balance of an unplugged magazine with heavy-duty slug loads.

Bear-Inflicted Wounds

When grizzly and polar bears attack, they most frequently bite at the head and face. It is common for parts of a casualty's scalp to be torn away, hanging in flaps and exposing the skull. In addition, punctures, fractures, tears (lacerations), and bruises of the face, arms, and legs are common.

While the scalp wounds are often spectacular and bloody, they may be the least serious except for later infection. Look for puncture wounds into the skull itself. Be alert for breathing problems due to facial injury and bleeding into the mouth. Watch for neck and back fractures. A complete and careful examination must be done after your ABCDEF's (see Chapter 2), because the casualty is commonly covered with blood from scalp wounds, which may keep you from seeing other injuries.

Wounds from black bears are often claw scratches, bites on legs and arms, or deep flesh wounds if the bear has attempted to feed. In the latter case, blood loss and shock will be major.

Bears often roll or drag their victims while mauling them, so wounds are commonly full of dirt, grass, and leaves as well as the bear's foul-smelling saliva. Infection is almost certain, even with medical treatment. When cleaning such a wound, you must not only irrigate it, but scrub it thoroughly, even though it may be extremely painful and will cause bleeding. Pain and subsequent infection will be less if you do this as soon as possible. Get out every trace of dirt. If any painkillers are available, give them before starting, allowing some time for them to act.

Scalp flaps should be washed thoroughly and laid back in position on the well-cleaned skull. They may be held loosely in position with tape or bandages, but *do not close any contaminated wound.*

If antibiotics are available, start them immediately as prescribed. Keep the casualty well fed and watered, and get him to medical help quickly. Change dressings twice daily and watch for signs of infection. If it occurs, clean the wound aggressively as described in Chapter 11.

Dog Bites, Maulings, and Rabies

As with bear attacks, prevention is important. Groups of dogs should not be allowed to run loose. Pets or sled dogs that are perfectly friendly may become dangerous when they "pack up" with other dogs.

Dogs most often bite adults on the hands and arms, sometimes legs. Children are often bitten in the face. Dogs lack the power of bears so fractures are rare, but if a person goes down in a dog attack, serious facial injuries, often including the eyes, are common.

With facial injuries, watch the casualty's airway. In children especially, be alert for shock.

Rabies should always be considered because it is fatal once the disease develops. The virus lives in the saliva of an infected animal. Dogs are common carriers, as are foxes, wolves, coyotes, raccoons, skunks, and bats. Squirrels, rabbits, mice, and rats may become rabid but rarely transmit the disease. Their bites often carry other infections.

Bites should always be well scrubbed with soap and water, irrigated, and left open to the sun for a time. Puncture wounds should be allowed to bleed freely, then scrubbed and well irrigated. Deep punctures should be soaked in hot salt-water several times a day for two days.

Immediate first aid will not prevent rabies. If rabies is known to be in the area, casualties must be taken *immediately* to medical care, even for minor bites, as lifesaving (and relatively painless) vaccinations must be started within a few days. A pet that acts strangely and bites for no apparent reason should be caged and observed for 10 days. If it is rabid, it will get very sick or die during that time. If it gets sick, it should be destroyed, and the head carefully removed and sent in for analysis. If it remains healthy or recovers, there is no danger of rabies.

Pets or working dogs that are bitten by others may take days or months to develop the disease, so confining the bitten animal for ten days will not tell you if it is infected. You must, if possible, confine and observe the animal that did the biting, as well as the bitten animal. If you cannot confine the biting animal, there is the unavoidable risk that the bitten pet may develop the disease later. If there has been any bite by a questionable animal, safety dictates that the casualty receive rabies vaccinations, and the animal be destroyed and the head sent in for testing.

Wild animals that bite humans or dogs should be shot (avoid head shots, which may affect rabies testing) and the head sent in.

If you must remove a head, wear rubber gloves and take every precaution not to get any blood or saliva on your skin. Burn the used gloves and anything with blood or saliva on it, and boil the cutting tools. Seal the head in several layers of plastic bags in a box and take it to the local nursing station, Royal Canadian Mounted Police (RCMP) office, or the Renewable Resources or Conservation Officer, who will send it to the appropriate authority to be checked for rabies.

Bites of Smaller Animals

Any bite or animal scratch, no matter how small, is likely to cause infection. Treat bites and scratches as badly contaminated wounds.

Snakebites

Rattlesnakes are the only poisonous snakes in Canada, and bites are rare. Rattlers are easily identified by the spade-shaped head, thin neck, thick body, and blunt tail tipped by a rattle. Newly born rattlers may not yet have noticeable rattles, but are capable of biting and injecting venom (poison).

Rattlesnakes will always try to escape. Bites occur when they are touched or stepped on, or when someone places a hand very close. Heavy boots will generally protect the wearer.

**Rattlesnake bites in Canada are rarely fatal,
so you may reassure the casualty with sincerity!**

How to Tell

People usually know when they have been bitten, but sometimes if the snake is hidden in a crack or under a rock, or if the casualty is crashing through brush and does not hear the warning buzz, he may not realize the source of the sudden pain.

There will be distinct fang marks, usually two, sometimes only one if the snake has a broken fang. If the strike is on bare skin, there may also be smaller scratches from other teeth. (Fang marks do not indicate a full dose of venom. If the snake has recently struck something else, the venom remaining may be little.)

The casualty will see and feel:

- immediate sharp burning pain
- swelling at the site within 5 to 10 minutes, spreading rapidly
- numbness and tingling of lips, face, and scalp 30 to 60 minutes after the bite (if they occur *immediately*, this may be due to overbreathing – hyperventilation – from fear).

From 30 to 90 minutes after the bite, the casualty may experience twitching of the mouth and eye muscles and a rubbery or metallic taste in the mouth. After about an hour there may be weakness, sweating, vomiting, and fainting. In about 2 or 3 hours there will be bruising at the site, and later, large blood blisters. In serious bites, breathing difficulties and collapse occur after 6 to 12 hours.

What to Do

Your main objective as a first-aider is to slow the spread of the venom and get the casualty to medical aid. You should:

- calm and reassure the casualty to slow circulation and reduce shock
- place the casualty at rest, and keep him from moving to slow the spread of the venom
- wash the bite area gently with soap and water
- splint the limb to prevent movement – but watch the advance of swelling to be sure that the bandages do not get too tight
- keep the limb level with the heart
- transport urgently to medical aid, by air medevac if possible.

There are some important "do nots" in snakebites:

- Do not give alcohol.
- Do not cut the fang marks.
- Do not try to suck out venom.
- Do not apply a tourniquet.
- Do not apply cold to the site.

All of these have been considered correct treatment at some time, but have been found to be dangerous in some way. In most cases, the casualty will recover, with some loss of tissue, and scarring at the bite.

Non-Poisonous Snakebites

These usually occur only if a snake is handled. They will produce only a row of scratches without any fang marks. Scrub them well with soap and water and treat them like any contaminated wound. An injection of tetanus toxoid should be given.

Bone Punctures and Cuts

Punctures or cuts by sharp, broken animal and fish bones have the same dangers as animal bites and should be treated similarly. The most dangerous is a bone cut from a trapped furbearer that has been dead for some time before skinning. Bacteria multiply in the carcass, and terrible infections can result. Clean all such injuries aggressively and seek medical help as soon as possible.

Insect Stings and Bites: Allergic Reactions

Both bees and wasps are common in the north, but more so farther south. Wasps such as the "mud-dauber," "paper wasp," or "yellowjacket" are common, and often gather where fish, meat, or fruit is found.

Most stings produce only a quick, sharp pain with some swelling and itching. However, a few people are allergic to insect stings and some may die within minutes if the proper medication is not available. This allergic reaction is called anaphylactic shock. Most people who have this problem carry a kit, containing an injectable drug called adrenaline and some pills. Instructions are provided in the kit.

How to Tell

A person who is stung and has an allergic reaction will usually show signs within seconds or minutes, although sometimes it may take up to two hours. He may have:

- difficulty breathing
- nausea and vomiting
- swelling of the tongue, nose, and mouth
- hives (red, itchy swellings)
- no pulse
- loss of consciousness.

What to Do

This person is in great danger of having his airway closed by swelling. If he is carrying a kit of medications, you should:

- Help him to take the medication (usually an injection and a pill).
- Watch his breathing and aid his breathing if he is not getting enough air.
- Gently scrape the sting and poison sack (if any) away with the edge of a knife. Do not try to pinch it with fingers or tweezers, as you will squeeze more poison into the sting. (Wasps do not leave a poison sack attached to the sting.)
- Apply cold to the site (apply ice packs, a plastic bag full of cold water, or submerge the limb in cold water).

What to Do – For Non-allergic Casualties

First-aid treatment is usually not needed. You may apply certain common materials which may help to neutralize the venom and sooth the sting. **For bee venom** (which is acid), apply a paste of baking soda and water. **For wasp venom** (which is alkaline), apply vinegar, lemon juice, or try the juice of wild cranberries, wild rhubarb, or sorrel.

If there is a large swelling, itching, redness, and pain, non-prescription antihistamines may be given according to directions. (These are commonly called "cold tablets.")

For stings in the mouth, give the person ice to suck, or have him flush his mouth with cold water. For a bee sting, give him a glass of water with a teaspoon of baking soda in it and ask him to rinse his mouth and hold it for several minutes.

Leech bites are not serious but may become infected if the leech is pulled off by force. Remove leeches by applying heat from a match or cigarette to them, or apply a drop of gas, oil, or kerosene. Any of these will cause leeches to drop off. Wash the bite. Apply baking soda paste to soothe it. If bleeding continues, finger pressure will stop it quickly.

13

Internal Bleeding

When we think of blood loss, we usually think about bleeding that is visible. But we can also lose blood inside our bodies, and this may be even more serious, because while we can almost always stop blood loss through the skin, it may be impossible to stop internal bleeding.

Internal bleeding is often caused by *blunt trauma,* which simply means that the body strikes or is struck by something so violently that blood vessels, bones, or organs are damaged, even though nothing penetrates the skin. We usually think of internal bleeding in the belly or chest, but it can occur inside the muscles, under the skin, even inside the skull. Hunters who shoot big game are familiar with the way blood spreads out between muscle layers near a gunshot wound. The same thing happens in humans. Even though the blood stays inside the body, it no longer performs its job and the effect on the body is the same as if the blood were lost.

Internal bleeding may also be caused by the sharp edges of broken bones. Because the large arteries lie near major bones, any serious fracture of the bone may damage them. When the femur (upper leg bone) is broken, it may cut the huge artery that lies just beside it, and as much as two litres or quarts of blood may be lost into the spaces between the muscles. An equal amount of blood can be lost from the marrow of the femur or pelvis. Shock usually results. Before intravenous fluids were available, broken femurs were often fatal.

Severe internal bleeding can also result from peptic (stomach) or duodenal (intestine) ulcers.

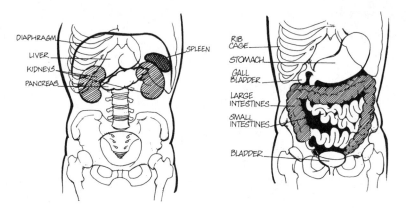

Fig. 13-1a: Location of solid organs.

Fig. 13-1b: Location of hollow organs

Bruises are internal bleeding which shows through the skin. Large bruises may indicate blood loss under the skin, and may be serious.

Some of the worst internal bleeding happens when the spleen, kidney, or liver is damaged by a hard blow. These organs lie high in the belly, just under the edge of the ribs. (**Figs. 13-1a,b**) A person struck there, whether front, back, or side, should be put at rest and watched carefully for signs of shock, which indicate internal bleeding. This casualty *must quickly have medical attention.*

How to Tell

Carefully examine the casualty. Signs and symptoms may not appear immediately, so watch the casualty for several hours if you suspect internal injury.

He may have one or more of the following:

- **shock**
- **tenderness and pain** over the injury
- **rebound tenderness** (pain occurring when a hand pushing gently on the belly is suddenly released)
- **rigidity** (tightness or hardness) of the belly muscles

- **nausea and vomiting**
- **bloating** (swelling) of the belly
- **bruises** indicating blood loss
- **blood from a body opening** that takes time to appear. (Blood in the urine often indicates urethra or bladder damage, but it may take six hours or more to show. It may not appear red, but simply as dark or "smoky" urine.)

What to Do

- **Treat for shock.**
- **Keep the casualty at rest.** Handle him gently. Raise his head and knees slightly for comfort.
- **Arrange urgent air medevac.**
- **Give the casualty nothing by mouth** except small sips of water. If the casualty cannot be evacuated, continue to give sips of water so that he does not dehydrate, but beware of vomiting!

With a femur fracture, internal bleeding into the thigh may be reduced by prompt splinting, application of a cold pack, and elevation.

If evacuation has been impossible and the casualty of internal bleeding begins to recover, *he must rest for 10 to 14 days* before starting normal activity. The casualty should be seen by a physician before starting normal activity because he is at risk of rebleeding.

If in doubt, assume there is internal injury and evacuate the casualty.

14

Chest Injuries

Because the chest contains the heart, lungs, and major blood vessels, any chest injury may be serious.

Chest injuries most commonly seen in wilderness situations are fractured ribs (which may or may not involve the lungs), massive bruises, gunshot wounds, and penetrating wounds caused by sharp objects.

General Care for Chest Injuries

- Cuts which do not penetrate the rib cage are treated simply as cuts.

- Injuries which penetrate the rib cage may cause a lung to collapse or blood to build up in the chest cavity. The objectives of first aid are to reduce these effects and maintain adequate breathing.

- Bruising may be superficial or indicate internal blood loss, and the objective is to prevent or reduce the effects of shock.

In any chest injury requiring air evacuation, ask the pilot to fly at the lowest level that is safe.

Major Bruising to Chest

This injury is common in the far north, where heavy sleds with rope hitches ride over snowmobiles and strike the driver. Drivers are also thrown off and run over by sleds. In these accidents, the casualty is commonly struck on the back, and may suffer rib fractures or major bruising. If the lowest "floating" ribs are involved, suspect damage to kidneys or spleen. Kidney injury usually shows as blood in the urine, which will be red-tinged or smoky in colour. Either kidney or spleen injury may produce major shock. Falls from ATV's are responsible for many chest injuries.

Any impact strong enough to produce major bruises to the rib cage is usually strong enough to break ribs and cause damage to blood vessels. The primary concern is shock due to internal bleeding (see Chapter 13). **The first-aider should always check for spine or neck injury in these cases**, both at the point of impact and at the neck, where a "whiplash" may occur.

How to Tell

- **Check for spinal injury.** Feel for irregularity and point tenderness over the spine; ask the casualty for any symptoms like tingling, loss of feeling, or inability to function. Treat as a spinal injury if there is any suspicion of it, even if you are not sure.

- **Check for broken ribs.** Does the casualty feel pain on breathing or movement? Is there tenderness at that point? Does pressing on the sternum (breastbone) cause pain anywhere on a rib? If so, there is a fracture at that point.

- **Check for lung puncture** (closed pneumothorax). Is there difficulty breathing, coughing-up of blood, rattling breath sounds, or blueness of lips, fingers, or fingernail beds?

If there is bruising but neither rib nor lung damage, place the casualty at rest in his most comfortable position and watch for signs of shock. Encourage coughing to reduce fluid build-up in lungs. If shock signs appear, treat for shock and **evacuate urgently**, by air medevac if possible.

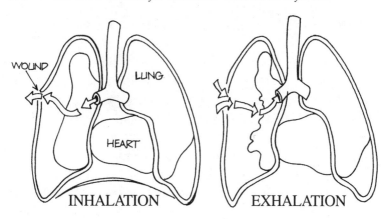

Fig. 14-1: Collapsing lung.

Punctured Lungs

Punctured lungs may be caused by penetration from the outside (open pneumothorax), or by a sharp broken rib (closed pneumothorax). Sometimes a lung will rupture by itself (spontaneous pneumothorax, also closed).

The lungs are expanded by negative pressure within the chest. Any leak of air into the chest cavity will cause the lung to collapse proportionately. (**Fig. 14-1**)

Punctured Lung – Closed Pneumothorax

How to Tell

If the puncture is due to a broken rib, the casualty will have been struck in the ribs. He may have:

- **pain at the site**, on breathing and to touch
- **difficulty breathing or shortness of breath**
- **coughing-up of blood**
- **signs of shock** (weak, rapid pulse, rapid breathing, fear, pale skin, etc. These signs will not appear in spontaneous pneumothorax.)
- **uneven chest expansion**.

It may be difficult to tell if one lung is not expanding as well as the other. Place your hands gently on either side of the rib cage and carefully compare what you feel, as well as what you see.

(If the puncture is due to a simple rupture of the lung with no apparent cause, the casualty will feel a sudden sharp chest pain and experience shortness of breath, which may increase and be mild to severe. The pain will be sharp, not "crushing" as with a heart attack. Treatment is the same as for a puncture caused by a broken rib.)

What to Do

- **Put the casualty at rest, semi-sitting, leaning to the injured side.** If he prefers another position for ease of breathing, let him take it.

- **If the casualty cannot get enough air, assist him with rescue breathing.** Time your breaths with his, and breathe gently to aid him.

Penetrating Chest Injury – Open Pneumothorax

How to Tell

In stabbing incidents, there is usually a mixture of slashes and stabs. The slashes may look terrible and bleed heavily but are often not life-threatening, while the dangerous straight-in stabs may bleed little externally and be obscured by the blood from the slashes. **It is critical to look carefully for penetrating wounds *and treat these first.***

Chest penetrations are usually easy to locate *if the casualty is conscious.*

If he is unconscious, you should check immediately, front *and* back, if there is any possibility of chest penetration. Early sealing of the wound is critical. Watch for:

- painful and difficult breathing

- bloody bubbles at the wound when the casualty exhales
- sucking sounds when he inhales
- crackling sounds (crepitus) on touching the chest wall near the injury, due to air bubbles in the chest wall being pushed about.

The casualty may be short of breath, pale, frightened, shocky, and have blueness of lips and fingernail beds.

What to Do

- **Seal the opening immediately** with any airtight substance. Use a bare hand temporarily if nothing else is available. Make an airtight seal of plastic or foil, and tape it in place on three sides.

- **If an object is stuck in the chest, do not remove it.** Pad around it, cover with airtight material, and tape it in place on three sides.

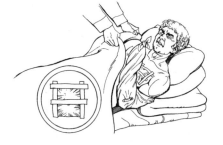

- **Support the arm on the injured side with a sling,** with hand high.

- **Place the casualty at rest in a semi-sitting position, leaning to the**

Fig. 14-2: Semi-sitting position for a casualty with lung injury. The sling is applied to take arm weight off the injured side.

injured side. (Fig. 14-2) Watch his breathing carefully, and do not leave him alone.

- **If the casualty cannot get enough air, assist him with rescue breathing** (see Chapter 21). Time your breaths with his, and breathe gently to aid him.

- **Call for urgent air medevac,** or evacuate by other means if necessary.

Crushed Chest – Flail Chest

If a section of ribs is broken so that it does not move with the rest of the chest during breathing, the casualty will be unable to inhale and exhale properly. When he inhales, the section is sucked in. When he exhales, it is pushed out (paradoxical breathing), so that there is no normal flow of air. Also, the movement of broken ribs causes great pain, which reduces the casualty's efforts to breathe.

You must reduce the movement of the loose section immediately, which will increase efficiency of breathing and reduce pain. If you cannot reduce the paradoxical movement enough to allow sufficient breathing, you must breathe for the casualty using rescue breathing, because **positive pressure going into the lungs will work far better than the casualty's own efforts to breathe**. You might have to continue this all the way to medical help.

An injury hard enough to fracture this many ribs will commonly do damage to the lungs below. Watch for signs of a punctured lung. Shock is likely.

How to Tell

The casualty will have sustained a heavy blow to the chest (**see Fig. 14-3**). You will note that:

- he will have great pain at the injury
- he struggles to breathe properly and to get enough air
- one section of the chest will move in opposition to the rest
- the casualty may be pale, and have blue lips and nailbeds.

What to Do

This is a critical emergency, requiring fast action.

- Immediately have the casualty lie on the injury to "splint" it against the paradoxical movement, OR have the casualty hold

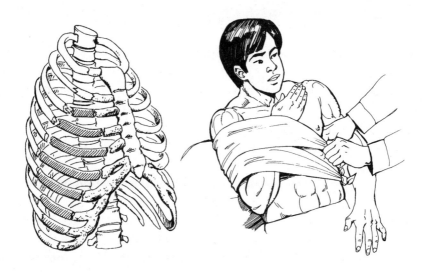

Fig. 14-3: Flail chest.   Fig. 14-4: First aid for flail chest.

a thick pad of cloth or even his arm against the injury to stop the movement.

- If the casualty still cannot get enough air, assist him with gentle rescue breathing.

- Tape a firm pad of cloth the size of the injury right on the injury, place the casualty's arm over it, and bandage tightly in place. (**Fig. 14-4**) Instruct the casualty to use whatever pressure with his arm gives the most comfort.

- Call in an urgent air medevac, or transport by other means if necessary, never leaving the casualty alone.

- Transport the casualty semi-sitting, leaning to his injured side.

- Assist the casualty with rescue breathing whenever he cannot get enough air.

- Treat for shock if it appears.

15

Joint Injuries

Sprains

Sprains are among the most common injuries. They may be so minor as to require no treatment, or more incapacitating than a fracture.

A sprain is a tearing or stretching of ligaments around a joint.

Ligaments are the tough fibres that hold joints together. Most hunters have seen these whitish fibres while butchering big game. When a joint is put under severe strain, as from a sharp twist, some of these fibres may tear or stretch. A sprain will also tear small blood vessels so that the area becomes swollen and discoloured. Sometimes it is difficult to tell a sprain from a fracture.

If in doubt, treat unknown joint injuries as fractures.

The most common sprains are to the ankles, fingers, knees, and wrists. Most sprains are caused by forces that move the joint beyond its normal range.

How to Tell

Review what happened. Has it happened before? Has the casualty a known weak joint? Was the joint twisted a particular way?
Have the casualty at rest and ask him to move the joint

through its normal range of motion. (Do *not* do this if you suspect a fracture or dislocation.) Compare it carefully with its companion joint on the other extremity.

Assess joint injuries immediately, before swelling starts, because swelling makes assessment difficult.

Look for the following signs and symptoms:

- **pain**, which increases on movement
- **loss or decrease of function** (the casualty is sometimes unable or unwilling to use the joint)
- **swelling and discolouration**, which appear slowly with sprains, rapidly with fractures
- **unnatural range of motion.** (When gently compared to the companion joint, the joint with a severe sprain has greater movement and feels "loose." If pain is minor and there is no unnatural motion, minimal treatment may be needed.)

What to Do

The objectives of first aid for sprains follow.

- Prevent or reduce swelling. Swelling slows healing and may disable the casualty.
- Support the joint. Artificial support with tape or elastic bandages will reduce pain, limit movement, and reduce further injury.

For best results, control of swelling should start immediately and continue for 2 hours. To control swelling, you should:

- apply gentle pressure (compression) with bandages to slow the flow of fluids into the injured area
- splint (immobilize) and elevate the part
- apply cold to the joint to reduce pain and slow the swelling.

You can remember these three steps by thinking of the word ICE, which stands for:

Ice
Compression (pressure)
Elevation.

There is a popular saying that "the best thing for a sprain is to keep using it so it doesn't stiffen up." This is *wrong*. Early first aid will reduce the amount of time lost in healing.

Knee Sprain

Knees are often sprained by the same forces that cause leg fractures or hip dislocations. Usually, there is an outward twist involved. The most common sprain is on the inside of the knee. This occurs easily when carrying a heavy pack.

How to Tell

The usual signs and symptoms of sprains will be present. Tenderness to pressure is often on the inside of the knee. If the cartilage within the knee is affected, the knee may not straighten fully, it may give way, or it may make clicking sounds when moved, and it probably cannot be used.

What to Do

For a mild or moderate sprain, you should:

- apply compression (with an elastic stretch bandage) and cold, and elevate and rest.

For a severe sprain:

- Give first aid as above. Apply cold frequently for 2 days. After 2 days, apply heat for 20 min., 4 or 5 times a day.

- If the sprain is severe or if there are signs of cartilage injury, splint it as a fracture in a position of comfort and transport the casualty to medical help.

Dislocations

Sometimes a joint is forced apart so violently that the two bones *remain* out of normal position. This involves stretching or tearing of ligaments.

A dislocation is the continuing separation of parts of a joint.

Sometimes, a joint under strain may "pop out" of position and back in again (subluxation). This will be painful, but may not require first aid. In severe cases, cold packs and support are desirable.

Dislocations are most common in the shoulders, fingers, thumbs, patella (kneecaps), and jaw. Hip dislocations are rare, and cannot be **reduced** – returned to position – by the first-aider. (See "Hip Fracture or Dislocation," Chapter 16.) Some dislocations, especially in the shoulder and patella, happen repeatedly because the ligaments are permanently stretched. Through experience, the casualty may know what to do about it.

Fractures and dislocations sometimes occur together, and there may be reduced circulation beyond the area. You may rightly hesitate to act.

It is best to seek medical advice by radio. If this is not possible and you are far from help, ask yourself: "Is the limb beyond the injury cold, blue or pale, numb, or without pulse? Is the casualty in severe pain which cannot be allowed to continue until help is reached?"

If the answers are no, treat as a fracture, splint in the position of most comfort, and transport the casualty to help or call in a medevac.

If the answers are yes, you may have to attempt to reduce the injury, recognizing that returning the part to position is dangerous and may cause damage to blood vessels or nerves at the site.

Basic Principles of First Aid for Dislocations

- Compare the injured joint with the uninjured one to help determine if there is a dislocation.

- If reduction must be attempted, do it immediately before muscles spasm (tighten).

- A very long, continuous pull may be required to tire and stretch tight muscles.

- If reduction must be attempted, fingers, thumbs, knees, and elbows require a straight pull in line with the normal limb.

- After reduction, treat with cold, compression, and elevation to reduce swelling, and splint if required.

First Aid for Specific Dislocations

Finger or Thumb: It will be obvious that finger bones are not in line. People who have this injury often reduce it themselves, immediately and instinctively.

What to Do

Simple dislocations are usually reduced by a straight, firm, steady pull in line with the finger or thumb. Do not attempt this more than twice; if this method is not successful, splint the joint and seek medical attention.

If there are signs of a fracture, treat the injury as one, and do not attempt to reduce the dislocation.

After reduction, splint the joint in the position of comfort until the casualty feels comfortable using it again.

Kneecap (Patella): This injury sometimes happens repeatedly, and the casualty may know how to deal with it himself. The kneecap will appear to be to the outside of and somewhat below its normal position.

What to Do

To reduce this dislocation, you should:

- warn the casualty of pain
- straighten his leg slowly while gently pushing the kneecap back toward its normal position
- apply cold, compression, elevation, and bandage the knee to stabilize the kneecap before he walks on it again.

Jaw: The lower jaw may dislocate during a yawn or while asleep. The two joints at its upper end slide out of their sockets and forward. The casualty usually cannot close his mouth and has pain at the jaw joints at the base of his ears. It looks and sounds funny, but is not for the casualty!

What to Do

This is usually easy to reduce.

- Wrap your thumbs well with gauze or strips of cloth to provide better grip.

- Place your thumbs on the surface of the casualty's lower molars, grip his jaw with the remaining fingers. Press firmly and steadily downward with the thumbs until his jaw pops into place. When the jaw "pops" back into place, it may snap shut on your thumbs – another important reason to pad them well.

Leave a supporting bandage in place until the casualty feels the jaw is comfortable and stable. (Be careful to leave it loose enough so that the casualty can vomit if necessary.)

Shoulder: Shoulder dislocations are common, painful, and rather frightening. Some individuals have a history of them and may tell you exactly how to help.

Compare the injured shoulder to the good shoulder. The

injured shoulder will have lost its normal rounded appearance and look angular. The front part of the shoulder may appear rounder than usual, and the ball joint may be felt forward of and below its normal position. The injured arm is usually supported by the opposite hand.

If you can get the casualty to medical help, splint the injury in the position of most comfort and transport immediately. If medical help is not available, you must act quickly because pain and muscle spasm will increase with time and may make it impossible to reduce the injury.

What to Do

There is one common first-aid procedure – the Stimson method. Create a flat surface; e.g., by placing a dogsled, komatik, or boat floorboards across some rocks.

Stimson Method (**Fig. 15-1**):

- Lie the casualty face down, with the injured arm hanging.

- Attach a weight approximately 10 kg or 22 lb to his wrist with wide bandages and leave it there for 15–30 minutes.

- When the muscles are stretched and tired, the joint may pop back in, but if it doesn't, turn the arm gently outward (thumb rotating outward, palm toward head) as you remove the weight.

Fig. 15-1: The Stimson method is used to reduce a dislocated shoulder.

The casualty should not use that arm again until he has had medical attention. Painkillers are useful during and after the first aid.

Hip Dislocation (see also "Hip Fracture" in Chapter 16): Hip dislocations are extremely rare but sometimes happen when a snowmobile driver or passenger on a sled puts out a leg. There is nothing you can do for this casualty except to treat shock, immobilize in the position of most comfort, give painkillers (as prescribed), and either transport to medical aid or call in an air medevac.

16

Broken Bones

Fractures (broken bones) and joint injuries (sprains and dislocations) are among the most common wilderness injuries, and are often mistaken for one another. In this chapter some fractures will be described, with how to recognize them and how to deliver the appropriate first aid. Fractures of the spine, skull, and of ribs involving the lungs require more specialized treatment and are described in other chapters.

A fracture is any break or crack in a bone.

Fractures may be caused by a blow, a fall, or a twisting force on a leg or arm. Many fractures occur when a person puts a leg out from a moving snowmobile, sled, or ATV. Some are caused by crushing. They are rarely caused by a severe muscular effort.

Bones may break completely or partly through. They may or may not move out of line. Sometimes it is difficult to tell if a bone is broken. Any fracture can become worse if the casualty is allowed to move it, so *if in doubt, treat as a break.*

Types of Fractures

Open fractures are those which have a break in the skin over a fracture, or a bone protruding through the skin. **Closed fractures** are those which show no break in the skin over the injury.

A closed fracture can become an open fracture if it is not handled carefully.

The broken ends of some bones, especially ribs, may damage internal organs, such as lungs, liver, spleen, or major blood vessels. Any movement of the broken bone ends increases the damage.

How to Tell

Sometimes the casualty will hear the bone snap. He will know it is broken, and will tell you so.

If you have seen the accident, you may have a good idea that a bone is broken.

When a bone breaks, the thin covering of the bone (periosteum) and surrounding tissues may be cut and will often bleed. This may cause pain and swelling at the site, and often the blood lost inside will show through the skin as bruising. If much blood is lost internally, or if there is great pain, shock results. If a bone is badly broken or if it moves after it is broken, its sharp ends will often do more damage to the muscles, blood vessels, and nerves around it. This will cause pain, more bleeding and swelling, often increased shock, and sometimes permanent damage. This is why splinting a fracture to keep the ends from moving is so important.

The common signs and symptoms of a broken bone are:

- **pain and tenderness** (*point* tenderness means pain on touching the point of injury)

- **swelling** from blood leaking into the tissues around the break

- **deformity** – an abnormal shape or position of a limb

- **loss of function** – the casualty is unwilling or unable to move the part

- **crepitus** – the sound of broken bone ends grating together (don't test for this!)

- **unnatural movement** – the limb moving or bending in ways it normally would not

- **shock**, which occurs commonly – but not always – with fractures. The worse the fracture is, the worse the shock.

Swelling at a fracture site increases the pressure in the tissues, compressing blood vessels and reducing circulation. Since healing requires good circulation, swelling slows the healing process.

An important part of first aid is *prevention* of swelling. This is done by *elevating* (raising) the injured part and applying *cold* to the injury. Both of these will reduce bleeding into the tissues.

If you only look at one arm or leg, it may be difficult to identify swelling or unusual shape. *Always compare paired body parts to identify swelling or deformity.*

Swelling or discoloration may take time to develop.

What to Do

The objectives of first aid for fractures are to:

- prevent further injury
- reduce pain
- minimize swelling.

The following steps will help to achieve this:

- **Remove clothing,** when practical, to look at the injured part.

- **Provide first aid before moving the casualty** unless it is dangerous to do so. If you must move the casualty before splinting, steady and support the injured part and move it as little as possible.

- **Support the injured part** until you can splint it.

- **Stop bleeding, clean and dress wounds.**

- **Immobilize (splint) the fracture.** Be sure to splint the joints above and below the break. *Immobilization is the key to preventing further injury and reducing pain.*

- **Elevate and support the injury,** if possible, to reduce further swelling.

- **Apply cold** directly over the injury to reduce swelling unless the environment is extremely cold and risk of hypothermia is great.

- **Check circulation** to areas below the fracture. Compare the warmth of the opposite hand or foot. If the fractured side is colder, the splint or bandages may be too tight. Keep checking! *This is critical in extremely cold weather as the hand or foot may easily freeze if blood flow is reduced.*

If these things have been done properly, pain should be reduced or eliminated. If pain gets worse, it is probably due to swelling or circulation problems; check the position of the casualty and his injury, location of bandages, tightness of knots, and circulation below the injury.

Traction (Pulling and Straightening of the Broken Bones)

When a bone breaks, the muscles attached to it contract (get tighter and shorter). This may cause the sharp bone ends to slip past each other and dig into muscle, blood vessels, and nerves, causing further damage, pain, and increased shock. (This happens mostly in leg breaks, where muscles are large and strong. It is rare in other parts of the body.)

Sometimes a broken limb will be angulated (bent) at the break. This may reduce blood flow and cause continued pain. When you are far from help, you will have to straighten the limb so that blood flow is restored, pain is reduced, and transport is possible.

The method of correcting these problems is called **traction**, which is the process of pulling the limb carefully back to its normal position and length before splinting it.

Traction must be used with great care. If incorrectly done it can increase damage. Correctly done, traction will reduce pain, reduce further damage, and may even save the limb if circulation has been cut off.

How to Use Traction

Some basic rules apply to all traction:

- **Do not start traction until splints are ready.** Holding traction steady for very long is quite difficult.

- **Once traction has been started, hold it steady until the break is immobilized.** If traction is released before splinting, there may be more damage and pain. The person applying the traction must be in a comfortable position, because once traction is started he may not be able to move.

- **Hold and support the limb above the break** so that the casualty will not be moved when traction starts. This is especially important on snow or ice, and is easiest with two persons.

- **Pull gently to lengthen *before* straightening.** If straightening is needed, pull gently lengthwise before straightening the limb. Never simply bend the limb back to normal without pulling, or great pain and damage will result.

- **Pull only to normal length.** *Be sure the body is straight* before starting, then compare the length of the broken limb to the normal one as you pull. When the heels (not the toes) are equal, a leg is at normal length. If the break is a femur, it may take a little time before the large muscles tire enough to allow this.

- **Splint firmly to maintain length and position.** A loose splint may allow contracting muscles to shorten the leg again.

- **Do not apply traction to fractures near the shoulder, knee, elbow, or wrist,** *unless* circulation is impaired and the part may die or freeze if you do not make the attempt. There is a chance of serious damage to nerves and blood vessels at these points. If circulation is adequate beyond the break, splint these fractures without straightening.

Casualties will be afraid of the pain and reluctant to have you apply traction. Tell them that it may hurt at first, but then the pain will be greatly relieved – and it almost always will. However, if pain is greatly increased or continues, or if the limb resists straightening, splint it in the position of most comfort.

About Splints

Since the objective of splinting is to keep the broken bone ends from moving, anything that does this can be called a "splint," and almost anything can be used as a splint as long as it is not too tight, heavy, or clumsy. (See Appendix A for improvised splint materials.) Splints must be:

- stiff enough for good support
- long enough to immobilize the joints at either end of the break, without being clumsy
- wide enough to be stable and comfortable when well padded
- light enough not to put a strain on the limb or body.

About Splinting in General

- **Prepare everything you need before you start**, especially if traction is required.

- **Test the splint on an uninjured limb** to be sure that it will go on easily and fit well. There is usually no rush in splinting, and the splint may be on for a long time, so take your time and be absolutely sure it is comfortable, will not loosen, and does not restrict circulation.

- **Pad splints carefully** so there are no pressure spots. Put extra pads in the natural hollows of the body. Good padding will also help keep the injured part warm in cold weather. Use fabrics if possible. If closed-cell foam padding is used, put a layer of cloth between it and the skin to prevent irritation from sweating.

- **Leave access to fingers or toes** to check circulation. Remove boots, unless freezing is a danger. Check circulation every 15 minutes for about the first 4 hours because swelling may cause the bandages to tighten. Watch for coolness, pale colour, or numbness. Compare with the warmth and colour of the uninjured side.

- **In cold weather carefully cover and insulate** the injured part because it will freeze more easily than an uninjured part.

- **Bandages must be wide** and should not dig into the skin.

- **Bandages must be knotted over the splint** or in a place where knots cannot press against the skin. If this is not possible, pad under the knots.

- **Splints should be tied first at the most stable end** and then at the unstable end; then work from the stable end. Test ties afterward so that each is equally tight.

- **Tie splints to either side of the break**, but *not* directly over it. Leave the injured area clear for observation and application of a cold pack. (**Fig. 16-1**)

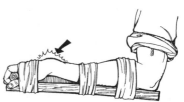

- **If possible, raise and support the injured part** immediately after splinting.

Fig. 16-1: Splints are tied above and below a break, not over it.

- **Apply cold packs** over the break immediately after splinting *if* cold injury is not a problem.

Handling Open Fractures

Open fractures are an infection hazard. Ordinarily, they should be handled only by a physician. If you are far from help, do your best.

If the injury is dirty it must be cleaned as well as possible. Use boiled and cooled water with soap. Irrigate with clean, clear water, as for a contaminated wound (see Chapter 11). You must not try to push the protruding bone back in, *but it must not be allowed to dry out or the exposed tissue will die.*

When the skin and surrounding area are clean, splint the fracture. The bone will probably be drawn back in when traction is applied.

Leave no bandages around the limb under the splint, as swelling may make them tight. Dress the wound, and place the bandage around the splint and wound together. If the bone still protrudes, it must be covered with a sterile dressing and kept damp with boiled and cooled water. *Do not let it freeze!*

Other Special Problems

In extreme cold weather and strong winds, do not expose the injured part for examination until the casualty is in a warm place. It may be necessary to identify fractures by touch through the clothing, place splints *over* the clothing, and move the casualty to a warm camp where a better job can be done. This is contrary to first-aid procedure in a city or town.

Using cold packs to reduce swelling also presents problems in cold weather conditions. The cold of the weather may be so severe that adding cold to the injury could cause frostbite or hypothermia.

Do not apply cold packs unless the casualty is comfortably warm. Remove them if they make him feel cold.

Cold packs can be made from plastic bags of very cold water, or from bags of snow. If snow is used, keep fabric between the bag and the skin. Bags should be filled loosely so that they can be shaped around the limb. Check often to prevent cold injury.

Splinting Without Splints

The quickest, easiest, warmest, and most comfortable leg splint is the casualty's other leg. (**Fig. 16-2**) If well padded and carefully tied with wide bandages, this will often be all the splinting needed for simple lower leg breaks, and will usually stabilize a femur (thigh) fracture until a warm camp can be reached.

Important points to remember are:

- remove boots *if* feet can be protected from cold
- apply gentle traction to align leg during splinting

Fig. 16-2: Splinting a fractured leg with the uninjured leg. Good padding between the legs is essential.

- pad well between legs, with padding thicker near ankles
- use wide bandages, none directly over the break
- finish with a figure-8 to prevent feet from flopping
- if he has a femur fracture, the casualty must not bend at the hips.

An arm sling acts as a sort of splint. It binds the arm to the casualty's chest and supports it. In cold conditions, it is often easiest and best to pin or tie the casualty's parka sleeve in a position that supports the arm in comfort, and then use a wide bandage to hold the arm to the chest. **(Fig. 16-3)** Padding may be placed against the chest. Keep the mitt free so that it can be removed to check circulation.

Fig. 16-3: A jacket sleeve may be pinned to serve as a temporary sling. Pin the sleeve high to remove weight from the shoulder on the injured side, or to reduce swelling in the hand and wrist.

First Aid for Common Wilderness Fractures

Foot and Toe Fractures

Small bones in the feet and toes are often fractured when something is dropped on them, when they are crushed, by falls from a height, and sometimes – when wearing soft footgear such as moccasins – just by stepping onto a sharp edge.

How to Tell

There may be point tenderness, a bump at the injury, sometimes swelling and discoloration. These injuries are often thought to be bruises, but the pain persists. These fractures are painful but not serious. The casualty can usually limp on them and get by until medical help is reached.

What to Do

Immediately following the injury, elevation and application of cold to the foot may reduce swelling. A stiff boot makes a good splint. If the break is severe, use a pillow splint.

If toes are crushed and skin is broken, treat the injury as a contaminated wound, separate toes with non-stick dressings, elevate the foot, keep the casualty at rest, watch for infection, and evacuate.

Ankle Fracture

The two "bumps" on the inside and outside of the ankle are the ends of the long bones of the lower leg (tibia and fibula). **(Fig. 16-4)** They overlap the smaller ankle bones slightly. When the ankle is twisted, the outer one (the lateral malleolus of the fibula) sometimes cracks. This is the most common leg fracture. The inner "bump" (the tibia) rarely fractures. Often the casualty will think that the ankle is sprained, and continue to use it. A high boot can act as a splint, and will allow use of the limb for some time, although there is the danger of a further twist causing the fractured part to be displaced. When the boot is removed, swelling

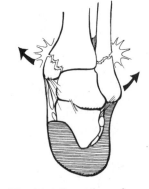

Fig. 16-4: Rear view of the ankle bones, showing typical breaks at the "bumps" (malleoli) caused by twisting. The outside of the foot is to the right.

may be immediate and dramatic, and the fracture becomes obvious.

How to Tell

The cause of this injury is often a twist. The casualty will feel and show:

- pain
- tenderness *over the bump itself* (gentle pressure directly on the bump will produce pain)
- swelling and discoloration, occurring quickly.

If the fracture is not obvious, *gently* tap upward under the heel of the affected foot. Pain at the site suggests a fracture rather than a sprain.

What to Do

For the first two hours, treat as for a sprain (see Chapter 15):

- **apply compression** by wrapping the ankle with an elastic or other snug bandage
- **apply a splint** to prevent movement
- **elevate the injury**
- **apply a cold pack** unless environmental cold is severe.

After two hours:

- **check** again to confirm the fracture
- **splint** with a pillow or other soft splint (a folded sleeping bag or foam sleeping pad would work well)
- **evacuate** to medical care, keeping the foot elevated, if possible.

The casualty must not walk on the injury, unless a life-threatening danger exists, and then he may be able to hobble to safety.

Lower Leg (Tibia and Fibula) Fracture

The most common fracture location is just above the boot top. One or both bones may be broken. If only one is broken, the other will help to splint the fracture. Careless handling can create an open fracture because the bones are just under the skin.

How to Tell

This break is usually easy to identify. You may observe that:

- pain and point tenderness are severe
- swelling and discoloration are rapid
- deformity, angulation, or protruding bone are unmistakable if present
- grinding sounds (crepitus) may be heard if both bones are broken
- shortening of the injured leg may be evident if both bones are broken.

What to Do

The casualty will be in great distress and possibly showing signs of shock. Reassure him, and keep him warm and at rest. Prepare all splinting materials before you start. If in severe cold and the casualty must first be moved to a warm camp, do not remove his clothing. If necessary, apply traction to realign his leg, and maintain the traction while another person pads well between his legs and ties them together with wide bandages. Then transport him to camp as quickly and gently as possible for a complete examination.

If this arrangement has been comfortable and circulation is good below the fracture, no further splinting may be required, and evacuation can be arranged. If pain is severe or the foot is cold or pale, then:

- prepare inner and outer board splints, well padded, crotch to foot

- apply stabilizing traction while you expose the injury, doublecheck leg alignment and length, and check circulation

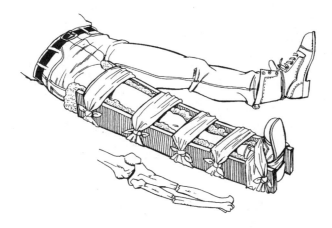

Fig. 16-5: Splinting a lower leg fracture.
It is essential that splints are well padded.

- splint with inner and outer splints over good padding; be sure to tie a figure-8 or otherwise support the foot, so that it cannot flop during transport (**Fig. 16-5**)

- elevate and apply cold to the site (unless cold injury is likely), keep the casualty in shock position, and arrange for evacuation.

If evacuation will be long or delayed, remove pants before splinting to simplify matters when the casualty has to urinate.

Knee Fracture: Kneecap (Patella) or Ends of Long Bones (Tibia, Fibula, and Femur)

A fall on or a direct impact to the knee is the usual cause. Pain is usually severe. Circulation to the lower leg may be reduced. The fracture and its exact location may be difficult to identify.

How to Tell

Examine the injury early because swelling may make diagnosis difficult. There is often deformity. If unsure, gently feel both knees to compare. If still in doubt, treat as a fracture.

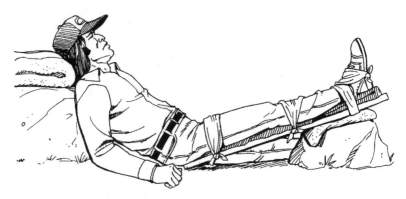

Fig. 16-6: Splinting a fractured kneecap (patella).

What to Do

Prepare a well-padded splint to fit underneath the leg from the buttocks to beyond the heel. Place extra padding under the hollows of the knee and ankle. **(Fig. 16-6)** You should then:

- gently realign the limb into the position of most comfort
- secure the splint with wide bandages at the upper end, thigh, and lower leg
- secure the foot with a figure-8 bandage
- elevate the leg
- check circulation often.

It may be necessary to arrange elaborate cushioning and padding for transport. Beware of cold injury if circulation is reduced – especially if the part is elevated.

If the knee cannot be straightened without great pain, immobilize it in the position of most comfort with rolled sleeping bags, extra clothing, or other padding.

Upper Leg (Femur) Fracture

This is a serious fracture, often involving internal bleeding and shock. The powerful thigh muscles may contract, shortening the leg and causing severe pain as the bones override. Internal bleeding in severe cases may be fatal. This fracture is usually easy to identify, although it may be less obvious in children and elders.

How to Tell

Any or all of the usual fracture signs and symptoms may be present. The foot may fall outward and the leg may be shortened. The casualty often hears or feels the bone break. Shock signs are common.

What to Do

In severe cold, control shock, apply gentle traction, splint the legs together, and keep the casualty on a board or flat surface so that he cannot bend at the hips during transport to a warm camp. Once in camp:

- prepare a well-padded board splint from the armpit to below the foot (see Appendix A for improvised splints)

- apply gentle stabilizing traction while the original bandages are removed, and hold the traction until a new splint is in place

- remove or adjust pants so that elimination can be managed during long transport

- apply a board splint with wide bandages at the chest, hips, ankles, above and below fracture, knees, and lower legs (**Fig. 16-7**) – be sure the feet are stabilized with a figure-8 bandage

- check tight spots and circulation, and adjust as needed.

Ground transport will be painful and awkward, especially if the splint protrudes much past the foot, and should not be attempted if the casualty is in shock, or if bouncing causes severe pain. Air medevac is preferred.

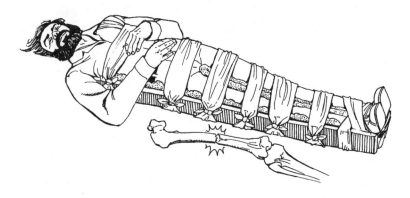

Fig. 16-7: Splinting an upper leg (femur) fracture.
Pad well between the legs.

Hip Fracture or Dislocation

Fractures of the upper end of the femur, or joint socket, and hip dislocations may be hard to identify, produce similar problems, and are treated the same.

Seniors may fracture the neck of the femur from a minor fall, and the break may not be obvious. Dislocations are caused by any strong force that drives the knee toward the pelvis, or by a twisting force on the leg. A leg thrust out from a moving snowmobile or sled is the most common cause of this injury.

How to Tell

You will observe:

- **pain** which is usually severe

- **deformity at the site** – if it is a dislocation, the ball-joint may show as a hard lump in the buttock (rear dislocation) or in the groin (front dislocation)

- **abnormal leg position** – it may be shorter, turned inward, and bent (rear dislocation), or longer, turned outward, and bent (front dislocation)

- **inability to move the leg.**

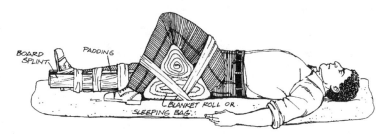

Fig. 16-8: A left hip dislocation secured in the position of most comfort to a splinted right leg. The right leg provides the rigidity.

What to Do

Do not attempt to correct a hip dislocation. It is difficult even in the operating room, and the chance of injury is great, especially if there is a fracture. Immobilize the injured leg in the position of greatest comfort, even if bent. This may require either a splint like a femur splint (**see again Fig. 16-7**), or it may require that the *uninjured* leg be splinted and the injured leg padded with large soft objects and tied to it. (**Fig. 16-8**)

Watch circulation in the leg. If it is reduced, it may be necessary to place warm (not hot) water bottles on the foot to prevent cold injury.

Arrange for urgent air medevac. Package the casualty on a well-padded board if one is available. Transport by sled or trailer will usually be too painful. Transport by boat may be feasible if the boat does not pound.

Fractured Pelvis

This is often a serious injury, caused by major force. A fall from a moving vehicle or from a height, being run over by a sled, or being crushed by a boat are all common events in the wilderness that may cause this injury.

There is always the danger that the organs cupped by the pelvis will be damaged, especially the urethra or bladder. Internal blood loss may be slow, with the casualty collapsing later from shock.

How to Tell

With a fractured pelvis, there may be pain in the hip or lower back and difficulty in walking. Pressing gently on the pointed tips of the pelvis in front at the belt line may produce pain. Watch for developing shock. If the urethra is damaged, watch for pain in the crotch, and possibly blood at the penis tip or meatus. The casualty may be unable to urinate, or may pass bloody urine.

What to Do

Call for an *urgent* air medevac, especially in the event of urethra laceration. If a pelvic fracture is severe, pain and the danger of increased shock may make it impossible to move the casualty by land over rough country. Pelvic fracture is especially dangerous for a pregnant woman.

Lay the casualty in his most comfortable position. If he wishes his knees bent, support them. Then:

- pad between legs and support feet with a figure-8 bandage

- support the pelvis with 2 wide overlapping bandages with the widest part on the injured side, or tighten pants and lace or pin them together to provide the same support (**Fig. 16-9**) – loosen or remove if support causes pain

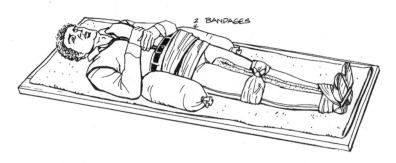

Fig. 16-9: Immobilization of a pelvic fracture.

- support further with padded weights beside the hips

- place a wide bandage around the knees

- transport, if the casualty's condition permits, on a well-padded, firm surface or board.

If the urethra is torn, withhold fluids except for tiny sips or ice chips.

Fractures of the hand

Most fractures of the hand are caused by crushing. Support the hand in the natural relaxed position and protect it from impact and cold. Leave fingertips accessible so that you can check circulation and cold injury.

For first aid:

- cup the hand over a roll of soft material
- place dressings between fingers if skin is broken
- place on a well-padded elbow-to-fingertips splint (**Fig. 16-10**)
- support in a sling with the hand elevated.

A pillow splint may also be used and pinned or tied across the chest with the hand elevated.

Fig. 16-10: Splinting of hand fracture.

Fractures Near the Wrist

When a break is near the wrist and causes deformity, no attempt should be made to straighten the arm *unless* circulation has been cut off and the hand may die. There is a risk of nerves or blood vessels being cut when straightening is attempted. However, if help is more than an hour away, if there is no radial pulse, and the hand is turning blue and cold, you must apply gentle traction to straighten it. If the pulse does not return, get to help with all speed.

First-aid procedures involve:

- fitting a padded splint under the wrist, hand, and forearm

- bandaging at the elbow, hand, and above the fracture (apply no pressure to the fracture)

- supporting the arm in a sling or pinning the jacket sleeve in sling position with the hand slightly raised (**see again Fig. 16-3**).

Forearm Fracture (Radius and Ulna)

How to Tell

The forearm has two bones, the *radius* and *ulna.* One or both may be broken. The usual signs and symptoms of breaks may be present. Point tenderness at the break is probably the best indication, unless deformity is obvious. The casualty may support the arm in a position of comfort. Such breaks are usually caused by direct blows or by falling on the outstretched arm.

What to Do

First aid depends on the location of the break. In all arm fractures:

- leave fingers accessible so that circulation can be checked often, and beware of cold injury

- when the casualty is transported lying on his back, you may place the well-cushioned arm beside his body if it is more comfortable that way.

For fractures along the length of the bones, prepare a splint to fit along the palm side of the arm from the elbow to the base of the fingers. An excellent U-section splint that will protect the arm from accidental impacts may be cut from a plastic fuel can. (**Fig. 16-11**) In cold weather, try to identify the fracture and position the arm without removing the jacket. Be sure to protect the fingers from cold. Arm fractures usually require only gentle traction for initial positioning. Pad the splint well, then:

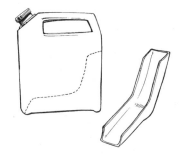

- tie the splint above and below the fracture
- apply a sling, or pin the splint to the jacket with hand slightly elevated
- check circulation often.

Fig. 16-11: A rigid U-section arm splint cut from a 5-gallon plastic fuel can. The well-padded splint must be supported by a sling.

Fractures of the Upper Arm (Humerus)

No splint is required, but if the casualty must travel, it is desirable to rig some sort of light shield over the injury to prevent accidental impacts. Closed-cell foam, animal hide, cardboard, or bark serve well. For first aid:

- place the forearm in a sling across the lower chest, or pin the jacket sleeve in this position
- pad well between the chest and upper arm
- bandage the upper arm to the chest, using wide bandages above and below the fracture
- check circulation often.

Fractured Humerus Near the Shoulder

Do not try to straighten a break near the shoulder joint *unless* there is no radial pulse. If there is none and you are more than an hour from help, you must try to gently straighten the arm. If no pulse returns, get to help as soon as possible. No splint is used for shoulder fractures, but the entire shoulder must be immobilized. This is best done by supporting the weight of the arm in a tubular sling or by pinning the sleeve in this position, with the casualty's fingertips at his shoulder. For first aid:

- support the injured arm, with the hand near the uninjured shoulder

- pad between the upper arm and body
- secure the arm to the chest with a wide bandage. (**Fig. 16-12**)

It may be desirable to improvise an impact shield over the injury if the casualty must travel.

Fracture of the Collarbone (Clavicle)

The collarbone is often fractured by a fall on the outstretched arm, a blow to the shoulder, or direct impact.

How to Tell

The casualty will usually support the elbow on the injured side and tip his head to that side. He will not use that arm. Look for pain and tenderness at the break. A bump may be felt or seen there.

What to Do

The objective is to support and immobilize the arm, and take the weight off the injury. You should:

- pin the sleeve of the injured arm across the chest, with the fingertips near the opposite shoulder, or use a tubular sling
- bandage the arm to the body using a narrow bandage, with the widest part near the elbow. (**Fig. 16-13**)

Fractures of the Shoulder Blade (Scapula)

These are rare, usually caused by a direct blow or a fall onto the back, and are hard to identify. The shoulder blade will heal itself as ribs do. If pain persists, relieve it by slinging and bandaging as you would a fractured clavicle, but use a wide bandage to secure the arm to the body.

Rib Fractures

Ribs are often fractured by a direct blow or by falling onto some hard object. In rare cases they may be fractured by hard coughing. Severe rib fractures can be dangerous because broken ends

Fig. 16-12: Immobilization of a fractured upper arm near the shoulder.

Fig. 16-13: Immobilization of a fractured collarbone.

can puncture the lung. (For rib fractures that involve lungs, see Chapter 23.) Fractures of the lowest ribs may injure the spleen if they occur on the casualty's left side, his liver if they are on the right. Injuries to either side will cause severe internal bleeding.

How to Tell

Sharp pain may be felt at the break, and it is made worse by breathing or movement. Pushing on the sternum (breastbone) will almost always cause pain at the break. There may be no other visible sign. In severe breaks, a large bruise could indicate significant internal bleeding.

What to Do

Broken ribs will heal by themselves in three to six weeks, but will be painful during this time. Try to reduce movement to limit pain. Non-prescription painkillers may help.

17

Head, Face, and Spine Injuries

Injuries to the head and spine are especially dangerous because both contain nervous tissue. The **skull** protects the **brain**, which allows us to think and controls all our activities and automatic body functions. The **spine** protects the **spinal cord**, which carries the commands of the brain to the rest of the body.

The brain and spinal cord are soft and delicate, and do not heal like other tissues. When the skull or spine is damaged, the brain and spinal cord may also be injured. Sometimes the spine may be damaged without injury to the spinal cord, but later movement may injure the delicate cord and cause partial or full paralysis. Rarely can this be corrected. First-aiders must handle head and spine injuries with the greatest of care.

Any blow hard enough to cause significant injury to the head is likely to damage the neck and because of unconsciousness or decreased alertness, the casualty may not be aware of the neck injury.

The first-aider should always immobilize the neck of a head injury casualty before moving him or administering other first aid.

In the north, the most frequent causes of head and spinal injuries are falls from all-terrain vehicles (ATV's), snowmobile collisions or accidents in rocky areas, falls, and blows from hard objects. Three-wheel ATV's, still in use in some areas, are especially dangerous because they tip easily and it is difficult for the rider to jump clear. Many casualties of off-road-vehicle crashes are children, who do not have the strength, skill, or judgement to handle these machines.

A good protective helmet is essential for safety on ATV's and snowmobiles. A good helmet will also keep the wearer warm even in severe cold, and compact helmets can often be worn under a large parka hood.

Head Injuries

The most common head and face injuries are **concussions** ("knockout" blows), **increased pressure within the skull** (compression, intracranial pressure), **fractures**, and **soft tissue injuries** (which are covered in Chapter 11, "Cuts, Bleeding, and Infection").

All head injury casualties should be watched closely for 48 hours for any of the following signs or symptoms. These indicate serious injury within the skull, and show that there is a critical emergency demanding immediate medical care.

Signs and symptoms are:

- decreasing level of consciousness
- headache, becoming worse
- flushed (red) face and raised temperature
- vomiting
- stronger, slower pulse
- difficulty seeing clearly
- changing personality (e.g., unusual aggressiveness)
- abnormal breathing rate or pattern
- weakness, twitching muscles, or seizures (convulsions)
- unequal pupil size or reaction to light.

While transporting the casualty or awaiting evacuation, check for these signs every hour, and record your findings on the Consciousness Record (see Appendix D) for use at the hospital.

Concussion

Concussion is a condition of widespread but temporary disturbance of brain function following an injury to the head. A person who "sees stars" after a head injury has a concussion. He may recover quickly or his condition may get worse.

How to Tell

A person with a concussion may show:

- immediate partial or complete loss of consciousness, usually of short duration
- loss of memory of the events immediately before and following the injury
- shallow breathing
- cool, pale, clammy skin
- nausea and vomiting upon recovery.

What to Do

(See *Increased Pressure Within the Skull*.)

Increased Pressure Within the Skull (Compression, Raised Intracranial Pressure, Subdural and Epidural Haematomas)

Compression of part or all of the brain within the skull is caused by collections of fluids within or outside the brain (**Fig. 17-1**), or by a piece of fractured skull pressing upon the brain. The condition may occur immediately following concussion with no return to consciousness, or it may develop many hours after apparent recovery from concussion as a result of a gradual pressure build-up. It is very important to monitor the casualty's vital signs and the reaction of his eyes to light for hours after a concussion to look for signs of compression.

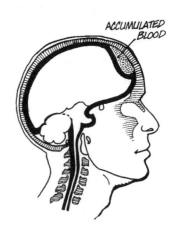

ACCUMULATED BLOOD

Fig. 17-1: Bleeding within the skull may put pressure on the brain.

How to Tell

The following signs may be present:

- **immediate unconsciousness** or later progressive **drowsiness** leading to unconsciousness
- **slowing of the pulse**
- **inequality of the pupils of the eyes** (One or both pupils may be dilated and unresponsive to light. Changes observed in the pupils should be recorded for the physician.)
- **twitching of the limbs** or **convulsions** caused by brain irritation or damage
- **weakness of one or both sides of the body**, especially if progressive, recorded for the physician.

What to Do

The casualty with concussion or increased pressure within the skull should be treated as any unconscious person. Be sure to:

- open the airway
- check breathing
- start rescue breathing if required, using jaw thrust instead of head tilt (see Chapter 21)
- check circulation
- stay with the casualty to monitor his airway.

Skull Fractures

Skull fractures happen most often at the temple, which is thin. But with enough force, fractures may occur anywhere on the skull. There is always a history of a hard blow or fall, and the casualty will often be dazed or unconscious for a period.

**Any force strong enough to cause head injury may
also be strong enough to damage the bones of the neck
(vertebrae), so spinal injury should be assumed and
the neck immobilized immediately.**

How to Tell

A fracture of the *upper* skull (cranium) may show:

- a depression, scalp cut, bruising, or swelling.

   A fracture at the *base* of the skull (basal) may show:

- blood or slightly yellowish fluid at the ears or nose
- black eyes ("raccoon eyes"), and bruising or swelling behind the ears.

   These signs may take several hours to develop.

For suspected cranial or basal fractures, you should:

- carefully apply a neck (cervical) collar to immobilize any spinal injury
- check breathing, guard the airway, and start rescue breathing if needed
- lightly apply a sterile dressing over ear(s) if blood or fluid appears
- gently cover injuries (cuts, bumps, depressions) with thick, soft dressings and hold them gently in place with bandages
- watch the casualty for signs of serious injury and record changes as they occur (use the Consciousness Record in Appendix D)
- do not leave the casualty alone
- call urgent air medevac, or transport the casualty in a semi-sitting position to medical help.

Be prepared for vomiting, which is common with head injury, even if the casualty is unconscious. Warn the casualty not to blow his nose if it runs blood or fluid. Hold dressings there to absorb it, but do not block the flow.

Common facial fractures involve the nose, the eye socket, cheekbone, and the lower jaw.

Penetrating Injuries

If an object penetrates and remains embedded in the skull, do not attempt to remove it. Cover it with a loose sterile dressing and protect it with a cup-shaped object that will keep it from being touched or moved. Treat the casualty as for skull fracture.

Spinal Injuries

Spinal injuries in the wilderness will usually require an air medevac, because it is difficult to immobilize (splint) the spine well with improvised materials. These injuries are usually caused by violent falls or blows, with falls from ATV's and snowmobiles being a major cause. The rapid "whiplash" motion of the head may also fracture neck bones. Remember that any blow hard enough to cause significant head injury may also cause injury to the cervical (neck) spine. *Always assume neck injury with any major head injury and use an immobilizing collar.*

Note that packaging the casualty and the use of a backboard are essentially the same for neck fractures and fractures lower in the spine. Neck fractures are especially difficult because the neck offers little bony or muscular support.

Injuries to the spine may or may not cause damage to the spinal cord within. Damage to the spine itself (the bony structure) is shown by:

- pain at the injury, especially to touch (pain may radiate to the front of the body or down the arms or legs)
- deformity at the injury
- bruising, cuts, or swelling at the injury
- muscle spasms around the injury.

When any of these signs are present, take no chances. Further movement could cause the sharp broken bones to damage the soft spinal cord within, possibly causing paralysis or death. If the casualty is awake and alert and wants to move or walk, and signs of injury are questionable, he is probably not badly injured.

When the spinal cord is also damaged, some of the following signs may be present:

- full or partial paralysis
- numbness or tingling (especially in the arms or legs)
- unexplained weakness or heaviness in the limbs
- difficulty breathing
- shock.

The aims of first aid for spinal injuries of either the neck or trunk are the same:

- prevent further spinal damage
- care for life-threatening conditions (especially respiration)
- slow the progress of shock.

The spinal casualty will be especially vulnerable to cold, and must be carefully protected from exposure.

Fractures of the Neck (Cervical Spine)

These are especially dangerous, and may result in full paralysis or stoppage of breathing. Watch the casualty continuously and be ready if breathing stops. If you feel there is a spinal injury in the neck, you should:

- watch breathing closely and give artificial respiration if needed, opening the airway using the jaw thrust without head tilt
- steady and support the head to prevent any movement
- protect the casualty from cold
- apply a cervical collar (neck collar) immediately, and package the casualty to prevent accidental head movement during first aid and transport
- without bending the neck, place the casualty on a flat, padded surface (backboard) for transport
- be prepared to give first aid for shock.

Because each of these steps must be done correctly to reduce the chance of spinal cord injury, each will be explained.

Fig. 17-2: The casualty's boots may be used to immobilize his head while a spine board is being improvised.

Rescue breathing is presented in Chapter 21. The head must *not* be moved when the airway is opened; the jaw thrust without head tilt is used.

Steadying the head should be done immediately to prevent accidental movement during first aid. Any heavy, padded objects may be used temporarily. Bags of flour, sugar, beans, or rice are excellent. The casualty's boots, soles out and uppers slid under the neck (**Fig. 17-2**), may work well. Two well-padded plastic fuel cans could be used. Mounds or bags of snow or sand could be used if well padded to protect the casualty from cold. This will be a temporary measure, used only until you can improvise a cervical collar.

A cervical collar *must prevent any head movement* to be effective. To do this it must be sturdy enough to support the weight of the head, large enough to surround the neck and fill the space between chin and collarbones, and padded well enough to fill the spaces and be comfortable. (See Appendix A for some improvised collars.) In a wilderness situation, it may be necessary to move the casualty slightly in order to apply the collar. **Do not tip his head forward!** With one person controlling his head and two at the shoulders, move the casualty only enough to place the collar and secure it, *taking great care to keep the head and neck* *in exact line with the body.* If it is necessary to straighten the casualty's head in order to place the collar or transport him, do this just before applying the collar and maintain a slight lengthwise traction in line with the spine, while straightening.

A backboard is critical because movement of almost any part of the body will tend to move the spine, possibly causing further damage. A backboard must be stiff enough so that it won't bend under the casualty, long enough to support him from head to feet (protruding slightly beyond the head so that it is protected), and at least as wide as the hips. If it is much larger, it will be clumsy to handle and transport, and may not fit into aircraft.

Backboards may be improvised from boat floorboards, cabin doors or planking, the plywood sides of passenger komatiks, or even from small poles lashed across larger poles to form a rigid stretcher. The latter must be flat and well padded. (**See Fig. 3-13, p. 31**)

It is much easier to fasten a casualty securely to a narrow board than to a wide one. A narrow board and casualty may fit together into a sleeping bag, which is much easier than trying to get the casualty alone into a sleeping bag.

Padding the Backboard

If a casualty is likely to be on a backboard for several hours before getting to medical help, the board must be padded for comfort, for insulation against cold, and to prevent pressure sores. The best padding is a closed-cell foam sleeping pad, about 1 cm (3/8- to 1/2-inch) thick, cut to shape and taped to the board. Several thicknesses of blanket may also be used. If only soft, thick open-cell foam is available, it should be split with a knife to about 2.5 cm (1-inch) thickness, because the usual 7 to 10 cm (3- or 4-inch) thickness will allow too much movement. Besides the basic padding, the natural hollows behind the neck, the small of the back, and under the knees and ankles should be padded separately with whatever padding is available. Do this *before* the casualty is moved to the board, and secure the pads in place with tape near the edges of the board so they can be untaped and adjusted later.

"Packaging" the Casualty

It is necessary to package the casualty into a compact bundle in order to move him without bending his spine. You should keep his head steadied and apply the cervical collar as the first steps, then:

- place soft padding between his legs and feet while supporting the feet
- tie the ankles and feet together using a figure-8
- place wide bandages around the thighs, knees, and lower legs
- gently tie the wrists together to keep the arms from flopping.

The casualty is now ready to be "log-rolled" onto a backboard. (**Fig. 17-3**) If the casualty is likely to be on the board for many hours, try to get him to urinate into a convenient container before starting. Then cut away or remove his trousers before placing padding between his legs, and place some absorbent material in position to soak up any urine or feces.

Fig. 17-3: A neck-injury casualty "packaged" and ready to log-roll onto a board.

Placing the Casualty on a Board

It is best to have at least two people, and preferably four, to do a log-roll safely. If it has not been practised, the rescuers should practise on an uninjured person before making the move.

The leader should station himself at the casualty's head, and give directions. If there is one helper, the helper should kneel at

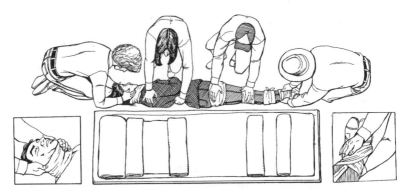

Fig. 17-4a: Log-rolling a spinal-injury casualty onto a padded board.

the casualty's hips, leaving room to roll the casualty toward him. He will grasp the casualty's clothing at the shoulder and hip to make the roll. The board must be within his reach.

If there are two helpers, one grasps the clothing at the casualty's shoulder and waist, and the other at the hip and knee.

If there are three helpers, the last one controls the feet. (**Fig. 17-4a**)

The object of the log roll is to keep the casualty's spine perfectly straight while getting him onto the board.

- The leader controls the head by cupping one hand beneath the casualty's chin and placing the other at the base of the skull, *being especially careful not to tip the head forward.* He gives the directions, but follows the roll of the body, rather than leading it with the head. He maintains a slight traction on the head during the roll, as does the rescuer (if there is one) at the feet.

- The helpers kneel on one knee and reach across the casualty's body to grasp his clothing, allowing room for the casualty to roll clear onto his side and rest against their legs.

- On the leader's signal, the helpers slowly roll the casualty toward them, being careful not to twist the body. The leader follows them exactly so that the head and neck remain exactly in line with the body.

- When the casualty is fully on his side and resting against the rescuers' legs, the helper closest to the feet moves the padded board into position under the casualty, being sure that the smaller pads match the hollows in the body shape, and slides the board in as close as it will go.

- On the leader's signal, the casualty is carefully rolled back onto the board. The leader should maintain the position of the head while the helpers gently adjust the final position, being careful not to bend the body.

If the casualty is conscious, take this opportunity to check his comfort. If he must be on the board for many hours, eliminate all bumps or hard spots before securing him. Cover him well, because he will be more vulnerable to cold than most other casualties.

Securing the Casualty to the Board, Supine (on the Back) Position

Because you will probably be using an improvised board without the convenient holes and straps, there is no single best way to do this. The objective is to fasten the casualty comfortably but so securely that neither his head nor his body can move if the board must be tipped on its side to allow for vomiting.

If straps or wide strips of strong cloth or hide are available, use them rather than rope. Strong tape (duct or filament tape or several thicknesses of electrical or white tape) works very well, except that it does not stick well in cold weather and must be cut to be removed or adjusted.

You should:

- as leader, maintain control of the head while the body is being secured

- place rolled blankets, sleeping bags, or other fabric along each side of the body and cover the casualty with a blanket or other cover to pad the ties

- securely tie high across the chest just under the armpits

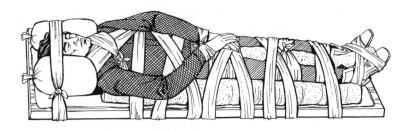

Fig. 17-4b: A spinal-injury casualty immobilized on an improvised spine board.

- tie across the lower abdomen, hips, thighs, knees, and lower legs, crossing the ties whenever possible

- leave the arms free, both for the casualty's morale and so that you can take pulses and check the temperature of the hands

- place bulky padding or food bags on either side of the head, and tie pads and head into place with a wide bandage, or use a strip of tape across the forehead to secure all. Do not remove the cervical collar. (**Fig. 17-4b**)

If this has been well done, you should be able to move the board into any position without significant movement of the casualty. If the casualty vomits, you must *immediately* tip the board so that the vomit will drain and not get into the airway. This is especially likely to happen when a casualty regains consciousness or when he is being transported.

He should be taken to medical care with all urgency.

When There Is No Backboard

Sometimes in the field, especially north of the tree line, there is nothing that can be used for a backboard. Then the first-aider will simply have to remember his objective – to keep the spine from bending – and use whatever means necessary to limit this movement.

If it is possible to make a warm camp and wait for help, do so. If it is necessary to move the casualty for safety, use whatever rigid material is available to splint the spine. A single board about 1 metre or 3 feet long, such as the crosspiece from a komatik, can be used to make a neck splint. It is best held in place with tape. (**Fig. 17-5**) A couple of tent poles may be used if necessary.

For other improvised backboards, see Appendix A.

Fig. 17-5: Use a short board to immobilize a neck fracture when no full-length board is available.

18

Eye Injuries

Although the wilderness may seem like a safe place for eyes, it is not. Flying chips from woodchopping are a common hazard, as are bits of stone flying from carving or quarrying tools. Hunters may suffer powder burns to the eyes from incorrectly hand-loaded cartridges or explosions from plugged gun barrels. Anyone may get sand, dirt, or sawdust blown into his eyes, or scratch the cornea – the clear covering of the eye. Snow-blindness is common in most northern areas but especially in the treeless Arctic in springtime.

Prevention

Because eye injury is so dangerous to vision and so difficult to correct, extra care should be taken to prevent it.

- In bright conditions, wear high-quality sun glasses that are rated to block out ultraviolet light. Choose ones that also prevent mechanical injury. Carry spare sun glasses, or know how to improvise slit-type goggles. (**Fig. 18-1**)

Fig. 18-1: Improvised slit-type goggles.

- Wear protective glasses when chopping, carving, or chipping.

- Use only those handloaded cartridges that are loaded exactly to written specifications.

- Don't rub the eyes, especially with dirty hands.

Scratchy, painful eyes irritated by sun, wind, or dust may be soothed with tea, which contains tannic acid. Simply squeeze a few drops of tea from a clean, cool, used tea bag into the lower lid. Repeat for as long as it seems to help. Do not use tea if there is a possibility of a penetrating injury.

Particles in the Eyes

Tears often wash away particles from the eyes, but when they cannot, the eye becomes irritated, teary, and pink. The particle is usually caught beneath a lid.

In all cases, contact lenses should be removed before particles. Have the casualty do this himself; he knows best how to do it.

What to Do

To locate the particle, you should:

- wash your hands well
- seat the person facing a bright light
- gently draw the lower lid downward while the casualty rolls his eye upward. (**Fig. 18-2**)

Fig. 18-2: Removal of a particle from the lower eyelid.

If a particle or turned-in eyelash is visible, gently wipe it away with the corner of a moistened tissue or clean soft cloth. If it is not visible, then check the *upper* eyelid as follows:

- have the casualty pull the upper eyelid out and down over the lower, so that the lower lashes brush the inside of the upper lid.

If this does not work:

- place a matchstick or something similar at the base of the upper lid

- grasp the upper lashes and pull the lid gently back over the stick, turning it inside out while the person looks down (**Fig. 18-3**)

- if the particle is not stuck to the eyeball, remove it as above. Have the casualty blink to replace the lid.

Fig. 18-3: Turning back the upper eyelid.

Particles on the Cornea or Sticking to the Eyeball

If the particle is on the eyeball, shine a light *across* the eyeball, not straight into it, to see best the particle with the least irritation to the casualty.

You should *not* try to remove these immediately with a moistened cloth. Instead:

- lie the person down, head tilted to the injured side
- hold the upper and lower lids open and flush the eye gently but well with lots of clean water.

If this does not remove the object, make one attempt to remove it with the moistened corner of a clean cloth, using a cautious "pushing" motion from the side. (Do *not* "dab" straight in, as this may embed the particle.) If it will not budge, then:

- close the eyelid
- use a bandage (not tape) to hold several gauze pads firmly in place on the eye, using just enough pressure to prevent blinking
- transport to medical aid.

An eye patch held on with tape alone becomes loose and uncomfortable, and does not apply enough pressure to prevent blinking.

Do not bandage both eyes unless the casualty is in severe pain, because he will be unable to help himself and his morale will suffer greatly.

If a baby's eyes must be flushed, it may take several adults to hold him motionless with lids open during the flushing.

If pain continues after particle removal, take the person to medical attention.

Objects Embedded (Stuck) in the Eye

Do not try to remove anything stuck into or near the eye. Take the casualty to medical care immediately. You should:

- treat and transport the casualty lying down, with his head supported and braced to prevent movement
- place a dressing around (not over) the object, and cover the object and eye with a paper cone, cup, etc., to protect it from any contact
- bandage without putting pressure on the object (**Figs. 18-4a,b**)
- reassure the casualty and explain to him that his eye is bandaged to prevent further injury during transport.

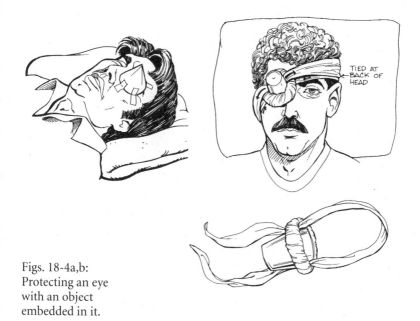

Figs. 18-4a,b:
Protecting an eye
with an object
embedded in it.

In the rare and horrifying case of an eyeball forced from its socket, do not try to replace the eyeball. Cover the eyeball gently with a moistened sterile dressing, protect it with a cup, and call for an air medevac or transport. To keep the moistened dressing from freezing in winter, it may be necessary to keep the casualty's head inside his sleeping bag.

If transport is long, keep the casualty well fed and watered. Having difficulty seeing and in great pain, he will be frightened and unhappy, so talk with him as often as possible.

Penetrating Injury to the Eyeball

If the eyeball itself is penetrated, fluid may leak out. Infection is likely, and loss of sight in *both* eyes may later occur. You should:

- tape a disposable cup over the eye and bandage as you would if an object were imbedded in the eye **(see again Figs. 18-4a,b)**
- if antibiotics are available, give as prescribed
- evacuate to medical help with all urgency.

Scratched Eyeball (Cornea)

The clear covering on the front of the eye is called the cornea. It is easily scratched, and will be very painful for 24 to 48 hours. This may be caused by an inturned eyelash, or almost any impact or brushing touch. If careful examination shows no particle, and pain persists after something touches the eye, you may assume that the cornea is scratched. You should:

- soothe the eye with drops of tea squeezed from a cool tea bag
- give the casualty dark glasses
- apply an eye patch and bandage if it helps relieve pain.

If the casualty has Aspirin or Tylenol (acetaminophen), he may take them for pain. The injury should heal in one or two days. If pain continues, there may be an infection or ulcer, either of which calls for rapid evacuation.

Cuts, Bruises, and Fractures to the Eye Area

If there is any possibility of injury to the eyeball, or if there is serious injury to facial bones or soft tissues near the eyeball, you should:

- control bleeding of the eyelid or cheek with gentle pressure, being careful not to put any pressure on an injured eyeball
- gently replace the damaged or torn eyelid, to prevent eyes from drying out
- cover the injury with a dressing, held lightly in place with tape or bandage
- transport the casualty lying down, with head supported and braced to prevent movement.

Rough transport, as on a sled over broken sea ice or rough snow, is not advisable, and if possible an air medevac should be called. Be sure that the casualty's face and head are well protected from cold, and guard against exposure. In all serious eye injuries you should keep the casualty at rest, as activity may cause more bleeding, with possible serious consequences.

Burned Eyes or Eyelids

Burns may be from heat, chemicals, or intense light (snow-blindness).

Chemical burns may be caused by battery acid, fuels, or various dry chemicals. The casualty will have intense pain and may be unable to stand light. Urgent medical aid is needed. You should:

- immediately brush away any dry material from around the eye
- flood the eye for at least 10 minutes with clean water (cool or slightly warm).

This will require that the casualty be placed lying down or sitting with his head back and tilted slightly toward the injured side to allow the water to run off. Gently pour a steady stream for the required time. The eye will probably have to be held open by the casualty or first-aider. If the casualty is a child, it may take several adults to hold him in position. NOTE: In the northern winter, water may not be quickly available. If a strong chemical, such as battery acid, is burning the eye, it would be better to use liquids such as coffee or tea from a thermos than to take the extra time to melt snow. However, the hot liquids must be cooled to body temperature by adding snow. Once this is done, snow can be melted and the eye flushed more completely with clear water.

Thermal (Heat) Burns to the Eye

Eyelid reflexes are so rapid that the eyeball or cornea is usually spared contact with flame. Explosive fires, as from gasoline, may redden the lids. They should be immediately cooled with the rest of the face, using a gentle stream of cold water or gently applied cold, wet cloths. If the lids are reddened or blistered, cover both eyes gently with gauze, bandage it in position, and transport the casualty to medical care.

Remember that any flame that burns the eyelids could also easily cause life-threatening inhalation burns, and these are far more dangerous.

Snowblindness (Photophthalmia)

Intense light, as caused by the sun or by welding torches, may cause "snowblindness." Snowblindness can occur on an over-cast day, and some Arctic people have recorded snowblindness occurring even inside a white tent in direct sunlight. This is questionable, and it is probable that the injury occurred before entering the tent and did not show up until later. Severe symptoms may not appear for several hours. *Prevention* is the key. Dark glasses should be worn in bright sunlight, especially on sea ice and anywhere in the spring before the snow is gone. (Tell your storekeeper that you want glasses that filter at least 90% of UV-B radiation.) Goggles or glasses with side shields are better than normal glasses. Some casualties have reported snowblindness from bright light entering from below and around the sides of glasses.

Because glasses are so easily lost or damaged, an inexpensive spare pair should be carried in the field, or the traveller should be able to improvise slit-type goggles, which are quite effective if the slit is made thin enough (**see again Fig. 18-1**). Make it only wide enough to provide essential vision. Blackening the upper edge of the cheekbones with charcoal and wearing a baseball cap pulled low over the eyes will also help, but will not substitute for sunglasses, as the most dangerous light is that reflected from the snow surface.

How to Tell

Many northerners are familiar with snowblindness. If you are not, look for:

- a history of exposure to bright light, usually 6 to 12 hours earlier
- eyes that are irritated, itchy and dry, feeling "full of sand"
- extreme sensitivity to light
- intense pain, made worse when lids move
- red watery eyes, swollen eyelids.

Snowblindness may occur in only one eye if the light has been mostly from one side for a long period. Remember that poor sunglasses may not prevent this problem.

What to Do

This injury usually heals itself within 24 hours. Still, the casualty will be in great pain and unable to see, so he will require care.

You should make camp and:

- get the casualty into a dark or shaded area
- have the casualty remove contact lenses

- keep him at rest and tell him not to rub his eyes
- apply cold wet cloths for temporary relief of pain.

You may squeeze a few drops of tea from a clean, cool, used teabag (no sugar!) into the lower eyelids as often as he feels it is of help. If the casualty has Aspirin or Tylenol (acetaminophen), he may take them for pain. Healing occurs naturally in a day or two.

19

Gunshot Wounds

Safety With Guns

Guns are essential tools for northern people who live close to the land, and almost every household has several. The fact that they are familiar and taken for granted leads to many deaths and injuries. All are preventable.

Children and Guns

Children often learn by imitating their parents and elders. The mechanics of working actions and safety catches, aiming and firing, are often within the abilities of four- or five-year-olds who do not understand the danger of what they are doing.

The only way to prevent tragedies is to keep guns out of children's reach.

Hunters should:

- keep guns unloaded unless they are hunting
- keep guns locked up or out of reach of children
- keep ammunition separate and locked.

Accidental discharges are common, mostly while hunting. In very cold weather, fingers are often cold and numb or covered with heavy mitts, which make it difficult to handle guns correctly. The most common unplanned discharges occur:

- when a gun is pulled from lashings on a sled, or removed from a vehicle
- when a gun leaned against the side of a boat or vehicle falls over

- when a gun is being loaded or unloaded and the action is worked
- when someone falls while carrying a gun.

In all such cases, there must be a cartridge in the chamber before the gun can discharge. Some hunters claim that it is necessary to carry a cartridge in the chamber so that they can shoot quickly if game is sighted, but it takes only *one second* – or less – to work the action and chamber a round, so *there is no real reason to carry a cartridge in the chamber, even while hunting.*

Mistaken identity is another common cause of death.

Never shoot at anything not positively identified.

Carelessness and excitement account for many injuries, and the range of rifles is often forgotten.

Effects of Gunshot Wounds

The kind of damage done by a bullet depends upon its speed, size, and type.

.22 calibre bullets in short, long, or long rifle cartridges tend to expand very little and make a penetrating wound. They often do not exit. These bullets often "tumble" and wander from their original path once they enter the body, so the most serious injury may not be in line with the entry.

Unless large blood vessels or bones are struck, bleeding may be slow and may show very little on the outside. However, the tiny, non-bleeding entry wound may hide serious internal bleeding, especially in the head, trunk, or abdomen.

High-powered rifle bullets cause massive damage. Much of this is done by the explosive force of the bullet striking at high speed. This sends an immediate shock wave through the body, which may fracture bones even without bullet contact and rupture blood vessels some distance from the impact. Bones that are struck may be shattered into small fragments.

All bullet impacts – except possibly very light grazing wounds

– require the earliest possible medical care. Unfortunately, any solid hit in the neck or head from a high-powered rifle may prove fatal before help can arrive, but the first-aider should not give up. Wounds of the chest or abdomen have a surprisingly good survival rate if the casualty can be moved to a hospital within about six hours. Maintaining the airway, minimizing blood loss, successfully fighting shock, and ensuring prompt medical attention increase the survival rate from wounds that do not penetrate body cavities, the neck, or the head.

First Aid for Gunshot Wounds

Each wound must be cared for according to the damage it causes. (Refer to chapters on fractures, internal bleeding, shock, bleeding control, etc.) Internal bleeding is almost a certainty, except in grazing wounds. Rapid shock should be expected.

For all gunshot wounds, check immediately to discover both entry and exit of the bullet.

Wounds in specific areas follow.

Chest

For bullet wounds in the chest:

- clear and protect the airway
- seal bubbling chest wounds immediately with airtight material taped on 3 sides (use a hand at first if nothing else is available), and be sure to also seal any exit wound
- place the casualty in a sitting position, leaning to the injured side
- support the arm on the injured side with a sling
- raise the legs to help control shock
- call urgent air medevac and request life support with the flight
- give only tiny sips of water if medevac is delayed.

Abdomen (Belly)

High-powered rifle shots into the abdominal cavity may be rapidly fatal, but .22 calibre wounds may not be. With .22 wounds, there may be internal bleeding but little or no external bleeding. The casualty will complain of severe abdominal pain and will be in shock. He will probably be extremely thirsty and demand something to drink, *which he must not have*. For shots penetrating the cavity:

- guard the airway and watch for vomiting
- dress the wound and wrap it firmly with bulky dressings
- treat for shock
- give nothing by mouth (If medevac is delayed, give the casualty tiny ice chips or bits of snow, or a wet cloth to suck on.)
- call an urgent air medevac with life support.

Head, Neck, and Face

Here, a solid hit is often quickly fatal. Bleeding may obstruct the airway. Maintaining an open airway is the first-aid priority.

- Place the casualty in the drainage (recovery) position to reduce bleeding into the airway.
- Clear any obstructions from the airway.
- Dress and bandage the wound to control bleeding.
- When the airway is no longer threatened by blood, place the casualty horizontal, face up, and watch him carefully. Raise his legs into shock position unless it increases bleeding.
- Call an immediate urgent air medevac, with life support.

Extremities

High-powered bullets may shatter long bones and cause great tissue damage. If a major artery is cut, bleeding must be controlled immediately or the casualty may die within minutes or go into irreversible shock. Place the casualty at rest, elevate the injury if possible, and apply direct pressure. A tourniquet may be necessary, but do not use it unless you are certain the casualty will otherwise die.

If long bones are shattered, it may be difficult to elevate the unstable part to aid in bleeding control unless the limb is supported on some rigid object.

For first aid, you should:

- place the casualty at rest, control bleeding with elevation and pressure on bulky dressings
- stabilize and splint any fractures
- place the casualty in shock position and give first aid for shock
- call an urgent air medevac with life support.

No matter how serious the wound, do not give up. Reassure the casualty and do your best.

20

Burns

We tend to think of burns happening most often at home or work, but at least as many occur in camp, where we may be far from medical assistance. People who have seen the terrible effects of bad burns are cautious, but burns are still among the most common wilderness injuries.

Some of the most frequent causes are related to the use of camp stoves and lanterns, gasoline fuels, tent and cabin fires, spilled hot liquids, campfires, and forest fires. Rope burns are a nasty combination of heat and mechanical injury.

Handling Liquid Fuels (Gasoline, Naphtha, and Kerosene)

Gasoline fuel for vehicles and naphtha fuel for stoves and lanterns are almost identical, and will be referred to here as gasoline. Both are highly volatile, and trigger the most liquid-fuel accidents. Kerosene is less volatile, except when vaporized.

Many people still do not understand what makes gasoline so dangerous. At normal temperatures, liquid gasoline evaporates, turning to an invisible gas which is heavier than air and will flow downhill. This vapour burns explosively when it ignites (catches fire). Gasoline actually contains more explosive power for its weight than dynamite. The exploding vapour, contained within an engine cylinder, is what produces the power to drive a machine.

Gasoline vapours will collect in an invisible "pool" in any low place, or on the floor of a cabin or tent. Or they may flow down-hill. If they are concentrated enough, and if they reach a spark

or flame, they will explode and flash back to the gasoline container. Almost every adult has heard the familiar "whump!" of
gasoline vapours exploding in the air.

The warmer the temperature, the more vapours are produced and the more easily they ignite, and vice versa. At around
−40°C, gasoline vapours are hard to ignite, which makes motors
hard to start.

Naphtha is just as volatile as gasoline, and must be handled
with the same care.

Here are some well-proven suggestions for handling gasoline
and naphtha safely.

- **Do not refuel any appliance (stove or lantern) inside a tent
  or building.** It may not be comfortable to go outside, but it
  would be even less comfortable to find yourself badly burned
  and without shelter.

- **Be sure appliances are completely out and cooled before
  refuelling.** Gas lanterns are especially treacherous because a
  tiny, almost invisible flame often remains high in the mantle
  after the lantern "burns out," *even with the valve off.*

- **Be sure no ignition source (flame, stove, cigarette) is near
  when you are fuelling.**

- **Do not allow fuel spilled on an appliance tank to burn off.**
  Wipe it off before lighting. Flame on the tank will greatly
  increase inside pressure and may cause the tank to explode.

- **Do not allow appliance tanks to get hot.** Some people have
  used a small stove inside a 5-gallon can to make a sort of
  heater. The heat will build up inside the can, heating the fuel
  tank and increasing pressure to the point where the stove
  may flare up or explode.

- **Do not open an appliance filler cap near an ignition source.**
  The rush of pressurized air carries explosive fumes with it.

- **Use only the fuel specified for an appliance.** Using naphtha
  in a kerosene stove is a common cause of fire and explosion.

- **Do not refuel a running engine.**

- **Wipe spilled fuel off an engine before starting.** It is easy to spill fuel on a snowmobile engine while refilling. Any electrical problem could destroy your machine in minutes. (They burn very quickly once started.) If you discover even a tiny fuel leak, fix it immediately for the same reason.

- **Keep children away from fires and cooking areas.** It is still common for children to fall into fires or tip over stoves or lanterns, or to tip pots onto themselves.

- **Never pour or throw liquid fuels on fires**, even if no flame is visible. The fuel may flash back to the container quicker than you can drop it. Even if it doesn't catch immediately, the fuel will be warmed and vaporized and spread out, then may suddenly flash. If in an emergency you must use fuel to start a campfire, use only a few spoonfuls in the centre of the pile, then toss a match into it from upwind and uphill.

- **Keep matches, cigarettes, and lighters away from children.**

- **Do not smoke in bed – even in camp.** This remains a major cause of fires.

Propane and Butane

The vapours from these fuels behave like gasoline vapour. They are heavier than air, invisible, and explosive. Treat them with respect.

What a Burn Does

When heat comes in contact with flesh, the skin and the tissues beneath will absorb some of the heat. As the body is mostly water and water holds heat very well, this heat will stay in the tissues for a time until it is lost from the surface and the circulating blood below carries some away. The longer the heat stays in the tissues, the deeper it will penetrate, the more it will hurt, and the more tissue it will destroy. This is why rapid cooling is so important in first aid.

In severe burns, the area will quickly swell. The fluid that causes swelling is drawn from the plasma (clear) part of the blood, so the blood loses volume and blood pressure drops. Soon after the burn, the burned skin will start to "weep" drops of clear or yellowish fluid, and a great deal may be lost this way. This fluid is also from the blood, so the volume is further decreased. If enough fluid is lost, the casualty will go into shock, just as if he had lost blood through a wound. The amount of fluid lost and the speed with which a casualty goes into shock depends mostly on the size and depth of the burn.

**In any major burn, shock is the
first great life-threatening hazard.**

Because the burned, surface tissues are dead and lack circulation, they form a breeding ground for bacteria.

**In major burns in the wilderness,
infection is the second great hazard.**

All burn casualties other than those with small local burns should be evacuated to medical care. **Those with major burns should be evacuated urgently by air.**

How to Identify and Describe Burns

You must be able to tell how serious a burn is in order to give the proper first aid, or to give the correct information to medical help by radio. Remember that size and depth of a burn are not the only criteria for seriousness; any significant burn of the face, hands, or groin is serious.

First-Degree Burns

Mild heat or very quick high heat will cause tissues to redden and swell. There is no blistering. Some surface skin cells may be killed and will peel off later. Sunburn is an example, as are most spilled-coffee burns or small grease spatters. If they are not too large, first-degree burns will generally heal themselves with little difficulty.

How to Tell

In a first-degree burn:

- the skin is red and sensitive to touch
- there may be slight swelling
- there is no blistering.

If you are in doubt, you may sterilize a pin with a flame and gently prick the burned area. If the pinprick is felt, it is a first-degree burn.

Second-Degree Burns

Higher heat will penetrate part way through the skin layers, and will kill more tissue. The skin will be red and blistered. There will be severe pain because nerve endings are damaged but not destroyed. Burns from hot liquids are often second degree. These burns are serious. They take some time to heal, often become infected when blisters break, and may leave scars.

How to Tell

In a second-degree burn:

- the skin is red, sensitive to touch, and very painful
- there will be swelling
- blisters appear soon after the burn
- pain is severe
- burns may be "weeping" or wet.

Third-Degree Burns

Still higher heat will penetrate and kill tissues clear through the skin to the fatty tissues below. The skin may look pale, dry, and white, or it may be brown and charred. There may be less pain in the third-degree area because nerve endings have been destroyed. However, a third-degree burn is usually surrounded by painful second- and first-degree burns.

Third-degree burns are often caused by direct contact with flame or embers, burning clothing, or longer exposure to a lower heat. There is much tissue destruction. Later infection is almost certain in a camp situation. There will be bad scarring and disfigurement, which may require skin grafts. Healing is long and tedious.

How to Tell

In a third-degree burn:

- the skin is pale, dry, and white, OR brown and charred
- the surrounding area will likely have first- and second-degree burns
- the third-degree area will not be painful.

Size of Burns

Since the seriousness of a burn depends on a combination of its depth (degree) and size and location, you must be able to judge accurately how much of the body area it covers. This is done by *percent*.

There are two ways to estimate the *percent* of body surface area (BSA) burned.

Estimating by the Casualty's Palm Size. The surface of the casualty's palm is usually about 1-1½% of his BSA. If the casualty is small or slender, the area may be closer to 1%. If he is an adult male who does hard physical work, his palm may be closer to 1½%.

You can estimate the size of a burn by estimating how many of the casualty's palms it would take to cover the area. Do *not* touch the area while estimating.

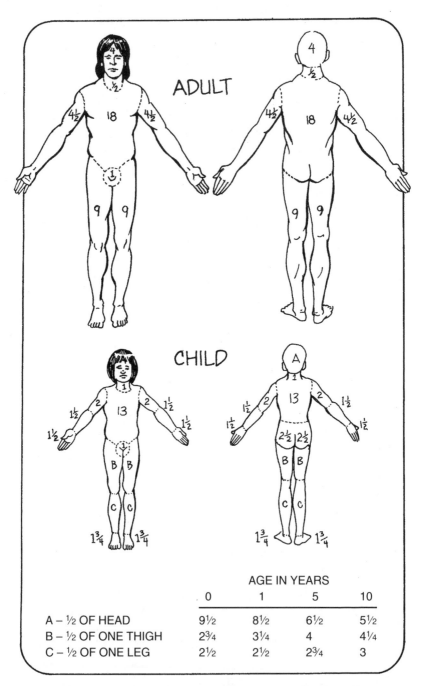

	AGE IN YEARS			
	0	1	5	10
A – ½ OF HEAD	9½	8½	6½	5½
B – ½ OF ONE THIGH	2¾	3¼	4	4¼
C – ½ OF ONE LEG	2½	2½	2¾	3

Fig. 20-1: Estimating burn size. Figures show percent of body surface area.

Estimating by the Rule of Nines. The body may be divided into areas of about 9%, as follows (**Fig 20-1**):

- head and neck   9%
- each arm and hand   9%
- front of trunk, each half   9%
- back of trunk, each half   9%
- front of each leg   9%
- back of each leg   9%
- genital area   1%

Total BSA   100%

Use either palm size or the Rule of Nines to calculate the size of the burn, or use both calculations to cross-check your estimate.

A burn which is very likely to produce rapid shock is:
- 15% of BSA of second- or third-degree burns on an adult
- 10% of BSA of second- or third-degree burns on a child
- second- or third-degree burns of face or hands.

In all such burns, expect rapid shock and start immediately to prevent or reduce it. Do not wait until after the burn is dressed. **As soon as the burn is cooled**, get the casualty into the shock position and start giving fluids as described below. Only then should you worry about the injury itself.

First Aid for Burns

In dealing with major burns, you must deal with the injury and shock. Use the **"three C's"**, which stand for **cool**, **clean**, and **cover**, to remember the basic rules for dealing with burn injury.

- **Cool** a burn as quickly as possible. This will remove the heat from the tissues and prevent continuing damage, reduce swelling, and greatly reduce pain. Plunge the injury immediately into cold water, and keep it there for 10 to 15 minutes or until the burning pain stops. If you cannot place the burn in water, *gently* place cold, wet cloths on the burn, wringing them out in cold water as they warm up.

If it is winter and all water is frozen, sprinkle snow *gently* onto the burn, allowing it to melt as you sprinkle, or gently place a thin layer of snow on the burn. Stop this cooling as soon as pain is reduced and the burn is no longer hot.

Do not rub the burn with snow or ice, or pack thick snow or ice onto it. This may cause damage to dead and injured tissue, may break the skin allowing infection to start later, and may freeze some of the injured tissues.

Do not try to cool extensive burns (burns over much of the body). CAUTION! It is easy to cause exposure (hypothermia) when cooling large burns. Keep the casualty well covered and warm except for the burn, watch him carefully, and **stop the cooling if the casualty starts to shiver**.

For any serious burn, place the casualty in the shock position immediately after cooling.

- **Clean** the burn if it is necessary to remove bacteria which may cause later infection.

  For minor burns, wash the area gently with hand soap and water, rinse it well, and let it air dry. For serious burns, carefully pick off any burned clothing not stuck to the skin. Leave the rest; it has probably been made sterile by the fire. Do not touch or break the skin. Do not breathe on or cough over the area.

  If a hand is burned, remove rings and bracelets immediately before swelling locks them on.

- **Cover** the burn with a clean, preferably sterile, lint-free cover. Do not use flannel or woolen material, which will stick. For second- and third-degree burns, cover the dressing with thick, clean absorbent fabrics and bandage firmly.

An excellent dressing for all burns is called Spenco Second Skin. It may be used on any burn, relieves pain, and its sterile covering absorbs fluid from the burn. It is a valuable addition to first-aid kits, but it is expensive.

Shock from Burns – Prevention and Treatment

Minor burns will probably not produce shock, but it may appear rapidly in major burns because of the rapid loss of fluid into the tissues and weeping from the burn. Hospital care would include intravenous fluids. Since these are not available out on the land, an attempt must be made to replace these fluids by mouth.

There is some risk in doing this as there is the chance of vomiting, **but the risk of severe shock is greater if no fluids are given.** Oral fluids may save many casualties with 20% to 50% BSA burns.

Fluids for Burn Casualties

A "recipe" for an excellent oral fluid is:

- 2.5 mL (½ tsp) salt
- 2.5 mL (½ tsp) baking soda (not baking *powder!*)
- 1 litre (1 quart) of water
- sugar to taste. **(Fig. 20-2)**

Another good and very simple solution, which can be used for most rehydration problems, is 5 mL (1 tsp) salt and 40 mL (8 tsp) sugar in 1 litre (or quart) of water.

Other good fluids are Gatorade mix, which can be purchased at many grocery stores, or WHO (World Health Organization)

Fig. 20-2: Fluids for burn casualties.

solution, which may be available from your nursing station or public health nurse.

If neither salt nor soda is available, broth from boiled game meat is good. Even plain water is better than nothing at all.

Salt and soda can be used for many things in first aid, so if you are adding them to your kit, carry at least 30 mL (6 tsp) each of salt and baking soda, and 60 mL (12 tsp) of sugar, if these are not carried in camp supplies.

How to Give Oral Fluids for Shock from Burns

Fluids should be started *immediately* along with first aid for shock, even if you do not yet see signs of shock. Even if he is nauseated, every effort should be made to encourage the severely burned casualty to take fluids.

Day 1:

- Give fluids in sips, as much as the casualty will tolerate.
- Give 3 to 5 litres (or quarts) in the first 8 hours.
- Give 3 to 5 litres (or quarts) over the next 16 hours.

Day 2:

- Give diluted fluids (salt/soda/sugar, Gatorade, etc.), OR
- flavoured, sweetened water such as lemonade mix or Tang, or just sugar water if that's all you have.
- Give light, easily digested foods if the casualty wants them.

Day 3:

- Give ordinary fluids as tolerated. (Avoid coffee, tea, alcohol.)
- Give lots of good food – proteins, carbohydrates.

If you have vitamin pills with you, give normal doses of multi-vitamins each day if the casualty is not vomiting. Do not give fruit juices for the first few days.

If Aspirin or Tylenol (acetaminophen) is available and the casualty is not vomiting, he may take them in normal doses for pain relief.

Throughout, watch the casualty's vital signs, and measure his urine output. Rapid pulse and respiration will indicate that he needs more fluids, as will a urine output of less than 1,000 mL (about 4 cups) per 24 hours.

Nursing Care for Serious Burns

Leave the dressings in place, but change the bulky outer dressings as they absorb fluids.

If infection appears:

- clean and irrigate the injury, and change dressings twice daily
- start antibiotics as prescribed if available
- keep the casualty well nourished and watered.

Special Burns

Airway (inhalation) burns may occur in a major building or tent fire, or if the casualty gasped as gasoline flashed. The interior of the nose, mouth, throat, and lower air passages may be burned or have been exposed to poisonous gases. The major danger is in the airway swelling. *Such a casualty is in great danger and must be evacuated urgently.* Oxygen should be brought in with the air medevac.

How to Tell

Anyone who has been exposed to a house or tent fire may have airway burns. If you are in doubt, evacuate the casualty immediately to medical help. Some indications of inhalation burns may be:

- singed nostril or moustache hairs
- burns around the nose or mouth
- cough, hoarseness
- soot in the mouth.

What to Do

Try to prevent swelling and get the casualty to help. You should:

- keep the casualty sitting if shock is minor
- give ice chips, bits of snow, or cold water rinses frequently for the mouth
- give assistance in breathing if it becomes difficult
- call priority air medevac, asking for medical aid and oxygen with the aircraft.

Facial burns should be treated as above, but do not dress them. Leave them exposed to air.

Eyelid burns threaten sight, as the eyelids may retract (shrink), exposing the cornea to drying. Cover the eyes and lids with sterile dressings, moistened with boiled and cooled, slightly salted water. Keep them moist.

Hand burns, if deep, will contract (shrink) and deform the hands. You should:

- cover the hand with antibiotic cream
- dress between the fingers
- place the hand in a plastic bag for protection
- elevate the injury
- keep the fingers moving constantly until medical care is reached.

Fig. 20-3: Bandaging a hand burn.

Encourage the casualty to maintain the hand as much as possible in the "position of function" with the fingers slightly cupped and the wrist slightly extended. (**Fig. 20-3**) A mitt may be worn over the plastic bag if it is cold.

21

Choking and Rescue Breathing (Artificial Respiration)

Any person who appears not to be breathing must be checked immediately for **airway**, **breathing**, and **circulation** (heartbeat) – the ABC's of first-aid care. Such a casualty may have:

- **respiratory and cardiac arrest** (no breathing or heartbeat) or
- **respiratory arrest only** (no breathing, continuing heartbeat).

If both breathing and heartbeat are stopped, **cardio-pulmonary resuscitation** (CPR) **must be started** if there is to be any chance of saving the life. (CPR training should be taken by all first-aiders.) If breathing only is stopped, rescue breathing alone must be started.

You can help another person to breathe in several ways, which taken together are called **artificial respiration**. The most efficient of these is **mouth-to-mouth breathing** – which is also called **rescue breathing** – assisted ventilation, or positive pressure ventilation. Because it can be given quickly in almost any position, results in full lung inflation, and does not require moving the casualty unnecessarily, it is the most important method and one that every first-aider should know well.

When to Use Rescue Breathing

A variety of things can cause breathing to stop in the wilderness setting. The most common of these are unconsciousness causing blockage of the airway by the tongue, near-drowning, and choking. Being struck by lightning and a number of different traumas and illnesses can also result in stoppage.

Sometimes, a few breaths given by a rescuer are enough to start the casualty breathing again.

More likely in the wilderness are situations that require the rescuer to **assist** another person to breathe when his own efforts do not provide enough air exchange. Among these are serious chest injuries, carbon monoxide poisoning, smoke inhalation, and some heart or lung ailments. Rather than memorizing all of these causes and situations, simply remember that *no matter what the cause . . .*

If anyone is unable to breathe well enough to sustain life, you must either help him to breathe, or breathe for him.

Rescue breathing is simple. But before you learn it, you should understand how the human airway is constructed and how it works.

How Normal Breathing Works

The lungs are completely contained within the chest cavity, which is enclosed by the ribs, the sternum (breastbone), spine, and the thin, sheetlike muscle called the **diaphragm**. When it's relaxed, the diaphragm is dome-shaped and fills the lower part of the cavity. (**Fig. 21-1**)

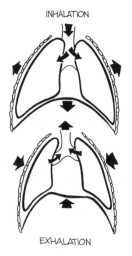

The **airway** to the lungs consists of the **mouth**, **throat**, and **windpipe** (trachea). At its lower end, the windpipe divides into two smaller tubes called **bronchi**, which enter the lungs and in turn branch into smaller and smaller tubes, or **bronchioles**. At the very ends of these are millions of tiny spaces called **alveoli**, where the exchange of oxygen and other gases takes place.

When a person inhales (breathes in),

Fig. 21-1: Mechanics of breathing.

his ribs lift somewhat and the lower edges flare out, creating more space in the chest cavity. At the same time, the diaphragm tightens and flattens, which also creates more space within the chest. The lungs expand. If the airway is open, air will rush in to fill this space. This is the process of breathing in, or **inhaling**.

Exhaling is the reverse. The muscles between the ribs relax, allowing them to drop back into position, reducing the space. At the same time, the diaphragm relaxes and rises back into its dome shape in the chest cavity, again reducing the space. Air is thus forced out.

Things that Prevent Normal Breathing

Normal breathing may be prevented by any blockage of the airway. Common obstructions are:

- the tongue
- a foreign object, blood, or vomit in the airway
- any material (water, sand, plastic bag, bedclothes) that prevents air from entering the airway.

Breathing may also be reduced or prevented by:

- a puncture in the closed rib cage, which leaks air into the system
- the puncture of a lung
- a major breakage of the rib cage, which allows part of it to be sucked inward during inhalation
- any pressure on the rib cage that keeps it from expanding normally
- a fluid build-up in the lungs
- a spasm (extreme tightness) of muscles in and around the airway
- swelling of the airway
- an illness, poisoning, drug overdose, or injury to the brain or nerves that affects the muscles of breathing.

A violent blow, heart attack, stroke, seizure, and smoke inhalation may also cause breathing to be abnormal or stop entirely.

Since the average person loses consciousness within a couple of minutes without air, and may die or suffer major brain damage in 4 minutes, **breathing is always the first concern of the first-aider.**

How to Identify Breathing Problems

If a casualty is not alert and cannot inform you, you must watch for signs of breathing distress. These are:

- movement of the chest cannot be seen, heard, or felt
- the casualty is struggling to breathe, or breathing is noisy or gasping
- breathing is abnormally fast, slow, or irregular
- breathing is unusually deep or shallow
- lips, nailbeds, and sometimes ears look bluish
- blood vessels of the head and neck are swollen with blood.

Sometimes several of these signs are seen at once. A casualty showing these is in danger of losing consciousness and dying of too little oxygen (asphyxia) *unless* artificial respiration is given to him. **If no oxygen is received for 4 minutes, the brain may be permanently damaged or the casualty may die.** You must help *immediately.* Every second counts!

Artificial Respiration for an Unconscious Person

If you think a person is unconscious and not breathing, you must check three things before starting. They are his:

- ability to respond
- breathing
- airway.

To check if he is responsive/conscious tap him on the shoulders and shout, "Are you okay?" If there is a possibility of neck or head injury, be careful not to move these parts. If he is conscious, he is probably breathing.

To assess his **breathing**, place your ear close to his mouth so

Fig. 21-2a: Airway closed.

Fig. 21-2b: Airway open using head tilt-chin lift method.

you can feel or hear his breath and watch his chest carefully for movement. Look, listen, and feel for 3 to 5 seconds. If breathing is gentle but there are no signs of a lack of air, artificial respiration may not be needed. If there is no breath, check to be sure his airway is open. If it is not, the casualty's tongue is often the problem.

To open the airway, one of two methods is used:

- **If you do not suspect neck injury**, place a hand on the forehead and, with your fingers under the bony tip of the chin, gently tilt the head back. This is called the **head tilt-chin lift** method. Tilting the head backward draws the tongue up and out of the airway. (**Figs. 21-2a,b**) Sometimes, this is all it takes to restore breathing. Immediately look, listen, and feel for 3 to 5 seconds to see if this has happened. If the casualty is not breathing, give one slow breath, allowing 1½ to 2 seconds for each breath.

  The most common mistake with adult casualties is not tilting the head back far enough. If the chest does not rise, reposition the head and breathe again.

  The head tilt-chin lift method is also used for opening an infant's airway. Be careful neither to press on the soft parts below the chin, nor to accidently close the infant's mouth during the lift. (**Fig. 21-3**)

- **If you suspect neck injury**, you must *not* bend the neck. To avoid this, you must lift the jaw forward and upward without bending the neck or moving the head. This is called a **jaw**

Fig. 21-3: Head tilt-chin lift method for an infant.

thrust (see again Fig. 2-1, p. 15), and using it lifts the tongue from the airway. To do a jaw thrust, you should:

- kneel at the casualty's head
- place your fingers behind the angle of his jaw and your thumbs at the ends of his lower lip
- strongly thrust his jaw forward (upward) with your fingers, while you
- draw his lower lip back with your thumbs
- steady his head with your palms and wrists.

Again, immediately look, listen, and feel for restored breathing.

A jaw thrust on an infant is done the same way, but only two fingers and the thumb of each hand are required.

(NOTE: the jaw thrust is difficult to practise on a conscious partner, as his jaw is not relaxed and often will not move forward.)

Ventilating (Inflating) the Lungs

If no breathing is detected, you must immediately start to ventilate. As your own lungs remove only a little of the total oxygen from the air you breathe, there is enough left in your exhaled breath to be effective. To give rescue breathing, you should:

- use one hand to maintain the chin lift and the other to pinch the casualty's nose shut

- cover his mouth with your own, making a tight seal (**Fig. 21-4**)

- breathe air slowly into his lungs, taking 1½ to 2 seconds to ventilate

- move your mouth away to let the air rush out again, and look, listen, and feel to be sure air is exchanged (**see again Fig. 2-2, page 15**)

- repeat the cycle every 5 seconds for an adult casualty

- check his pulse.

Check the carotid (neck) pulse in an adult or child (**see again Fig. 2-3, page 16**), the brachial (arm) pulse in an infant. (**Fig. 21-5**) If there is no pulse, you must begin CPR or get someone who can. (You should take a CPR class.)

If you are using the jaw thrust, you will not have enough hands to pinch the nostrils shut, so you must press your cheek against the nostrils to seal them.

Fig. 21-4: Mouth-to-mouth ventilation.

Fig. 21-5: Checking an infant's brachial pulse.

If the casualty is an infant, cover both his mouth and nose with your mouth and get a good seal. This is easy and quick. The **depth** (amount of air blown) and **rate** (number of breaths per minute) will be different for different size casualties. In all cases, deliver each breath slowly.

- For casualties 8 years and older: give a full breath every 5 seconds, or about 12 per minute. This is about normal breathing for an adult at rest.

- For children 1 to 8 years: take 1 to 1½ seconds to give a breath (enough to make the chest rise) every 3 seconds, or about 20 per minute.

- For infants under 1 year: take 1 to 1½ seconds to give a breath every 3 seconds, or about 20 per minute. Breathe just hard enough to make the chest rise. Remember always to look, listen, and feel for air exchange.

Some Important Details

There are several important points to remember in rescue breathing. **Blow air slowly and gently** into the lungs because rapid or hard breaths may force air into the stomach. **Listen and feel for air leaks** as you blow. Leaks will keep the lungs from inflating fully, and you will notice little or no air rushing out between breaths. Most often, leaks are around the edges of the mouth or through the nose. Some casualties have had surgery and breathe through a **stoma**, an artificial opening in the neck between the top of the breastbone and Adam's apple. If you discover a stoma, breathe into that instead of the mouth.

If air will not go in, you will feel great resistance. Reposition the head or jaw to adjust the tongue and try again. If air still does not go in, there is probably something else blocking the airway. Give first aid for choking. (See details that follow in this chapter.)

If air is forced into the stomach by hard or rapid ventilations, the stomach will start to inflate. This puts pressure from below on the diaphragm, making it harder to ventilate. It may also cause belching or vomiting as the air rushes out again. *Do not* try to force air from the stomach if you are getting good air exchange, as you will probably cause vomiting. If the stomach is becoming distended, reposition the airway and continue rescue breathing. If vomiting occurs, turn the casualty onto his side with his head down. Let vomit drain, wipe his mouth, roll him back, and continue rescue breathing as quickly as possible.

It is common for casualties to vomit just as they start to breathe again, so as unpleasant as it is, this may be your sign of success.

If the casualty starts trying to breathe on his own, let him. You have succeeded!

Complications

Several factors may make mouth-to-mouth breathing difficult or impossible. It may be that:

- the casualty's mouth will not open
- the casualty's mouth is severely injured and ventilation is difficult
- the casualty has no teeth and a tight seal is difficult (dentures should be left in unless they will not stay in place)
- the rescuer does not wish to come in contact with blood in the casualty's mouth.

Since the nose is also part of the airway, the rescuer may simply hold the casualty's mouth closed with his hand and ventilate through the nose instead. If the air does not rush out quickly enough for good exchange, the rescuer may help by opening the casualty's mouth for each exhalation.

Rescuer Health Concerns

Rescue breathing can be distasteful and could possibly transmit some minor illnesses, but very rarely does it result in dangerous infection. It is extremely unlikely that either HIV (the virus linked to AIDS) or HBV (hepatitis B) infection will be transmitted by mouth contact, *unless there is blood or an open wound or sore in either mouth.*

Most people will not hesitate to start mouth-to-mouth breathing if the casualty is a friend or loved one, and few hesitate even for a stranger. Each case is different, but you must always remember that **if a person is not breathing, he will certainly die within minutes, and his life is in your hands**.

Check with your local clinic or nursing station regarding HIV and hepatitis B in your area. You can obtain a pocket face mask, which allows rescue breathing without contact.

When Normal Breathing Returns

When a casualty starts to breathe again on his own, place him in the recovery position (**see again Figs. 1-1a,b,c,d, p. 3**), which will keep any fluids in the mouth from interfering with breathing. Watch him carefully, as problems may occur again.

Any casualty who has stopped breathing and has been revived should be taken to medical care.

How to Assist Breathing

If a casualty is breathing but cannot get enough air and is showing signs of distress such as struggling for air or blueness of lips and nailbeds, you may have to assist him to breathe.

Keep the casualty in his position of comfort with his airway open and use the technique of rescue breathing, but time your ventilations with the casualty's efforts. A hand on his chest will help you to feel and time his breathing efforts.

If the casualty rejects your help, let him breathe on his own. If he then becomes unconscious, start rescue breathing for him.

Choking

Food or small objects sometimes get caught in the upper airway, blocking it. If the object cannot be coughed up by the casualty, he may collapse and die. In adults, the problem is usually a piece of food, often meat. Infants and children often put small objects into their mouths and may choke on these.

Anyone of any age may choke. A choking person may be conscious or unconscious, standing, sitting, or lying. He may be too big to get your arms around, or a tiny infant that would be injured by methods used for an adult. But the basic problem is the same; the airway is blocked and must be cleared. Once it is cleared, if the casualty is not breathing, rescue breathing or CPR must be given.

Suspect choking whenever:

- a person is seen to clutch at his throat, is unable to breathe, cough, or speak, and turns red or blue
- a person of any age suddenly stops breathing and collapses
- a person is found not breathing
- a person silently and suddenly leaves the table without explanation.

The airway may be fully or partly blocked during choking. If it is only partly blocked, the casualty may be able to breathe and cough. If he is able to cough hard, he is getting enough air and will probably not need help. If he makes a whistling or crowing noise when trying to inhale, has only a weak cough, and is turning blue, he will need help just as if his airway were fully blocked.

People who suddenly choke while eating may be embarrassed and leave the table quickly so as not to be seen. This takes them away from help, and people have died in restaurant restrooms.

Whenever you suspect choking, approach the person and ask him, "Are you choking?" If he cannot speak and is clutching his throat and shows evidence of choking (**Fig. 21-6**), tell him you will help him, and proceed as described below.

Fig. 21-6: Typical appearance of a choking person.

If you place a cork in a plastic pop bottle and suddenly squeeze the bottle, the cork will fly out. Exactly the same thing happens to objects stuck in the airway when a sudden pressure is applied to the abdomen or chest. The best known technique is called the **Heimlich Manoeuvre**, or **abdominal thrust**. You can do this for a casualty regardless of whether he is standing, sitting, lying, conscious, or unconscious. The principle is the same in all cases, although you might apply the technique differently. Be sure each thrust is separate and distinct, not a continuous pressure.

Abdominal Thrust – Standing or Sitting

Ask someone to get medical help if it is available. Then, for a standing or sitting casualty:

- stand behind the casualty

- to determine the correct hand position for the thrusts, feel for the top of his hip bones with your hands, then move your fingers to the midline of his body (**Fig. 21-7a**); this step is called "landmarking"

- leaving one hand in its landmark position, make the other into a fist and place it midline on the body, thumb-side against the belly, just above the landmarking hand (**Fig. 21-7b**)

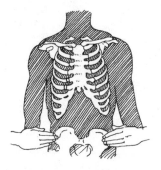

Fig. 21-7a: Abdominal thrusts – locating the hip bones.

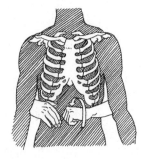

Fig. 21-7b: Abdominal thrusts – fist position.

Fig. 21-8a: Abdominal thrusts –   Fig. 21-8b: Grasp the fist.
conscious casualty.

- cup the landmarking hand around the fist and thrust quickly and strongly inward and slightly upward (**Figs. 21-8a, b**)

- repeat the thrusts until the object is forced out or until the casualty becomes unconscious.

It is common for the object to fly out with the first thrust. If it does not come out, the casualty will eventually collapse. Lower him gently to the floor, face up, call again for medical help, and continue the thrusts whether he is conscious or not. Now, however, you must use a different approach.

Abdominal Thrust – Lying Down

Ask someone to get medical help if it is available.

- With the casualty on his back, open his mouth, lifting the tongue and jaw upwards (tongue-jaw lift) by grasping the chin with your fingers and pressing on his tongue with your thumb.

- Sweep a hooked finger through the mouth, searching for an object (If the casualty is a child or infant, look first and remove only objects you can see.)

- Open the airway using the head tilt-chin lift method and give 1 slow breath; if air does not enter . . .

- reposition the head and try to ventilate again; if air still does not enter . . .

- kneel astride the casualty so that you can reach his abdomen comfortably when your arms are straight (**Fig. 21-9**),

- locate the top of the hip bones with each hand as you did before and slide your thumbs toward each other.

- When your thumbs meet at the midline, centre the heel of one hand above the other hand and place your other hand on top of it (keep fingers raised or interlocked so only the heel does the thrusts).

- Thrust inward and upward quickly and strongly, giving up to 5 distinct thrusts.

- Repeat the tongue-jaw lift and finger sweep.

- Open the airway and attempt to ventilate. If no air will enter, repeat the cycle. If air enters (shown by rising of the chest), continue rescue breathing until the casualty breathes naturally.

Fig. 21-9: Abdominal thrusts – unconscious casualty lying down.

Fig. 21-10: Chest thrusts – standing

Chest Thrust for a Pregnant or Obese (Fat) Person

Follow the same procedures, but place your thrusting fist on the lower half of the sternum (breastbone) instead of the abdomen. Thrust straight in, rather than upward. (**Fig. 21-10**) If the casualty collapses, *kneel beside her* and follow the procedures for giving abdominal thrusts, except place the heel of your hand midline on the lower part of the sternum rather than the abdomen, place your other hand on top, and thrust straight down. The chest should be depressed 2.5 to 5 cm (1½ to 2 inches) with each thrust.

Chest Thrust for an Infant (Under 1 Year)

Chest thrusts must be used for choking infants, as abdominal thrusts may cause injury. For a conscious infant, proceed as follows:

- Call for help.

- Check for breathing, crying, or coughing.

- Place the infant face down on your forearm, supporting his head and neck by holding his jaw, and keeping his head lower than his trunk, and deliver 5 back blows with the heel of your hand. (**Fig. 21-11**)

- Turn the infant face up on your forearm, firmly supporting the head and neck lower than the trunk.

- Locate the centre of the sternum along an imaginary line between his nipples. Place 3 fingers on the sternum just below the imaginary line. Raise the finger closest to the head, leaving the other 2 fingers in place for the chest thrusts. (**Fig. 21-12**)

- Deliver 5 thrusts, depressing the chest 1.3 to 2.5 cm (½ to 1 inch), pausing and removing all pressure between thrusts to allow the chest to recover.

- If the obstacle is not forced out, repeat the cycle of 5 back blows and 5 chest thrusts until successful or until the infant becomes unconscious.

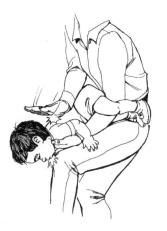 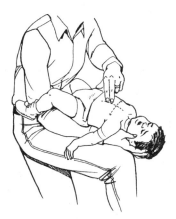

Fig. 21-11: Back blows – infant.   Fig. 21-12: Chest thrusts – infant.

If the infant becomes unconscious, you must:

- Call for help.

- With the thumb inside the mouth and the fingers under the chin, grip the tongue and jaw and lift them. Examine the mouth and remove with a finger sweep any visible object.

- Open the airway (head tilt-chin lift) and attempt to ventilate. If the lungs inflate, continue artificial respiration until the infant breathes normally. If they do not inflate, reposition the head and try to ventilate again.

If air still does not enter:

- Give 5 back blows.

- Give 5 chest thrusts.

- Use the tongue-jaw lift and examine mouth. Remove any visible objects.

- Attempt to ventilate. Repeat the cycle until successful.

If an infant is unconscious and his airway is blocked, the procedures are essentially the same as for an adult, except that:

- both the infant's mouth and nose are covered by the rescuer's mouth when attempting to ventilate

- when ventilating, give enough air to make the chest rise

- back blows and chest thrusts are given instead of abdominal thrusts

- a tongue-jaw lift and visual examination are made instead of blind finger sweeps.

Whenever a casualty of any age resumes normal breathing, stop first aid for choking. Watch him carefully to see that he has no further difficulties. Take him to medical care at the first opportunity.

Rescue Breathing: A Step-By-Step Review

Any time you believe that a person is not breathing, you should:

- **check his level of consciousness/responsiveness.** Tap his shoulder and shout, "Are you okay?" If no response . . .

- **call for help.** You will need it for immediate first aid or rescue. Then . . .

- **check his breathing.** Place your ear next to his lips and look, listen, and feel for breathing for 3 to 5 seconds. If no breathing, then . . .

- **open his airway.** You can give rescue breathing in almost any position if the airway is open, but consider the possibility of neck injury. Then . . .

- **again check his breathing.** Did opening the airway restore breathing? Look, listen, and feel for another 3 to 5 seconds. If no breathing . . .

- **give 2 slow breaths.** Watch to be sure that you are getting air into his lungs. Then . . .

- **check his pulse.** Feel for the carotid (neck) pulse in adults and children and the brachial (arm) pulse in infants. Take 5 to 10 seconds to do this. **If no pulse,** start CPR. **If a pulse is felt** . . .

- **continue rescue breathing.** Ventilate an adult every 5 seconds, a child or infant every 3 seconds. Look, listen, and feel continuously to be sure air is getting in. Continue until the casualty starts breathing on his own.

Part IV

How to Recognize and Handle Common Illnesses

This section looks at the common illnesses that may befall any of us when we are far from help. We must remember that no matter how certain we are about what an illness is, we may in fact be wrong, and a mistake could be very serious for the patient. If you have the slightest doubt, do not take a chance; **get the patient to medical care.**

Illnesses are often harder to identify than injuries, because there are often fewer *signs* (things the first-aider can **see**) and more *symptoms* (things the patient **feels** and must describe). It is extremely important that you ask the patient as much as possible about his problem, and **write it down** on the checklists in Appendix D, in order to be able to report completely and accurately to a doctor if a radio is available, or so that you can make a better judgement yourself if there is no help available. Use your checklists (Appendix D) to record your assessment findings.

22

Abdominal Complaints: "Bellyaches"

The abdomen, with its many organs, can produce a great variety of pains and problems. Some are common and not serious, and do not necessarily require travel to medical care. Some indicate serious illness and require evacuation.

Ailments That Do Not Require Evacuation

Gastroenteritis (Stomach Flu, Food Poisoning)

This common problem is usually caused by bacteria in food or water, but may also be caused by viruses or other agents. It causes inflammation of the gut, and the unpleasant signs and symptoms we all know.

Prevention

The bacteria that cause this problem are found everywhere that there are people, and are common in sewage. They grow and multiply on food at temperatures over about 4°C (40°F). Camp and personal cleanliness is the main prevention. In freezing conditions, the problem is greatly reduced as bacteria cannot multiply on frozen food or frozen dishes, and there are no flies to carry bacteria.

In above-freezing conditions or in a warm shelter, you should:

- Wash your hands before preparing or eating food.

- Keep game meat and fish cool and clean; while it is hanging cover it against flies.

- Wash dishes well in soap and water. A few drops of Javex (chlorine bleach) in rinse or dish water will kill most bacteria. Let them air-dry to reduce contact with bacteria on hands or towels.

- Maintain a separate latrine. Cover all waste immediately with dirt, sand, or ashes so flies cannot touch it. Touch a match to the paper. In a short-term camp where a latrine is not built, pull out a rock, use the hollow where it lay, and roll the rock back into place.

Gastroenteritis is usually brief, but it may be serious in very cold weather (remember the story in Chapter 1 about the campers), because it weakens and dehydrates the patient and may make it easier for exposure and frostbite to occur.

How to Tell

Signs and symptoms are:

- a general (not localized) bellyache that worsens
- crampy pain, often coming in "waves," with abdomen relaxed between cramps
- watery, gassy diarrhea, often explosive
- loud bowel sounds, often loud enough to be heard several feet away
- occasionally a minor fever, vomiting, small amount of blood in the stool
- duration of from 3 hours to overnight.

If the problem is due to bacteria in food, there will often be more than one patient. Suspect food contamination whenever more than one person gets sick at the same time.

What to Do

This illness will go away by itself, usually in less than 24 hours, although the patient may be weak and shaky until his food and liquid intake and his rest patterns are back to normal.

- Stop travelling if possible and allow the patient to rest.

- Keep him warm. He will need more coverings than usual. Warmers in the sleeping bag will be welcome.

- Give lots of clear fluids, continually, in small amounts. Salty soups or broths and fruit juices are both good. Give some of each if possible. The broth from boiled game meat is excellent. Or give one of the rehydration fluids described in Chapter 20.

- Hold solid foods until he is feeling better.

- If prescribed, Imodium (Loperamide HCL, an over-the-counter medicine) to reduce diarrhea, or other diarrhea medications, may be given if vomiting permits. Give no other medications.

- If the condition gets worse or does not improve in 24 hours, seek urgent medical attention. Keep giving fluids if the patient can tolerate them.

Giardiasis (Beaver Fever)

Beaver fever is common throughout the north. It is caused by a single-cell organism called *Giardia* and is transmitted through the wastes of many animals, including humans. It is usually caught by drinking untreated water from a lake, stream, or pond, and takes 1 to 3 weeks to appear as sickness. It may continue for several weeks.

Prevention

If giardiasis is found in your area, assume that all water is contaminated, and treat it in one of the following ways before drinking:

- **Boil water for 10 minutes.**

- **Add one of the iodine water purifiers according to directions.** Several types can be bought in outdoor stores or pharmacies, or obtained from your doctor or nurse. These give the water a slight iodine taste. To be absolutely sure *Giardia* are killed, you should allow the iodine 8 hours to work. (*DANGER: iodine is poisonous if taken in any quantity, and must be kept from children, but is not dangerous when added properly to water.*)

- **Use a specialized water filter.** These are found in outdoor stores or outdoor catalogues at various prices. Because *Giardia* are quite large, a very high-priced filter is not needed, but the holes must be 6 microns or less. An ordinary filter paper such as a coffee filter is not good enough. Remember that even though a 6-micron filter will remove *Giardia*, it will **not** remove bacteria and viruses.

How to Tell

Signs and symptoms are similar to stomach flu, but last more than two days. The stool is foul-smelling, often light coloured, watery and bulky, and may contain blood and mucus. The abdomen may be bloated. The patient is often tired or depressed. After an acute episode of less than a week, the condition may become chronic, with loose stools, lots of gas, and fatigue.

What to Do

Treat the patient as for stomach flu. He may eat solid foods if he wishes, but should avoid spicy foods, coffee, and alcohol, which will irritate the stomach.

While treatment is not urgent (unless the patient has blood or pus in the stool, or runs a fever), he should be taken to medical attention. The drug to combat beaver fever is a strong one, and is usually only given by medical personnel.

Gastritis, Esophagitis (Burning Stomach)

Several things may cause this. It may indicate a developing or existing ulcer. It may be caused by stomach juices coming up into the lower throat (esophagus). In this case, there may be a smell like vomit on the patient's breath. This is not usually an emergency, but merits early medical attention.

How to Tell

The patient complains of burning in his stomach, or "heartburn."

What to Do

- Give antacids (Rolaids, Tums, etc.). If antacids are not available, 1 mL (¼ tsp) of baking soda in a glass of water may be used, but should not be taken regularly because it could change the chemical levels of the blood. (If there is no relief with antacids, the patient may be experiencing a cardiovascular problem. See Chapter 23.)

- Avoid highly spiced or acidic foods (tomatoes, cranberries, rhubarb, vinegar), fatty foods, coffee, chocolate, alcohol, and cigarettes.

- See a physician or nurse on returning to town.

Mittelschmerz (Middle Pain)

Women sometimes get sharp abdominal pain midway between periods, when the egg is released from the ovary. It will be limited to one side, depending on which ovary is involved. If on the right, it may be confused with appendicitis, but will lack most of the other symptoms. It will go away by itself in about 24 hours, and no treatment is needed.

Ailments That Require Evacuation

The above ailments are uncomfortable but generally not serious. The following are more serious.

Botulism

Botulism is caused by poison created by bacteria growing in food which has been sealed airtight. It is difficult to identify and is often fatal. Common causes are meat or fish (including specialty items such as beaver tail) which has been kept above freezing in a plastic bag or wrapped in plastic, and home-canned meat or fish which has not been cooked long enough or is not tightly sealed.

Prevention

- Do not store any fresh or thawed meat or fish in plastic at temperatures above freezing.
- Throw away any cans with even slightly bulging ends or any jar with a poor seal or bulging lid. While the bulging may be caused by freezing, it may also be caused by gas built up by the bacteria – and you can't afford to experiment! (NOTE: do not feed these to dogs. While dogs are not affected by many bacteria which cause food poisoning, they *are* affected by botulism.)

How to Tell

Signs of botulism poisoning start suddenly, 16 to 36 hours after eating bad food. The earlier signs and symptoms start, the worse the poisoning. The patient may have:

- nausea, vomiting, cramps, diarrhea (these are sometimes the first signs)
- a dry mouth
- difficulty seeing well
- (later) difficulty swallowing
- muscle weakness, sometimes difficulty breathing.

What to Do

If there is the slightest possibility of this poisoning, you must arrange an immediate air medevac. Also watch others who may have been exposed, and send them out on the medevac as a precaution.

- Protect the patient's airway. Keep him in the drainage/recovery position, as he may be vomiting and he cannot swallow well.
- Call an immediate air medevac.

Appendicitis

Appendicitis is an infection of the appendix, which is a tiny fingerlike organ extending off the intestine. The appendix may or may not burst. If it does, it releases bacteria, pus, and intestinal contents into the abdominal cavity. The result is called "acute abdomen" and is critical.

Whenever a patient has indications of appendicitis, be sure to ask if his appendix has been removed. If it has, he has a different problem.

How to Tell

- **Appendicitis almost always starts with pain or discomfort *around the belly button* (umbilicus). The pain worsens, and may be increased by movement.**

- **In a few hours, the pain moves to the lower right belly.** (Notice this progression; it is a very important indication.)

- **Nausea and vomiting** are common. So is **constipation.** The patient will not want food.

- **The abdomen is tender. There is often rebound tenderness in the right lower quadrant.** (Rebound tenderness describes pain which occurs when a *gently* pressing hand on a tender area of the abdomen is suddenly removed. It is the most important sign of peritonitis.)

- **There may be fever.**

- **Breath may be foul and the tongue "furred"** (in perhaps one third of cases).

If the appendix ruptures, the local tenderness may suddenly disappear, only to return, generalized, after several hours as "acute abdomen" or peritonitis, a critical condition.

What to Do

You cannot provide any first aid which will really help this patient unless you happen to have the proper antibiotics, and even then he must be taken quickly to medical aid. Call in an air medevac if possible, and evacuate him in the position of greatest comfort. In the meantime, you must:

- protect the airway and watch for vomiting
- watch for and treat shock
- give nothing by mouth. (If transport is long delayed, give only ice chips, bits of snow, or a wet cloth to moisten a dry mouth.)

Peritonitis (Acute Abdomen)

This condition is commonly caused by a ruptured appendix, disease or infection of abdominal organs, blockage of the intestine, or bleeding into the abdominal cavity from injury. **It is a critical emergency**. The patient must be evacuated as soon as possible.

How to Tell

To examine a patient for acute abdomen:

- get the patient's story and write down what he tells you about how he feels

- press very gently with (warm!) fingers on the four parts (quadrants) of the belly **(Fig. 22-1)** to locate tenderness or rigidity

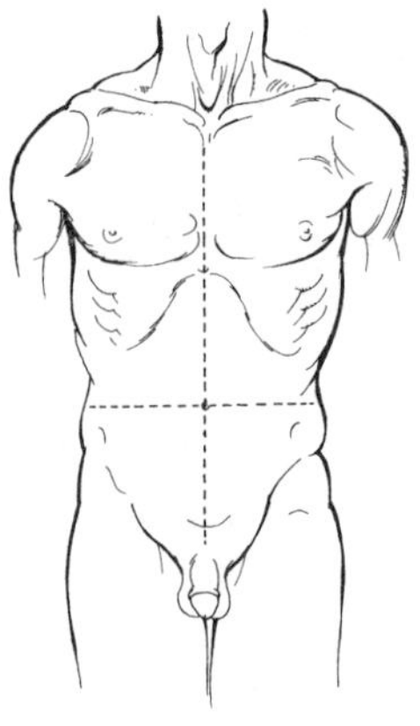

Fig. 22-1: The surface of the abdomen showing the four quadrants.

- check for rebound tenderness (This is the most important sign. Press the belly gently, then release suddenly. If pain flares over the area, evacuate immediately.)

- check for fever

- take the vital signs and record them.

Signs and symptoms are:

- severe pain; movement or rolling over often produces pain
- rebound tenderness
- belly that may be rigid and extremely painful (The patient may be afraid to move for fear of pain. He may keep you from touching his belly.)
- belly that may be swollen
- vomiting that is almost always present
- high fever
- shallow breathing, rapid pulse; shock is usually present.

What to Do

If several of these signs and symptoms are present, there is an emergency. There is nothing you can do but get the patient to help quickly. If a radio is available, get medical advice immediately.

- Call an urgent air medevac.
- Transport in the position of comfort. This may be on his back, with knees and body slightly flexed.
- Give nothing by mouth, except tiny ice chips or snow bits or *tiny* sips of water.
- Protect the airway, and watch for vomiting.

NOTE: If there is diarrhea, or if there is NO vomiting, the problem may NOT be acute abdomen. However, you should still evacuate the patient.

Renal Colic (Kidney Stone)

Sometimes a small "stone" builds in a person's kidney from

chemicals in the urine. When this stone passes down the narrow tube (the ureter) to the bladder, it produces one of the worst pains known. The patient may fear he is dying. The stone may take a long time to pass, and may obstruct the flow of urine. Fortunately, it is not life-threatening, and when the stone has passed the pain will stop. Rarely, the stone will not pass and the patient will require surgical intervention.

How to Tell

- The patient may have a history of this ailment.
- The pain starts suddenly.
- The pain is sharp, stabbing, in waves, and increasing.
- The pain starts in the back under the ribs, moves slowly downward around the side and into the groin.
- The patient will twist and squirm, seeking a position of comfort. (He won't find it.)
- The patient may have frequent urination, pain on urination, or bright red blood in the urine.
- The patient may have nausea, vomiting, cold sweats, fever, or chills.

What to Do

- Reassure the patient. Explain that it is not fatal and will go away by itself. The lower the pain moves, the sooner it will go away.
- Give painkillers if he is not vomiting.
- Give as much fluid as the patient can take (to flush out the stone).

There will be sudden relief when the stone passes. It may take 24 hours. If it continues for 48 hours, get the patient to medical care. NOTE: Even if a stone passes, the patient should see a physician or nurse when he arrives back in town.

Urethritis, Cystitis (Urinary Tract Infection)

This infection is more common in women. Those who have had it before will recognize the signs and symptoms. It is caused by a variety of normal body bacteria invading the urinary tract. It may cause great discomfort and distress. If it is allowed to continue, it may progress to kidney infection. The patient should be evacuated to medical care. She is usually able to travel or be transported, but urination will be very frequent.

How to Tell

The patient will show or tell you of:

- frequent urination, often every 15 to 30 minutes
- burning pain on urination
- cloudy, smelly, sometimes bloody urine
- high fever and chills
- pain and tenderness in the lower belly.

What to Do

If the patient has had the problem before, she may be carrying the correct medication. If so, she should take it as prescribed.

- Give the patient as much fluid as she can handle; the more the better. This tends to flush out the infection and slow its progress toward the kidneys.
- Take the patient to medical care. This does not usually call for an air medevac, but if it progresses to a kidney infection, it will.

Salpingitis (Pelvic Inflammatory Disease – PID)

PID is one of the most common causes of acute abdominal symptoms in the female, and occurs most commonly in young, sexually active women. It is caused by infection of the tubes leading from the ovaries to the uterus (the Fallopian tubes) and may include both organs. The infecting bacterium is usually transmitted by intercourse.

This is a severe, dangerous infection which may lead to infertility, and any person suspected of having this should be evacuated immediately, regardless of antibiotic availability.

How to Tell

The patient may be very sick, and will have:

- increasing, severe pain in the lower abdomen
- rebound tenderness
- tenderness on palpation of the abdomen (the patient will resist movement).

The patient may also have:

- fever
- abnormal vaginal discharge
- rigid abdominal muscles.

What to Do

Little can be done in the field if the proper antibiotics are not available. You should:

- obtain medical advice by radio if possible
- keep the patient at rest
- administer appropriate antibiotics by mouth if available and only if prescribed by a medical authority
- give the patient nourishing liquids and water if she wants and can tolerate them
- call for urgent air medevac.

Ectopic Pregnancy

Ectopic pregnancy is the development of a fetus in an abnormal location, often in a Fallopian tube. About six weeks after the egg is fertilized, the developing fetus ruptures the surrounding tissue, which may cause severe bleeding into the abdominal cavity, with pain, tenderness and rapidly developing shock.

This is a true medical emergency, and cannot be dealt with in the field. Internal bleeding usually continues and often becomes life-threatening.

How to Tell

The patient will be female, usually young, and will have:

- a history of sexual activity with 1 or 2 missed periods
- pain and tenderness in the lower abdomen
- indications of shock.

She may also have:

- a history of cramping pain and "spotting" (occasional blood from the vagina between periods)
- bleeding from the vagina
- rigidity of the abdomen.

What to Do

Again, little can be done in the field, and the patient must be evacuated quickly. The first-aider's primary concern is control of shock. You should:

- place the patient at rest
- treat for shock by raising her feet, and keeping her warm and reassured
- give fluids or rehydration drinks if the patient can tolerate them
- protect the airway from vomit
- call for an immediate air medevac.

Kidney Infection

This may accompany a kidney stone, or it may be from a urinary tract infection. It is somewhat similar to the latter, but the patient will be much sicker.

How to Tell

The patient will usually have:

- sudden high fever and chills (the patient will be very sick)
- moderate back pain
- tenderness over the lower ribs on either side
- (sometimes) burning on urination and traces of blood in the urine.

What to Do

The patient should:

- rest
- drink at least twice as much fluid as normal
- take antibiotics as prescribed if they are available, and continue them for 5 days after signs and symptoms have vanished
- get to medical care regardless of antibiotics or temporary improvement.

Gallstones (Gallbladder Disease)

The cause of this painful condition is the formation of a stone in the gallbladder, which is connected to the underside of the liver in the upper right part of the abdomen, just below the ribs. It is common in North American Indians, overweight people, middle-aged people, and more common in women. The patient has often had earlier attacks, and may recognize the symptoms.

How to Tell

Signs and symptoms are:

- pain and tenderness in the upper right abdomen
- pain that may radiate to the shoulder or back
- possible nausea and vomiting

- eyes that may show a yellowish colour (jaundice)
- possible fever
- duration of 1 or 2 days.

What to Do

Although the condition is not immediately life-threatening, it may become so. It is best to get the patient to medical care quickly, as surgery may be required. In the meantime, you should:

- keep the patient at rest
- give nothing by mouth until vomiting stops
- give clear fluids avoiding milk or anything with fats or oils
- give strong painkillers if available
- transport to medical care in a position of comfort.

If transport takes some time and the patient has stopped vomiting and wants solid food, he may eat lightly but must not have fats or oils. Often the attacks will pass, but sometimes may become complicated and progress to *acute abdomen.*

Hernia (Rupture)

A hernia occurs when a small loop of the intestine penetrates through a weakness in the muscular wall of the lower abdomen and into the groin or scrotum. It is often brought on by lifting, straining, or sneezing. Many patients have had earlier occurrences. The condition does not correct itself. Only surgery will prevent recurrence, and people who spend much time on the land should have this done.

How to Tell

- There is an obvious soft mass in the groin or scrotum. The patient will find it himself.
- The area may be swollen and tender.

What to Do

The patient may have experience in correcting the condition himself.

- Lie the patient on his back with head and chest lower.
- Hold gentle, steady hand pressure on the mass for 10 minutes or more. The protruding gut will often slide back in.

If the condition does not repeat, the patient may resume normal activity, but should avoid lifting or straining. It is likely to repeat. If it continues to repeat, get the patient to medical attention. *However, if the gut is pinched off and signs of acute abdomen appear, it becomes an emergency and the patient must be evacuated with all speed.*

Summary: Assessment of Serious Abdominal Conditions

Any abdominal condition could be serious and life-threatening. Many abdominal problems are hard to identify, and it is always best to evacuate or get medical advice. Any serious abdominal condition should be urgently evacuated to a medical facility. The following signs and symptoms indicate a serious abdominal condition:

- **rebound tenderness** (increased pain when the gently pressing hand is removed suddenly)
- **pain on rolling over**
- **persistent vomiting**
- **vomiting with constipation** and **no passage of gas** from the rectum
- **a hernia that cannot be pushed back** when the patient is lying down
- associated **shock**
- **any abdominal pain that gets worse** in 48 hours when the patient is taking only clear fluids by mouth.

23

Heart and Lung Problems

Heart Attack

Any sudden collapse is often – and often mistakenly – assumed to be a heart attack.

If the problem is sudden and unexplained, there is no indication of chest pain and the casualty is not able to function normally, the problem may be a stroke.

Heart attack is not the only cause of chest pain. For example, pleurisy, an inflammation of the lining of the chest, may cause sudden stabbing pain in the chest, belly, or shoulder on inhalation. Unlike a heart attack, it *will* be increased by movement, breathing, or coughing and *will not* be crushing in nature and *will not* cause shortness of breath.

Of actual heart attack casualties, about ⅔ die before reaching the hospital, even if they are near medical help, and they die within the first 2 hours after the attack. The first 2 hours are the critical period.

What a Heart Attack Is

The heart is a muscle. As any muscle, it needs a supply of blood and oxygen to live, and blood and oxygen are supplied by the coronary (heart) arteries.

These arteries may be narrowed inside by fat build-up. When they are so narrowed that the blood supply is cut down, the heart may not get enough oxygen during exercise and a pain like a cramp or pressure may be felt there (**angina pectoris**). It may radiate to the jaw, left shoulder, or arm. It is usually brought on by exercise and relieved by rest. It is sometimes mistaken for indigestion. This condition is NOT a heart attack, but often precedes one.

When a soft clot forms in and clogs a narrowed heart artery, that part of the heart gets no fresh blood and no oxygen. Then there is intense pain, and that part of the muscle may die. This is a true "heart attack." The heart may beat irregularly and stop, or if the attack is a minor one, it may recover.

While this often happens during or after exercise, it can happen at any time, even during sleep.

There is little the first-aider can do for heart attack except to keep the casualty comfortable, breathing easily, reassured, and to transport him or get medical help. Some heart attack casualties are saved by CPR when they are close to advanced medical facilities, but if a heart stops in the wilderness due to heart attack, CPR will probably be futile.

In the wilderness, do not start CPR unless it can be continued and the casualty can be delivered to a hospital within 1 hour.

How to Tell

In a heart attack, there is:

- sudden, extreme pain in the centre of the chest, which feels "crushing," "tight," or "burning"
- sometimes pain radiating to the shoulder, left arm, neck, or shoulder blade (**Fig. 23-1**)
- steady pain, usually for more than 30 minutes
- pain that is *not* increased by coughing, deep breathing, or movement

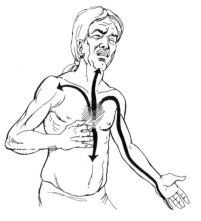

Fig. 23-1: Heart-attack pain is usually in the centre of the chest, sometimes radiating to the shoulder, neck, or left arm.

- great fear, a feeling of doom
- pallor and sweating
- shortness of breath
- nausea or vomiting
- sometimes a weak and rapid pulse, which may be irregular.

Sometimes the pain may feel like indigestion. The casualty will often deny that he is having a heart attack. He may not want to admit the possibility.

What to Do

Although there is little you can do about the condition, don't tell the casualty this. He will be terrified enough as it is. You should:

- reassure the casualty, keep him warm and comfortable
- keep him quiet and calm (do not let him walk AT ALL!)
- keep him semi-sitting if he is short of breath, horizontal if he is not
- guard his airway
- call for a most urgent air medevac.

While you are waiting for the medevac, you should:

- take his vital signs often and record them for the doctor
- not let him smoke
- give him sips of liquids if he asks, but *no* coffee, tea, or alcohol.

You should not try to evacuate the casualty of a serious heart attack by means other than air if it will involve much rough travel, bouncing, excitement, or exposure to severe cold.

If no evacuation is possible, then:

- keep him at absolute rest
- raise his legs if signs of shock appear, but if this causes shortness of breath, discontinue it
- give him liquids as tolerated, and light, mostly carbohydrate foods if he wishes them. (See the section on "Feeding Heat Foods" in Chapter 5.)

If the attack has been minor he may recover, but should be kept at rest until medical advice has been called or evacuation arranged.

Unusual Heartbeat
(Very Fast, Very Slow, or Irregular)

Most people have irregular heartbeats at some time. These often feel like "butterflies in the chest," or "something turning over in there." Usually there is no pain, rarely there may be weakness or dizziness. This is an occasional thing and usually lasts for less than five minutes. It may be brought on by coffee or tea, alcohol, tobacco, medicines, stress or anxiety.

The occasional irregular heartbeat is usually harmless, and will eventually stop if the casualty discontinues the things that cause it.

If pain is involved, it could be a heart attack. If in doubt, radio for medical advice or evacuate gently to medical help.

For very rapid or very slow heartbeats that do not correct themselves with rest, keep the casualty at rest while you radio for medical advice or evacuate to medical help.

Breathing Difficulties – Chronic (Continuous),
Chronic Obstructive Pulmonary Disease (COPD),
Emphysema, Chronic Bronchitis

Major lung problems are common among northern elders. These lung problems may be due to a combination of the very cold, dry Arctic air, a long smoking habit, stone dust from carving soapstone, and long exposure to smoke from other smokers, oil lamps, lanterns, and campfires.

The casualty usually has a history of the problem, and knows what aggravates it and what helps it. Attacks are often brought on by allergies ("hay fever"), smoking, exposure to other people's smoke, a cold or the flu, heavy exercise, or infections.

How to Tell

The casualty has:

- severe shortness of breath (SOB)
- a history of the problem
- wheezing or gasping breaths
- often a wet cough
- often blue lips or nails (cyanosis)
- usually NO fever (which pneumonia casualties *will* have).

The casualty will often insist on sitting up, slightly hunched forward with arms braced to allow full expansion of his rib cage and lungs, and will refuse to lie down, as this worsens SOB. **(Fig. 23-2)**

Fig. 23-2: Typical position and appearance of a person with breathing difficulties.

What to Do

To help this casualty, you should:

- calm and reassure him
- assist him to sit in a position of comfort and best air-exchange
- keep him at rest in a warm place
- encourage coughing to reduce fluid build-up in the lungs
- help him to take any prescribed medications.

Most people with chronic (continuing) breathing problems will be aware of them and carry their own medications. When the casualty can breathe better, evacuate him to medical help if he can be kept comfortable and sitting.

If evacuation is delayed or impossible, you should make a "steam tent" with a cloth over the casualty's head to catch the steam from a boiling kettle. Be careful to have the kettle far enough from the casualty's head and body to prevent steam burns, and arrange the kettle to prevent tipping.

**Safety note: the fumes from a camp stove or
kerosene heater or even campfire smoke can be
irritating and cause further problems, or may carry
carbon monoxide or other poisonous gases. Arrange it
so that *only steam* is caught by the steam tent. You may
have to rig some sort of spout for your kettle so that
invisible fumes from the stove are not included
in the steam tent. (Fig. 23-3)**

You may give the casualty lots of warm fluids. Broths are
preferable to coffee or tea. If he has Aspirin or Tylenol (acetaminophen), he may take these as directed for pain.

People should avoid smoking around the casualty.

**If a casualty has severe problems breathing,
cannot get enough air, and nailbeds and lips are
turning blue, use rescue breathing timed with his
own efforts, and continue this until he can breathe
by himself or until help is reached.**

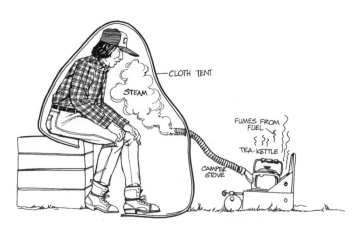

Fig. 23-3: An improvised steam tent for a person with breathing difficulties.
Be sure that no fumes from the stove enter the tent.

Pneumonia

Pneumonia is an infection in lung tissue caused by bacteria or viruses, and may follow other respiratory infections or illnesses. The lungs accumulate fluids, which reduce oxygen intake, and the infection produces toxins. If it progresses far enough, it is a killer.

How to Tell

The casualty is *very sick* and has:

- a cough, which may be dry at first, but later produces thick sputum that is rusty, green, or yellow, and may resemble pus
- a high fever, often with shaking chills
- pain on breathing or coughing
- rapid respiration and heart rate.

What to Do

To help this casualty, you should:

- call for immediate medical advice and air medevac, or evacuate by ground or water with all urgency
- keep the casualty warm and well nourished.

While awaiting medevac, assist the casualty to:

- take antibiotics, as prescribed
- breathe steam in a steam tent (**see again Fig. 23-3**)
- drink lots of fluids to reduce dehydration from fever and coughing.

Asthma

Asthma is a condition in which the muscles of the air passages go into spasm and constrict, making breathing (especially exhalation) very difficult. Attacks are most often triggered by allergies. Many sufferers are prone to sudden attacks at night.

How to Tell

The casualty will show the following signs:

- laboured breathing, especially breathing out
- wheezing
- anxiety
- difficulty with speech, which often is whispered
- blueness (cyanosis)
- (rarely) unconsciousness and respiratory arrest.

What to Do

The objective of first aid is to ease the casualty's breathing.

- Reassure and calm the casualty.
- Place the casualty in a sitting position so that he is leaning slightly forward and supported on something like a tabletop or a stack of pillows.
- Provide lots of fresh air.
- If the casualty has medication, in the form of a "puffer" spray, assist him to use it.
- Arrange for evacuation if the attack is long, does not respond to medication, or results in severe breathing difficulty.
- If the episode is mild, recommend that the casualty seek medical attention as soon as possible.

24

Seizures, Allergies, Substance Abuse, and Poisonings

Seizures (Convulsions, Epilepsy)

Seizures are fairly common. They are triggered by temporary, usually brief periods of intense electrical activity within the brain.

The mildest seizure may be hardly noticeable; the strongest may involve unconsciousness, violent jerking of muscles, difficulty in breathing, and loss of bladder control. They may be frightening to observe, but are usually short and are not dangerous in themselves. However, the unconscious casualty may injure himself during the seizure or his airway may become blocked.

A single seizure may have a variety of possible causes. These include alcohol or drug abuse (especially during acute withdrawal), high fever (especially in infants), head injury, diabetes, stroke, heart problems, meningitis (or other brain infections), carbon monoxide poisoning, or high blood pressure late in pregnancy.

Epilepsy

If seizures happen repeatedly, the condition is called epilepsy.

People with epilepsy (epileptics) usually know about their condition, and may know when a seizure is about to happen. They usually take medication to prevent or lessen seizures, and may wear Medic Alert bracelets or tags.

Epileptics often have seizures when their regular medication is interrupted. People who are drinking alcohol often forget medications, and the alcohol itself may also stimulate seizures.

How to Tell

Minor or Partial Seizures (Petit Mal): The casualty may stare into space, turn pale, and fail to respond to questions. He may be unconscious for a few seconds. This may resemble fainting, and is treated the same.

Major or Generalized Seizures (Grand Mal): The seizure has **convulsive** and **recovery** stages. When the convulsive stage begins, the casualty may:

- give a sudden cry, lose consciousness, and fall to the ground
- twitch, jerk violently, roll his eyes
- clench his teeth tightly (may bite his tongue), froth at the mouth, breathe and gurgle noisily, turn blue in the face
- wet his pants.

This stage may last one to several minutes, rarely more. When the **recovery** stage begins, the casualty may:

- go limp
- fall into a deep "sleep of recovery" for 10 to 30 minutes, during which he may be completely unable to respond.

Following this, he will slowly regain consciousness. He may be confused, with no memory of the seizure. He may be combative. He will eventually return to normal.

What to Do

There is little you can do for an actively convulsing casualty except to:

- keep him from hurting himself by removing objects which he may strike during convulsions, removing firearms or sharp tools if he is carrying any

- gently turn him onto his side (recovery position) to keep his airway clear of saliva, blood, or fluids (outside, place padding under his face to protect it from snow or rocks)

- loosen clothing around his neck

- protect him from cold (if he is outside in severe weather) by covering him loosely, but not so as to endanger his airway.

Do not try to restrain a convulsing casualty. If you think he may have injured himself seriously in the fall, you may have to try to stabilize the injured part as best you can while he convulses. *Do not place anything between his teeth or in his mouth.* Do not worry about minor bleeding from tongue bites, but keep any blood out of his airway.

When the convulsive stage is over, the casualty may fall into a deep, coma-like sleep for up to half an hour. During this time, you should:

- protect the airway and assist breathing if needed
- protect the casualty from cold, especially if he is outside
- treat any minor injuries which he may have received during the convulsion.

As he gradually returns to consciousness, speak of and treat him with consideration. He will probably be able to hear you long before he appears conscious. He may be self-conscious and embarrassed, or may get irritable and angry. Allow him to rest as long as he wishes and return to normal activity when he likes. Ask the casualty whether he recalls anything unusual before the seizure.

Continual Seizures (Status Epilepticus)

Rarely, convulsions will last 20 minutes or more, or a casualty may have two or more seizures without regaining consciousness in between. This is a life-threatening emergency and requires immediate transport to hospital care.

Recording Seizures

After providing first aid, you should record all your observations, as these may later prove useful to a physician. Make notes on the length, frequency, and nature of his convulsions, his level of consciousness, what he was doing before the attack, his colour, his medications, his recall of anything unusual before the seizure, and anything else you notice. Give this information to his nurse or physician on your return to town.

Allergies (See also "Insect Stings and Bites" in Chapter 12)

Many people have mild allergies to various things such as plant pollens, animal fur, even dust. These cause signs and symptoms similar to a cold and are usually only minor irritations. Allergic persons are often aware of their allergies and carry antihistamine tablets for relief.

If any person develops itching, swelling, or breathing difficulties after taking a medicine, after having unfamiliar food, or being stung by an insect, he should check with medical authorities on his return to town, as this may be the early sign of a severe allergy *which could be fatal next time he is exposed.*

Severe Allergy (Anaphylaxis)

A few people have allergies so severe that they may go into an often fatal shock-like reaction after receiving certain medications (especially penicillin and rarely Aspirin), an insect sting, or after eating food containing the item to which they are allergic.

Severely allergic people going into the wilderness should carry kits provided by medical authorities.

Without such medication, quick death is likely. Others in the party should also know how to use the kit, in case the casualty cannot help himself.

How to Tell

Immediately after contact with the offending item, the casualty may:

- show signs of shock
- choke, wheeze, or show other signs of breathing difficulty

- show blue lips and nails
- show blotchy skin weals (hives) and itch all over the body
- show local or general swelling
- collapse.

What to Do

Action must be immediate. You should:

- immediately give the medication in the emergency kit, following directions
- treat for shock and protect from the environment
- assist breathing if necessary
- call immediate air medevac.

If long-distance ground transport is necessary, the casualty will probably have either expired or recovered before it can be completed.

Poisoning

There are far fewer sources of poisonous materials in the wilderness than there are in town. The most probable poisoning incidents, in order of frequency, are:

- alcohol or illicit drug or prescription medicine overdose by adults
- accidental breathing of carbon monoxide in closed tents, cabins, or igloos
- intentional breathing or sniffing of fuel, glue, or aerosol fumes by young people
- swallowing of engine or stove fuels such as gasoline, kerosene, and methanol by children
- eating poisonous plants and contaminated foods.

Prevention

Most poisonings happen to children because adults have allowed them to get harmful items. Many small children, especially ages two to four, will eat or drink anything, no matter how bad it tastes.

**Always assume that a small child will
eat or drink anything he can reach.**

- Keep medicines, cleaners, and fuels locked up or away from children.
- Avoid putting fuels or other poisons in containers used for drinking, especially pop bottles.
- Alert children early to poisonous berries and mushrooms.
- Never call medicines "candy" to get children to take them.

Prevention for adults includes:

- awareness of the effects and hazards of drugs and alcohol
- awareness of the hazards of carbon monoxide
- proper labelling, dosage instructions, and containers for medications
- identification of naturally poisonous foods.

General Rules for Poisoning

If you suspect a person has taken a poison, act as follows:

- **Identify the poisonous material.** Look for the material itself, and for bottles or containers; examine any vomit to see what is in it. Sniff it to see if you can smell the odour of the material. Save a sample – even if it is in vomit – for analysis when medical care is reached.

- **Determine the amount taken.** You may simply have to guess, based on the amount left or from what the casualty or observers tell you.

- **Determine how it got into the body.** Was it swallowed, inhaled, injected, or absorbed through the skin?

- **Determine how much time has passed** since the poison was taken.

- **Watch for signs and symptoms** of poisoning to show, and record them. (Signs and symptoms are described under each poisoning type.)

General First Aid for Poisoning

Individual common poisons are discussed below, but some general rules are as follows:

- **Get medical advice immediately by radio if possible.** The nurse or doctor will probably call a Poison Control Centre to get exact information, but he cannot do this unless you have correctly identified the poison.

- **Get rid of or dilute the poison.**

- **Seek medical attention.**

Getting rid of the poison is done by causing the casualty to vomit. However, there are four important cautions here.

- **The casualty must be alert and able to control vomiting** if you try this; otherwise he may inhale some vomit and die.

- **Do not cause vomiting if the poison is gasoline or kerosene.** The liquid or fumes may get into the lungs and cause a fatal pneumonia.

- **Do not cause vomiting if the poison is a corrosive.** Corrosives include things like lye, drain cleaner, oven cleaner, and bleach. If someone has swallowed them, there may be burns on the lips and mouth. These materials will burn the throat as they come up, and cause more damage than if they were left in place and diluted.

- **Do not cause vomiting in infants** (less than 1 year) unless on medical advice.

HOW TO CAUSE VOMITING: Syrup of ipecac is highly effective. It is found in some advanced first-aid kits or may be provided by a health centre. If it is available, follow the instructions. Usually, instructions advise you to give it according to age:

- for casualties over 10 years: 30 mL (2 tablespoons)
- for casualties under 10 years: 15 mL (1 tablespoon)
- follow with 1 or 2 glasses of water.

Repeat (once only) if the casualty has not vomited after 20 minutes. Usually he will vomit two or three times. If he takes anything by mouth within the next hour, he will continue to vomit. *Guard his airway!*

If syrup of ipecac is not available, have the casualty lean forward and tickle the back of his throat with his finger until he vomits (don't use your own finger – it may get bitten). This method is not as effective as using syrup of ipecac, and may not completely empty the stomach.

Drinking warm water – several glasses – may also induce vomiting, and will also dilute the poison.

Diluting the poison is usually done only for **corrosive** poisons. Give the casualty a moderate amount of milk (canned milk is excellent) or water with egg white, or plain water if nothing else is available. Give it slowly enough and in small enough volume not to cause vomiting.

Getting the casualty to medical help is the final step in general first aid for poisoning. Because there is no way to tell how much has been absorbed or whether there will be later effects, evacuate even if the casualty appears to have recovered. Air medevac is best. Whatever the method, observe him carefully, give small amounts of fluids and food if he wishes them, and guard his airway.

Specific Poisoning Incidents

Illicit Drug or Medicine Overdose

While this problem is much more common in town than out on the land, it could occur there, especially if someone has prescription medications or is carrying illegal drugs. Occasionally, small children take medications, thinking the pills are candy.

Aspirin is especially dangerous, as it is common in camps and causes serious effects if taken in large amounts. All medicines should be kept from children's reach.

Overdoses sometimes occur with people who have trouble with the prescribing language. Mistakes in understanding directions are common, but almost as common is the mistaken idea that, "If one pill will help me, then six of them will work faster." This idea is wrong and dangerous.

Some medicines may make people sleepy and unfit to operate snowmobiles or other machines. Some may decrease blood flow to the skin and increase the chance of frostbite, or slow the body's vital functions and increase chances of exposure.

Alcohol should never be drunk while a medication is in the system; the combination is unpredictable, and has been responsible for many overdoses and deaths. Alcohol itself is a powerful drug.

Depressed persons may attempt suicide by taking every pill they can find.

How to Tell

There are so many medications and drugs that it is impossible to list here all the signs and symptoms. Suspect drug overdose whenever you observe unexplained "drunk-like" actions, strange behaviour, hallucinations (seeing or hearing imaginary things), a reduced level of consciousness, signs of shock, or collapse in any person who is:

- suspected of drug or alcohol abuse
- depressed and possibly suicidal
- known to be taking medications
- a small child who has had access to medications.

Drug abusers will probably deny their actions unless they are frightened by their condition. Suicidal persons often admit overdosing if questioned gently, or may even volunteer the information. Persons (often elders) who are confused about the medications they are taking are often vague, and their actions may have to be guessed from the contents of containers. Small children will often leave empty or spilled containers in plain sight, and may cry or complain about the taste.

What to Do

It is very important to get medical advice as quickly as possible. A search should be made for the drug container to confirm the overdose, and containers should be saved so that contents can be clearly identified. If reporting an overdose by radio, be sure to have the containers with you.

If you know or suspect drug overdose, you must do the following:

- Cause vomiting by one of the preceding methods if the casualty is alert. If you are not sure of the poison, save the vomit in a plastic bag and send it with the casualty for testing.

- Protect the casualty's airway. He may be semi-conscious or unconscious and still vomit. *Keep the casualty in the drainage (recovery) position and watch him constantly.*

- Assist breathing if it appears necessary.

- Keep the casualty warm. He could be extremely vulnerable to cold injury.

- Be calm and reassuring. Some drugs produce great restlessness, aggressiveness, or suspicious and fearful (paranoid) behaviour, and it may be necessary to "talk down" such a person for hours, in privacy, in a calm, friendly way.

- Call for medical advice by radio, reporting if possible exactly what the casualty has taken, and his pulse, respiration, and all signs that you observe.

If medical advice is not available by radio and an air medevac cannot be arranged, transport must be considered. If the casualty is in shock or vomiting repeatedly, you will be unable to transport. If the shock or nausea passes, transport gently by whatever means allows you to continue observation and the first aid above. Give the casualty frequent sips of water or clear fluids if he can handle them. If he is hungry, he may eat small amounts of light, nourishing food.

Poisonous Foods (Berries, Mushrooms)

There are few poisonous mushrooms or berries in the north. They are generally well known to adults, but children may eat them.

How to Tell

Indications of poisonous food ingestion may appear quickly or take up to 18 hours to appear. Signs and symptoms are:

- nausea and vomiting
- abdominal or muscular cramps
- shock
- diarrhea
- dizziness
- double vision
- convulsions.

What to Do

First aid is the same as for drug or medicine overdose. You should save a complete sample of the mushroom or berry for testing, or if this is not possible, save the vomit in a plastic bag for later analysis.

Inhaled Drugs (Glue, Gasoline, Propane, Spray Paints, Aerosols)

Many people experiment with inhaling these materials, and may do so on the land as well as in town. There are many dangers, ranging from death in the most severe cases to permanent damage to the brain, liver, kidneys, and other organs. As well, many people have been seriously or fatally burned when attempting to light cigarettes during propane or gasoline-sniffing episodes.

If someone is discovered sniffing gasoline or propane, it is critical that no open flame, cigarette, or gasoline lantern be brought into the closed area while fumes, soaked rags or bags are present.

Drunken behaviour lasting from five minutes to an hour, plus the odour of the abused substance, are clues to inhalant abuse.

What to Do

You should:

- get the substance abuser into fresh air
- protect his airway
- assist breathing if necessary
- call for medical advice, or air medevac if condition is serious.

Carbon Monoxide (CO) Poisoning

This is one of the great killers in northern climates. Carbon monoxide is a gas which is produced by incomplete burning of fuels, and cannot be seen, smelled, or tasted. Because it replaces oxygen in the blood, the brain gradually becomes short of oxygen and the casualty does not know what is happening. Frequently, he will become helpless before he realizes what is happening to him. In this way, its effects are somewhat similar to hypothermia or going to extreme high altitude. Each year, someone dies from CO poisoning in the north and many more are made ill but do not realize what has affected them.

There is probably as much or more CO poisoning in camp situations as in town, because there is more of a tendency to use camp stoves and heaters in small spaces with poor venting.

Prevention

In a field situation, CO is usually formed in one of three ways: by camp cook stoves and lanterns, by kerosene space heaters, and by any liquid-fuel engine. Charcoal is also a great producer of CO. Charcoal barbecues (hibachis) have killed many in recreational vehicles such as pickup campers, but fortunately they are used less often away from roads.

Camp stoves create the most CO where the flame strikes the cold bottom of a cook pot and is suddenly cooled. Experiments have shown that even in a well-vented two-person tent, CO can build to unsafe levels *within one minute*, then continue to increase more slowly. In most cases this is not fatal, but may produce dizziness, headache, and nausea. However, in a very tight tent, fumes can cause death.

The same experiments showed that CO from camp stoves could be greatly reduced (but not eliminated) by raising the pot supports an inch so that the flame did not directly touch the pot bottom. This results in slower cooking, but as camp stoves are often used to warm the tent while cooking, the delay may be welcome.

Poor burning of stoves, heaters, or lanterns, indicated by **yellow flame** or **strong smell of fumes**, also produces CO. Debris or moisture in the burners or poor fuel may cause this. In general:

- camp stoves should be used outside of tents, snow shelters, and cabins if possible

- if they must be used inside for heat or wind protection, pots should be raised so the flame does not strike them directly

- keep stove burners clean and use good quality fuel

- if dizziness, headaches, and nausea appear, especially in more than one person, suspect CO poisoning and immediately check stoves and heaters and get fresh air.

Kerosene heaters, especially the wick type, are notorious CO producers and are especially dangerous if the wick is not kept carefully trimmed and adjusted. *Yellow flames* and a *strong fuel smell* are danger signs. These heaters are often left on in wall tents day and night and used to melt water from snow or to bake bannock, so even an efficient one will eventually have some effect on the campers. When using kerosene heaters, you should:

- use them only when needed, and if possible, turn them off at night
- keep wicks well trimmed and adjusted so that there is no yellow flame
- keep a vent open during use.

Snowmobile and ATV exhaust fumes have poisoned people who have taken the machine into a cabin or tent to make field repairs, and let the machine run while tuning it. *Avoid this procedure.* Also avoid carrying people – especially children or elders – on sleds close to the exhaust fumes for long trips.

How to Tell

Because CO reduces the amount of oxygen going to the brain, people often do not recognize signs of poisoning, sometimes until it is too late. Most often it is not recognized until headaches appear. At this point, there is already a lot of CO in the blood.

A very high dose absorbed very quickly will produce rapid loss of consciousness.

A slow development of poisoning, most often seen in a camping situation, will show some or all of the following signs and symptoms:

- **low CO level**, often not noticed: shortness of breath, drowsiness, poor concentration, reduced sharpness of sight
- **moderate CO level**: headache, dizziness, sometimes nausea, irritability, sometimes "drunk" feeling (may feel like an "early hangover"), worsening vision and hearing, clumsiness, twitching.

As more CO is breathed, these symptoms get worse until the casualty has a throbbing headache and worse nausea.

Eventually, the casualty will experience:

- **high CO level**: confusion, rapid heartbeat and breathing, loss of bowel and bladder control, vomiting
- **very high CO level**: collapse, convulsions, coma, death.

What to Do

If the casualty is conscious:

- move him away from the CO source and into fresh air
- protect him from cold, as low blood-oxygen levels will mean less heat production
- keep him at rest and allow him to recover in fresh air – it may take several hours for the CO to leave the bloodstream.

If the casualty is unconscious:

- move him away from the source and into fresh air
- assist breathing or give artificial respiration or start CPR if required. It may be necessary to do this for hours. When he has started breathing on his own again, you should protect him from cold and keep him at rest until he has recovered.

25

Emergency Childbirth

Women have given birth in the wilderness as long as humans have lived on earth. But in recent years, most childbirth has occurred in the hospital, so birth in the wilderness is now uncommon. Non-medical people who are familiar with delivering babies are less commonly found than they once were.

Below are the basics of childbirth, in case an experienced midwife is not present during an unexpected wilderness delivery. *It is important that any expectant mother be within quick reach of medical help when delivery is due, in case there is an emergency that cannot be handled by traditional means.* It is unwise for expectant mothers to gamble on their delivery date.

How to Tell When a Baby Is Due

If the mother knows when her last menstrual period began, you:

- subtract 3 months, then
- add 7 days.

For example, if the last period began June 1, then:

> *June 1 minus 3 months is March 1,*
> *plus 7 days = March 8.*

Expect the baby about that time.

Remember that the first labour may be a long one, but that later babies may come very quickly, and catch even the mother by surprise!

Things to Avoid During Pregnancy

A mother who abuses alcohol while she is pregnant may cause her child to have fetal alcohol syndrome (FAS), which causes mental and physical damage to her child. Smoking during pregnancy causes reduction in birth weight and is also believed to cause other impairments.

Early Emergencies in Pregnancy

Many northern women stay in hunting or fishing camps for long periods while pregnant. Sometimes it is possible to identify those who are most likely to have problems, and return them early to a settlement where there is medical care.

Women who are most likely to have problems with childbirth are:

- those who are having their first pregnancy
- those who have had many other pregnancies
- the very young, teenage mother.

Danger Signs in Pregnancy

Bleeding

If a woman begins to bleed even a little during early pregnancy, she is at risk of having a miscarriage (losing the baby). Bleeding after six months of pregnancy is especially dangerous, and a woman may bleed to death without medical help.

What to Do

If any bleeding is noted, keep the woman at rest, and call in an air medevac.

Severe Anaemia

If a woman feels tired, weak, and has pale or transparent skin, she is at risk of dying from blood loss during childbirth.

What to Do

Take the woman to medical help well before the baby is due.

Swelling

If during the last three months of pregnancy, a woman has swelling of the hands, feet, and face, and has headaches, dizziness, and perhaps blurred vision, she may have a type of pregnancy disease called **toxemia**. (If only the feet swell it is probably not serious, but she should use little salt and watch for other signs of toxemia.) **Sudden weight gain** and **seizures** (convulsions) are other serious signs. *This person's life is in danger.*

What to Do

Call in an air medevac, or if air transport is not available, transport her as gently as possible to medical help. During transport, you must watch carefully for developing seizures, and protect her airway. If you must wait for the medevac, she must stay at rest and eat nourishing high-protein food but with little salt. (A little is okay.)

Certain other conditions make it important that a woman be attended by a doctor during pregnancy. She should not take long trips into the field if:

- she has a chronic (continuous) or severe illness
- she is under 15, over 40, or over 35 at her first pregnancy
- she is very short, or has narrow hips
- she has diabetes or heart trouble
- she has a hernia
- her blood does not clot normally
- she has had serious trouble or bleeding with other births
- she has had previous premature delivery
- it looks like she will have a multiple birth
- it seems that the baby is not in the normal position in the womb.

How to Check the Baby's Position

A baby normally lies head down, facing the mother's back, and will usually be born easily if he is in this position. **(Fig. 25-1)**

- **If the baby is lying sideways** with head on one side and feet on the other, a surgical delivery will probably be required. **(Fig. 25-2)**
- **If the baby is head up**, the birth will probably be very difficult, and should be managed in a hospital.
- **If the baby is head down but facing forward**, labour may be longer and more painful.

To check the position, the examiner – preferably another woman or the father – should have the mother lie on her back. Use a hand to push in gently on either side just above the pelvic bone. With the other hand, feel for the top of the womb.

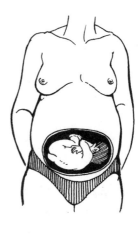

Fig. 25-1: Normal position of a baby in the mother's womb just before birth.

Fig. 25-2: Baby sideways in the womb, probably requiring surgical delivery. The head may be felt on one side.

The baby's head will feel hard and round. His bottom will feel larger and wider. His back is normally forward, and it will feel smooth and rounded. His arms are normally crossed and his legs drawn up, so these will not be felt unless he is face forward; then the mother's abdomen may feel lumpy. The attendant can also ask the mother where the baby was last kicking, and use the answer as a guide to determine the baby's position.

Signs of Labour

A few days to a few hours before birth, several things may show that birth is near.

- **The baby moves lower** in the womb. The mother breathes more easily but may have to urinate more often because of pressure on the bladder.

- **A small plug of mucus**, sometimes tinged with blood, may come out a few hours before birth. Or, a small amount of mucus, often blood-tinged, may come out 2 or 3 days before labour.

- **A few contractions** may happen but then stop, even weeks before labour.

- **Rarely, there is false labour.** Contractions are strong and close together, but then stop for hours or days.

Getting Ready for an Emergency Delivery

If it is impossible to get the mother to medical help, prepare a clean, warm, comfortable camp and get ready for the birth. Ideally, you should have the following:

- lots of very clean, soft cloths or rags, preferably cotton
- a clean bar of soap
- a brush for scrubbing hands and nails
- alcohol wipes for cleaning hands after washing
- latex, rubber, or vinyl surgical gloves

- a new, unwrapped razor blade, or good scissors, or a razor-sharp knife
- some sterile gauze dressings or pieces of very clean cloth for the navel
- two strips of clean cloth or gauze for tying the cord
- a soft blanket for the baby
- a plastic bag for saving the placenta (afterbirth) if medical help is not far away.

Cleanliness is very important, but do the best you can if you are caught by surprise. Hands may be scrubbed with soap and sand if there is no brush. The navel patches, strips for tying the cord, and cloths may be washed and dried if there is time, or lightly singed (not charred) over a camp stove or fire to sterilize them. The scissors or knife must be boiled for 10 minutes (at a rolling boil) and left in the water until used for cutting the cord. (There is no rush, so do it right.)

If you must assist in an emergency delivery and have never seen one before, be careful, but do not be frightened. It may look messy and painful, but most deliveries are normal, and need very little assistance. Helping to start a new life is an exciting, rewarding experience that you will take pride in and never forget.

First Stage: Labour Starts

The first stage of labour begins with strong, increasing contractions and continues until the baby's head enters the birth canal. This may last anywhere from 10 to 20 hours for a first mother, and from 7 to 10 hours in later births, but there is no real rule on this. Be prepared early!

It is normal for this stage to go slowly. Tell the mother not to hurry it and not to worry. Most women (and most observing men!) are concerned about the time this takes. The bag of waters may break at this time, or may break just before the baby is born. There will be some blood and mucus from the vagina; this is normal.

During this stage, the mother should:

- *not* push until the baby begins to move down; then she will feel she *has* to push
- keep her bowels and bladder empty, so their contents do not complicate things during delivery
- change position often, or even get up and walk a little. She should lie in the position of most comfort, usually on her left side.

The attendant (preferably a woman or the father) should:

- give the mother water or other fluids to drink (if she is nauseated, give sips)
- wash well the mother's belly, genitals, buttocks, and legs with soap and warm water
- spread clean cloths or papers on the bed and change them when they get soaked or dirty
- assemble the other materials ready for use.

The attendant should *not* massage or push on the belly, or ask the mother to push or bear down. If the mother is having much pain or is frightened, ask her to take slow, deep breaths during each contraction, breathing normally between them.

Second Stage: The Birth

Birth of the child occurs during the second stage of labour. Sometimes this begins when the "bag of waters" breaks. This stage is usually quicker and easier. If the mother has had children before, she will know the baby is coming. She may feel a desire to move her bowels, and some feces may be forced out. The vaginal opening begins to stretch (this is called crowning), and the top of the baby's head will appear. (**Fig. 25-3**)

During this stage (before the baby's head appears), the mother should:

- push (bear down) with all her strength during contractions.

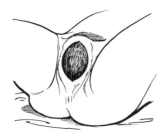

Fig. 25-3: When the top of the baby's head appears ("crowning"), urge the mother to push during contractions.

Fig. 25-4: The head will usually start to emerge face down. Tell the mother now to take short, fast breaths (pant). If the head is coming very rapidly, restrain it gently.

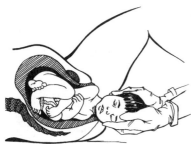

Fig. 25-5: The baby's head will turn to the side as it emerges. Lower the head slightly to help the upper shoulder emerge.

Fig. 25-6: If the cord is around the baby's neck, slide it gently over the baby's head with a finger to create slack.

When the baby's head starts to emerge, the mother should:

- try not to push hard, but take many short, fast breaths (pant). This will help to prevent tearing of the vaginal opening. The baby's head will usually come out face down, then begin to turn to the side. (**Fig. 25-4**)

The attendant should:

- support the baby's head, but *not pull on it*

- if the baby is coming very rapidly, tell the mother not to push, and gently restrain the baby until the head is delivered
- if the shoulders appear to stick, lower the baby's head to allow the upper shoulder to slip out. (**Fig. 25-5**)

It is possible for the bag of waters (amniotic sac) to be covering the head as it first emerges; the attendant may simply tear the membrane with his fingers and move it away from the face.

Sometimes the umbilical cord will be around the baby's neck when the head emerges. Simply slide the slippery cord over the baby's head or shoulder with a finger. *Do not pull on it.* (**Fig. 25-6**)

In a normal birth, the attendant should *never* put a hand or finger inside the mother. This often causes dangerous infections later.

The baby will emerge unbreathing and looking blue-white, covered with a slippery, waxy material. If you have not seen this before, it looks frightening, but is normal. He will usually start breathing, crying, and "pink up" very quickly.

Immediately after the baby is born, the attendant should act as follows:

- **Support the baby with his head lower than his feet. (Fig. 25-7)** Grip the feet with the index finger between the ankles and support the back, neck, and shoulders with the other hand. *The baby is very slippery; be careful!*

- **Keep the baby below the level of the mother** until after the cord is cut. This will give him more blood from the cord and placenta.

- **Hold the baby with his head lower** until the mucus drains from his nose and mouth. If it does not drain, wipe it away with a clean cloth around your finger. The baby should begin to cry and his face will become pink. **If the mucus is clear but the baby remains pale and limp and does not breathe for 1 minute**, begin artificial respiration (see Chapter 21) and continue until he breathes on his own.

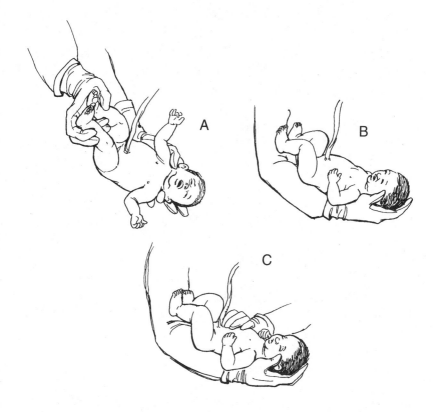

Fig. 25-7: Support the newborn head-down.

- **Wrap the baby immediately**, especially if you are in a tent camp. *It is important to keep him warm!* Use a clean, soft, warm blanket or cloth. Keep his face clear. You may place aluminum foil or a reflective "rescue blanket" around his blanket for extra warmth.

- **Lay the baby on his mother's abdomen**, head lower to assist drainage, or if he is active and crying well, place him to the mother's breast. The baby's sucking will cause the uterus to contract and the placenta to deliver sooner, reducing bleeding. Also, the earliest breast milk contains materials which will help the baby resist infection.

Third Stage: Delivery of the Placenta

The third stage of labour begins when the baby is born and lasts until the placenta comes out. You do not have to watch for this at first. Cover the mother and care for the baby.

Care of the Cord and Placenta

The placenta will deliver itself anywhere from five minutes to an hour after birth. *Do not* pull on the cord to speed delivery.

When the baby is born, the cord will be fat and blue and still pulsating. It is still delivering blood to the baby. Wait. There is no rush.

After a while the cord becomes thin and white and stops pulsing. Now tie it about 5 cm (2 inches) from the baby and again a little farther out with the sterilized cloth strips. Cut the cord between these two ties with the sterile scissors, freshly unwrapped razor blade, or sterilized knife.

If the placenta has not been delivered, gentle massage of the mother's abdomen will help.

- **If there is much bleeding either before or after the placenta is delivered**, firmly massage the uterus between both hands. It may be felt as a firm round mass in the lower abdomen. Massage it until you feel it contract and get hard.

There is normally some bleeding when the placenta is delivered. It usually lasts only a few minutes, and amounts to about a cup. A little bleeding is common for several days.

When the placenta is delivered, wrap it in a clean cloth until the cord is cut. Then, if medical care is available within a day, save the placenta in a plastic bag for examination by a doctor.

Care of the Baby's Navel

To prevent infection where the cord attaches to the baby, you must **keep the cord dry**. The air must get to it. In clean, warm surroundings, leave it open to the air. If the baby is to be wrapped, as it usually will in the north, cover his navel **loosely** with a sterile gauze pad or dry piece of soft cloth which has been sterilized.

Care of Haemorrhage (Serious Bleeding)

Sometimes the mother will haemorrhage from the uterus after delivery. While this is rare, **it is life-threatening**. Blood may emerge as a steady trickle from the vagina, and be obvious. Or she may bleed internally and not show much blood; in this case, watch for signs of shock. A rising, weak pulse, faintness, pale skin, and perspiration are the normal signs. You must:

- **treat for shock** in the usual way
- **give plenty of fluids**, especially broths or rehydration fluids
- **air medevac** with all urgency.

Serious haemorrhage may be rapidly fatal. If the mother is haemorrhaging, you should:

- **massage the belly** until you feel the uterus get hard.

If bleeding continues in spite of massage, you should:

- **press down with one hand over the other on the belly just below the navel, using all your weight.** Continue to press down long after the bleeding stops, to give the blood time to clot. Remove weight slowly, and replace it if bleeding starts again.

Breech Delivery

Sometimes the baby's buttocks, knees, or feet appear first instead of the head. This is a rare but dangerous situation, and calls for medical help to be flown in immediately with an urgent medevac flight.

If help is not quickly available, try to get radio contact so that a physician can talk you through the delivery. If this is not possible, you should:

- support the part which emerges first
- encourage the mother to deliver the extremities, abdomen, and chest.

When the abdomen and chest are delivered, and only then:

- pull very gently while lifting and rotating the baby toward the mother's abdomen.

This will usually help to bring the baby's mouth and nose clear of the vagina.

As soon as the mouth is within reach, you should:

- clear the baby's airway by wiping mucus from it with a clean cloth or finger.

If the umbilical cord is wrapped around the neck, slip it over the head or shoulder to loosen it during delivery. When the breech delivery is complete, treat the baby and mother as described previously.

26

Dental Emergencies

Prevention

Since most dental emergencies are hard to deal with in the field, the best first aid is prevention, which should start early in life.

One practice which destroys more teeth than any other is giving a child a bottle filled with pop, fruit juice, or other sweet drinks and letting him take it to bed. These sweet, acid liquids will cause tooth decay (caries) very quickly, and many children become "dental wrecks" in their first few years.

Teeth should be brushed after every meal, even when out camping. If a toothbrush is forgotten, the end of a pencil-thick green twig may be chewed until it is soft and fibrous, then used as a brush to rub the teeth and gums. Use a fresh one each time. Lacking this, a finger dipped in salt and baking soda will do a passable job, although some sort of toothpick will be needed to clean between the teeth. Toothpaste is not as important as careful brushing.

Game meat – especially moose and polar bear – is often somewhat stringy and sticks between the teeth. It should be removed promptly, as it may irritate gums and cause infection.

Working in the Mouth

The mouth harbours more dangerous bacteria than any other part of the human body. If rubber gloves are available, use them. Also wear glasses to keep saliva from getting into your eyes. Wash hands thoroughly both before and after any dental

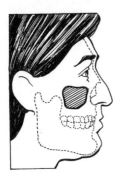
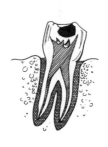
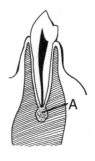

Fig. 26-1: Location of a sinus in the cheek. Sinus infection may be mistaken for toothache.

Fig. 26-2: A cavity near the pulp clamber ("nerve") may cause irritation and a toothache.

Fig. 26-3: An abscess (A) at the tip of the root will cause severe throbbing pain, and requires a dentist's care. Infection may cause the face or jaw to swell.

first aid. Do not work in a mouth with unprotected fingers that have any cut or scrape on them.

It is extremely difficult to see well in the mouth. Use a flashlight, or get the patient to sit or lie so that the sun shines directly on the problem teeth. A mouth mirror, found in some drugstore toothache kits, is a valuable first-aid tool.

Toothaches

Toothaches have several causes, and can be so severe that the patient cannot eat or sleep. Sometimes, sinus infections are confused with toothaches. The sinuses are hollows in the bone of the upper jaw just above the tooth roots. (**Fig. 26-1**) To tell the difference between sinus and dental problems, press or tap the cheek with the finger. If there is pain on one side only, it is probably dental. If on both sides, it is probably sinusitis, especially if the patient has a plugged or runny nose.

Toothache Caused by a Cavity

Cavities may be quite small on the surface, but bigger beneath, where the tooth material is softer. As a cavity gets deeper, it gets closer to the nerve and blood supply (the pulp chamber) in the centre of the tooth, and will start to produce a toothache. (**Fig. 26-2**)

How to Tell

This sort of ache may come on slowly, or it may be triggered by acidic food, cold, or heat.

There is often a cavity visible. The pain is usually steady (not throbbing), and may be made worse by cold water or air.

The exact source of the pain may be difficult to locate. Pain from an upper rear tooth may be felt in a different tooth or even in the lower jaw on the same side, and vice-versa. It is not felt on the opposite side, however. To locate the problem tooth, tap the teeth gently, one by one, with a small hard object, until a painful one is found.

What to Do

This kind of ache can often be relieved by using one of the toothache kits found in drug stores. They are an important part of a wilderness first-aid kit, and are inexpensive. They usually contain a mouth mirror, an instrument to clean out the cavity, some forceps, a liquid such as oil of cloves or eugenol which is soothing to the cavity, and some cotton pellets or temporary filling material to pack into it. If you have such a kit, follow the instructions. The steps usually are:

- locate the problem cavity
- gently clean out anything packed into it
- dry the tooth and cavity with cotton pellets
- coat the inside of the cavity with the soothing liquid
- pack the cavity with a cotton pellet soaked with the liquid, or with the temporary filling provided
- advise the patient not to chew on that side, and to keep cold away from it.

If this does not relieve the pain entirely, the patient may wish to take Aspirin or Tylenol (acetaminophen). He should see a dentist soon, or the cavity may progress to an abscess.

Do not place an Aspirin tablet or crushed Aspirin directly on any dental problem. It will not help, and may cause a burn or sore at the location.

Toothache from an Infection (Abscess)

If the pulp chamber is badly irritated, it may die, and infection may occur at the tip of the root. An abscess, or pocket of pus, is formed and may create pressure, swelling, and severe pain. This is called a *periapical* abscess. (**Fig. 26-3**)

A similar abscess may occur in the gums around the tooth when food gets packed into the crevices between gums and teeth, and bacteria grow there. This is called a *periodontal* abscess. In both cases, the pain is usually throbbing, in time with heartbeats. Since both are infections, antibiotics are desirable if they are available and prescribed.

Periapical Abscess – How to Tell

Signs and symptoms are:

- severe, usually throbbing pain
- pain that may be briefly relieved by clenching the jaw, then opening the mouth
- affected tooth painful to tapping with a small, hard object
- possible swelling of the gums near the root, or of the jaw or face
- possible fever
- foul-smelling breath.

What to Do

This person needs a dentist's help soon, as the tooth will have to be pulled or a root canal done. Infection can spread. If antibiotics are available, give them as prescribed. If they are not available there may be little you can do except get back to town, because painkillers may not be very effective.

You should:

- give antibiotics as prescribed
- give painkillers if available and as prescribed
- give warm salt-water mouth rinses often
- get the patient to medical help.

Tooth Extraction in the Field

It is usually not advisable to try to pull a tooth in camp. The wrong tooth may be pulled, the jaw or other teeth damaged, and infection may spread. Ordinary pliers often slip and damage other teeth, and will commonly crush the tooth, leaving the broken-off roots still in place.

Sometimes an unhealthy tooth is not firmly attached to the jaw, and may be removed by pushing from one side to the other with a finger, although it may take several days of this treatment to loosen. However, it is best to evacuate the patient to dental care. Even very bad teeth can sometimes be saved.

Periodontal Abscess – How to Tell

The pain will be similar to the periapical abscess, but there is more often a foul breath and bad taste in the mouth as pus drains from the crevice around the tooth. There may be an obvious swelling at the site. They are less common in children, more common with increasing age, and more common around back teeth. (**Fig. 26-4**)

Indications are:

- red, swollen gums in the area, oozing pus
- foul-smelling breath and bad taste in the mouth
- severe pain, usually throbbing
- possible swelling of the face and jaw
- possible fever.

Fig. 26-4: A periodontal abscess (A) is a pus pocket under the gum and against the root of the tooth. The gum at that point will be red and swollen.

Fig. 26-5: A periodontal abscess can be drained by releasing the pus and debris with a thin, smooth probe. Probe gently, and do not push against resistance.

What to Do

Because the infection is in a crevice between the tooth and gum, you may be able to use a thin, blunt instrument to probe into the area to allow pus and debris to drain. (**Fig. 26-5**) This may be painful, but will bring some relief. Probe mostly where the worst redness or swelling is, but also somewhat to either side. There will be some bleeding. Don't probe against strong resistance or great pain. Also check for bits of food stuck between the teeth, and remove them. *Do not use a knife or other sharp-edged instrument, because you will certainly cut the gums.* A good thin, blunt probe may be whittled from a clean, splinter-free wooden sliver. Something about the size of a toothpick, but flatter, would be good.

- Give antibiotics as prescribed if they are available.

- Give hot salt-water mouth rinses. Have the patient rinse vigorously, then later hold mouthfuls for several minutes to draw out infection.

- Probe gently into the crevice between tooth and gum at the infection site; try to release pus and debris. Hold the probe parallel to the tooth.

- Rinse again immediately. Continue rinses every few hours as long as there is infection.

- The patient may take Aspirin or Tylenol (acetaminophen) if needed.

- Get the patient to medical care. Normal travel is possible unless the infection is severe.

Infection Spreading from an Abscess

Either type of abscess infection may spread to involve a larger area. When this happens, the entire side of the face may swell. *This condition requires hospital care.* The patient is very ill. If it happens on the land, you should:

- give antibiotics (if available) as prescribed
- give Aspirin or Tylenol (acetaminophen)
- apply warm, wet cloths to the face
- keep the patient at rest, give lots of liquids and liquid foods
- evacuate to medical care.

If a swollen area inside the mouth forms a peak, it may be lanced with the sterilized tip of a razor-sharp knife to help drainage, and hot salt-water may be held in the mouth every few hours to draw infection. However, the patient must still be evacuated.

Broken Tooth

If a tooth is broken off and the pink, sensitive nerve is showing, it will be extremely painful to temperature change or touch. The patient may have to hold a pad of gauze or clean cloth in his mouth to protect it until dental care can be reached. If a toothache kit is available, a few drops of the soothing liquid can be placed on the gauze pad.

Knocked-Out (Avulsed) Tooth

When a tooth is knocked out cleanly, there is a chance that it may grow back in. If the tooth remains in the mouth after it is knocked out, simply place it back in its socket and avoid chewing on it until it gains some stability.

If it has been knocked out of the mouth and has become dirty, wash it off and have the patient keep it inside his lip while you make some warm salt-water. Rinse both the tooth and the socket with this, and replace the tooth as above. If this is done within a half hour, there is a chance that it will grow back in place.

Do not replace knocked-out primary (baby) teeth in youngsters under six years old.

Infected Wisdom Tooth (Pericoronitis)

As the last molars or wisdom teeth begin to come in on the lower jaw of young adults, a small flap of skin partly covering the tooth may form a pocket, which collects bits of food. (**Fig. 26-6**) Bacteria may breed there, and the infection will cause the flap to swell. It is then pinched when the jaws are closed, which increases swelling and infection.

How to Tell

The patient with pericoronitis will have:

- redness, swelling, and pain, and pus oozing from a skin flap over and behind the lower third molar
- foul-smelling breath and a bad taste in his mouth.

What to Do

- Have the patient rinse the area repeatedly with hot salt-water, forcing it under the flap with as much pressure as possible.

- Probe under the flap (as for periodontal abscess) to loosen and release pus and food particles. (**Fig. 26-7**)

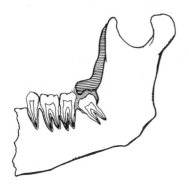

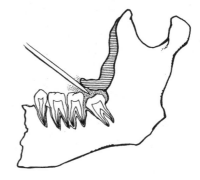

Fig. 26-6: An infected wisdom tooth occurs when food debris is trapped under a flap of gum over the partly hidden tooth.

Fig. 26-7: Pus and debris can be released by gently probing around the partly hidden tooth. Follow with many hot salt-water rinses.

- Have the patient rinse vigorously again. He should later hold mouthfuls of hot salt-water for several minutes to draw out infection.

- Continue hot salt-water rinses every few hours until swelling recedes.

- If infection is severe and antibiotics are available, give them as prescribed.

- Until the swelling is down, keep the patient on foods and liquids that do not require chewing.

Vincent's Infection

When mouth hygiene has been very poor, there may be a general infection called Vincent's Infection or "Trench Mouth."

How to Tell

This condition comes on quickly and shows the following signs:

- a whitish or greyish "skin" or deposit on parts of the gums, especially between the teeth

- swollen, red, and painful gums that bleed easily
- very foul-smelling breath
- more saliva produced than normal.

What to Do

To help the patient with Vincent's Infection, you should:

- have him rinse vigorously and repeatedly with hot salt-water
- using a cotton swab or gauze on a stick, gently wipe off as much of the greyish "skin" as will come easily
- for 1 or 2 days have the patient rinse hourly with hot salt-water
- keep the patient well fed and give plenty of fluids
- give pain medication if it is available.

After 24 hours, there is usually enough improvement to wipe off the rest of the greyish material. Continue rinses and increase tooth-brushing as he improves. Avoid smoking, which irritates the tissues.

Wash hands well after providing treatment and burn the cotton swabs. The patient should use only his own cup and eating utensils and should not share food.

Good tooth-brushing should prevent a repeat infection.

27

Other Common Problems

In this chapter we will describe a variety of other problems which may be encountered by the wilderness first-aider. Some of these, such as diabetes and psychiatric emergencies (severe mental or emotional problems), are generally recognized before the people who suffer from them enter the wilderness setting, so they should not surprise the first-aider.

Diabetes

All people normally have some sugar in their blood. It is the "fuel" that powers muscular action and maintains body heat. The amount of sugar in the blood at any one time is regulated by a chemical called **insulin**, which the body normally produces in the correct amount. Some people have too much or too little insulin, which results in too little or too much sugar in the blood. This condition is called **diabetes**.

Some diabetics must simply control their diet to avoid sugar problems. Others must do this and also take anti-diabetic pills or insulin injections daily, and always carry the medication with them.

If the amount of sugar or insulin swings too far out of balance, the diabetic will get extremely sick and may die in a fairly short time. Because either imbalance can cause confusion or unconsciousness, a diabetic may be unable to understand what is happening or to help himself. For this reason, a first-aider must be able to identify diabetic problems, and understand whether the problem is caused by *too little* or *too much* sugar.

Insulin Shock (Hypoglycemia)

Sickness caused by **too little sugar** (or sometimes too much insulin) is called **insulin shock**. *It is the type of diabetic problem most likely to happen.*

The most common cause is too much exercise and too little food. This combination is common during hunting and fishing trips and wilderness journeys, especially in bad weather when it is difficult to eat regularly.

Many diabetics take oral medications, and too many of these tablets can cause insulin shock. In rare cases, insulin shock can be caused by the casualty mistakenly injecting too much insulin.

How to Tell

Insulin shock usually comes on quickly. The casualty may look as though he is in shock. He may act drunk. He is often hungry. Sometimes he may be aggressive. He may fall unconscious. You will probably see or find:

- pale, sweaty skin
- unusual behaviour, such as confusion or aggressiveness
- slurred speech, shaking hands, clumsiness, dizziness
- rapid pulse, shallow breathing
- headache.

If the casualty is unable to tell you of his condition or is unconscious, check for a Medic Alert bracelet, necklace, or wallet card. Most diabetics carry them.

If you are in doubt, treat as a diabetic: it will not hurt if you are wrong, and it will be absolutely lifesaving if you are right.

What to Do

A person in insulin shock is in great danger, but the first aid is simple.

If the casualty is unconscious:

- protect his airway by placing him in the drainage (recovery) position (**see again Figs. 1-1a,b,c,d, p. 3**)

- place a small amount of syrup or honey inside the cheek or under the tongue, where it will be absorbed. You can speed this by gently rubbing it into the cheek and gums. If you have no syrup, place about half a teaspoon of sugar under the tongue, where it will dissolve and be absorbed.

When the casualty is conscious and fully alert again:

- give him a meal before he resumes activity.

  This is normally all the first aid required, but it is lifesaving.

If the casualty is conscious, at the first sign of abnormality:

- give the casualty sugar. This may be in the form of sweet drinks, candy, jam or jelly, honey or syrup, or just plain sugar if nothing else is handy. Remember to use foods and drinks with sugar, and not an artificial, low-caloric sweetener. You may have to coax him if he is confused or aggressive.

When he improves, you should:

- give the casualty a meal before he resumes activity.

In either case, if he does not respond, call for an immediate air medevac and be ready to assist breathing if necessary.

Diabetic Coma (Hyperglycemia)

If the casualty has **too much blood sugar** or **too little insulin**, he may suffer diabetic coma. This is quite unlikely in the wilderness setting, as diabetics are able to tell when they are getting short of insulin and will treat themselves. However, if a person gets too much food and too little exercise, or if he loses or uses up his insulin, it may develop to the point where he cannot help himself.

How to Tell

The problem will come on slowly. The casualty may be aware of it. The casualty:

- urinates a lot
- is always thirsty
- has normal or flushed, dry skin
- has a headache, nausea, or vomiting
- has a fruity or nail-polish (acetone) smell to his breath
- may act strangely, be dizzy or delirious
- may (rarely) fall unconscious.

What to Do

If the casualty is conscious:

- if he has insulin and knows how to take it, you should help him to do so
- give plenty of fluids to fight dehydration
- call an urgent air medevac if these signs are present and the casualty is unable to get insulin.

If the casualty is unconscious and you are in doubt, radio for medical advice or an air medevac. Do not attempt to give insulin unless you are completely familiar with the casualty and the procedure, for if he is suffering from insulin shock rather than diabetic coma, insulin will be fatal.

Hyperventilation (Overbreathing)

A person who breathes too rapidly for a short time may exhale too much of the gas (carbon dioxide) that controls his breathing rate, and become unable to breathe properly. He will breathe rapidly, yet feel as though he is suffocating, will probably be dizzy, have stabbing chest pains, and tingling and numbness in his hands and feet. He will be frightened – which only increases the problem.

You must speak to him firmly, but be reassuring. Tell him

what his problem is, and ask him to calm down. Ask him to take a breath and hold it for a few seconds. (It may take several tries.) This will increase the carbon dioxide in his blood, and may stop the problem right there.

If this does not work, have him breathe into a paper bag, if one is available, or else into a cloth bag like a food bag or pillowcase. You may also use a large plastic bag, but watch carefully to ensure that he gets enough air. If none of these is available, have him tuck his face down into his parka or jacket front and rebreathe his own breath for a while. This will usually return him to normal.

If it continues, he may fall unconscious and may appear to stop breathing. **Keep his airway open.** You may start rescue breathing, as the air from your lungs contains the needed carbon dioxide. Even if you do not, he will start breathing again on his own in a short time as the gases in his blood reach new levels.

If the overbreathing was not caused by anxiety or fear and does not respond to treatment, it has been caused by another problem. Evacuate the casualty to medical care rapidly.

Dizziness

A variety of conditions and medications may cause dizziness, sometimes so severe that the casualty cannot tell up from down, and the world appears to whirl around him. In the elderly, dizziness may be one symptom of a stroke. It may also be caused by an infection in the inner ear.

A severe case may be so terrifying to the casualty that he will hyperventilate (overbreathe).

You should reassure the casualty and put him at rest. Try to determine if he has taken any drugs or medicines or has other symptoms. If he is an older person, check for numbness, tingling, paralysis, difficulty in speech, sight, or hearing, any of which may indicate a stroke.

Dizziness often passes without ill effects. If it does not pass with rest, or if you suspect some illness, transport the casualty to medical care.

Illnesses Due to Heat

While heat stresses are less common in the north, the human body may become overheated from hard, continuous effort, especially if it is heavily clothed, if the temperature or humidity is high, if there is little wind, or if there is reflected heat and light from sand, water, or even snow. The primary problem is that the body cannot lose heat rapidly enough. Heat stresses are most likely to occur during spring warm spells, before the body has had several days (usually 5 to 10) to acclimatize to the increased heat.

Prevention

Heat stresses may "creep up" on the unwary northerner, who does not normally consider heat a problem. To prevent heat problems, you should:

- remove whatever clothing is necessary to keep comfortable
- drink plenty of water during exercise (in very hot environments, 0.5 to 1 litre or 2 to 4 cups each hour when sweating heavily)
- avoid excessive use of coffee, tea, or alcoholic drinks during warm weather, as they cause increased fluid loss
- watch elders or infants carefully during hot spells, as they do not adjust to heat well.

Until recently, salt pills were thought to be a useful preventive measure. They are not necessary, and can be harmful. Salting normal meals to taste has been found to be adequate for all but extreme heat levels, which are not usually found in the north.

Heat Exhaustion

Heat exhaustion is quite similar to shock. In order to cool the body, blood vessels in the skin dilate. Because skin heat is so high, dilation is so great that the blood supply to the brain and vital organs becomes inadequate. This is compounded by the loss of fluids through sweating and heavy breathing.

How to Tell

Indications are very like those of shock. The casualty may have:

- rapid heart rate
- dizziness or faintness (even loss of consciousness)
- nausea
- pale skin
- possibly a headache.

The casualty may or may not be sweating heavily, and his temperature may be low, normal, or even slightly high.

Do not expect the casualty to feel hot. If he is hot, heat exhaustion has probably progressed to heat stroke (sunstroke), which is a true medical emergency.

What to Do

Treat the casualty as though he were in shock. You should:

- place the casualty at rest with feet slightly elevated
- give water or salty fluids as soon as he can drink safely, 1 to 2 litres or 4 to 8 cups at a rate that is comfortable.

Water is the most important item here. If salt is available, add enough to make the water as salty as a soup, but if no salt is at hand, give water alone. Rehydration drinks are also very good. Recovery should be rapid, but keep the casualty at rest until he feels well.

Heat Stroke (Sunstroke)

Heat stroke is a true medical emergency and is fatal if not treated promptly.

After hours of hot work and continuous sweating, sweating decreases and may cease entirely, and the heat regulating process breaks down. Body temperature rises rapidly to around 41°C (106°F) and will continue to rise until brain damage and death occur.

How to Tell

Heat stroke may come on very rapidly. The casualty may quickly show:

- confusion, poor coordination, delirium, or unconsciousness
- hot skin
- no sweating.

Immediate action is critical!

What to Do

Cool the casualty immediately. The longer the delay, the more danger of brain damage or death. You should:

- move the casualty to shade or put up a shade for him
- remove his clothing and immerse his body in cold water (if you cannot place him in water, cool him by wetting him down and fanning him, by placing snow or ice in his armpits and in his groin, or by sponging and fanning him. (Do not rub him with alcohol.)

The critical action is to cool him as rapidly as possible. Continue cooling until his temperature reaches 39°C (102°F). If you do not have a thermometer, cool him until his skin or the inside of his mouth is about the same temperature as your own. Then remove him from the water and place him at rest.

You must observe him carefully, as his temperature may rise again and he will require further cooling. Evacuation is required, as his temperature regulation may be unstable for some time.

Heat Cramps

Loss of salt due to sweating may produce muscle twitching or severe cramps, especially in the legs or abdomen.

Stretching of the affected muscle is often helpful if done immediately. A cramp in the lower leg may be helped by extending the leg and pulling the toes up toward the body. Pounding or kneading the cramp may contribute to soreness afterward.

Several cups of salty fluids or slightly salted water should be given and the casualty allowed to rest for a time.

Low Back Pain

There are a variety of causes for low back pain, but the two most common are:

- back strain
- ruptured disc.

First-aid care is similar for both. In either case, pain on movement may be so severe that the casualty cannot travel by any means which involves bouncing, and may be confined to camp for days or even weeks.

Back Strain

Back strain is commonly caused by malfunction of the joints between the lower vertebrae or by injury, often very slight, to the tissues surrounding the lower spine. Either will cause inflammation of the tissues, which in turn causes the muscle to go into painful spasm. It may be brought on by carrying heavy loads, by working in a bent position, or even by bending over or sleeping in an awkward position. It is increasingly common in middle-aged persons, especially those who have done hard physical work or carried heavy loads much of their lives. Obesity (excessive fatness) often contributes, as the weight of the belly throws a strain on the lower spine.

How to Tell

The casualty often has a history of back pain and will know what the problem is. He will complain of:

- muscle pain in the lower back near the spine
- painful spasm (abnormal muscle tightness) of the muscles around the lower spine
- inflexibility of the lower back.

Pain is greatly reduced when the casualty lies face up with his legs slightly bent at the knees, but pain may be excruciating when he tries to get up or move. The muscles in spasm will be rigid to the touch when compared with a normal back. Back strain usually clears up in a few days with bed rest, but may take a week or more.

Ruptured Disc (Slipped Disc)

The bones of the spine are separated by discs or pads of material that are much like cartilage. As the tissues around the spine deteriorate, either from age or injury, one of these discs may rupture and be forced into the spinal cord canal or against the root of one of the large nerves that leaves the canal. Pain may be similar to back strain, but may be worse and may cause pain to radiate down the leg (sciatica). This condition may or may not clear up with rest, and the casualty may have to be evacuated. The type of evacuation depends upon the severity of the casualty's pain. Some may be able to tolerate evacuation by sled or boat; others may be in such pain that any movement is intolerable. A person in severe pain and muscle spasm who cannot be moved may improve with rest, so that ground evacuation becomes possible.

How to Tell

The casualty will complain of:

- muscle pain, spasm, and inflexibility in the lower back as with back strain

- pain radiating to the side, down through the buttock and down the back (or sometimes the outside) of the leg (sciatica).

The casualty will usually experience excruciating pain when trying to get up, and if he is able to walk will usually limp.

What to Do

It may be impossible for the first-aider to tell the difference between back strain and a ruptured disc, but the first aid is similar. You should:

- place the casualty at rest on his back or side on a firm support
- provide padding under his knees to flex them slightly, flexing adds comfort
- provide pain killers and anti-inflammatories (Aspirin, ibuprofen, naproxen) as directed on the container, or the non-prescription back pain medications available in drug stores (not both at once).

In camp, any firm, flat surface will do as support for the casualty, provided it is well insulated from cold. One or two thin, closed-cell foam sleeping pads or a couple of skins will provide a good firmness.

Heat from hot towels or hot water-bottles may be comforting and reduce spasm.

Encourage the casualty to remain at rest until the condition improves, as attempts to start normal activity too soon may result in worsening the condition. Lifting and bending forward should be avoided.

People who are familiar with back strain may carry non-prescription medications that contain mild painkillers, muscle relaxants to reduce spasm, and agents to reduce inflammation. Sometimes one can prevent a severe episode of back strain by taking these and lying down immediately at the first sign of back pain, remaining totally relaxed or asleep for an hour or more until all sign of spasm has passed.

If evacuation is attempted, the casualty must be firmly

fastened to a well-padded board so that the spine cannot move as the vehicle bounces.

High Altitude Medical Problems

Trekkers, climbers, skiers, and tourists may develop medical problems related to altitude exposure at altitudes above about 8,000 feet, although people with cardiac or pulmonary disease may experience increased symptoms at lower altitudes. As altitude increases, the atmospheric pressure decreases. Although oxygen molecules continue to constitute 21% of the total atmosphere, as at sea level, the pressure exerted by these molecules decreases as the overall pressure decreases at altitude. Symptoms of altitude illness develop as a result of lack of oxygen (hypoxia), and other factors such as intense sunlight and cold may cause concurrent problems such as snowblindness or frostbite.

With continued exposure to altitude, the body gradually adapts to hypoxia by a process of acclimatization which serves to increase oxygen uptake and delivery to the body. Acclimatization includes increased respiration, increased blood flow to certain organs such as the brain, increased resting heart rate, and a gradual increase in the level of haemoglobin in the blood. When observing vital signs at altitude, remember that an increased resting heart rate and respiration rate are a normal part of acclimatization, and at altitudes above about 14,000 feet, some cyanosis (bluish discoloration of lips and finger nailbeds) can be observed in most people.

With a gradual exposure to increasing altitude, humans can climb high attitudes without needing to breathe extra oxygen. However, people often do not have, or do not take, the time to gradually ascend to altitude, and serious and even fatal medical problems related strictly to altitude exposure can occur at altitudes as low as 8,000 to 10,000 feet. In general, the higher the altitude and the more rapid the exposure, the more likely an individual is to develop medical problems.

Medical problems particular to altitude include acute mountain sickness, high altitude pulmonary edema, and high altitude cerebral edema.

Acute Mountain Sickness (AMS)

How to Tell

The casualty will have one or more of the following symptoms:

- persistent headache that is not relieved by medication
- marked fatigue or weakness
- nausea and sometimes vomiting
- dizziness or light-headedness
- difficulty sleeping.

These symptoms develop on the first or second day at altitude and generally resolve after several days. Symptoms become more severe at higher altitudes (above 12,000 feet), and with rapid ascent, and may be so incapacitating that the individual can barely stand or walk and must rest in bed. Symptoms are generally worse in the morning.

What to Do

First-aid treatment includes:

- keeping the casualty warm
- encouraging fluid intake
- having the casualty sit up, if possible, or at least propping up his head
- giving Tylenol (acetaminophen) or Aspirin for headache.

Symptoms generally lessen over several days. However, mild AMS may become severe AMS and blend into HAPE and/or HACE overnight, so that the casualty is found in serious condition in the morning. For this reason, never underestimate any level of AMS. It is wiser for the casualty to descend and rest at a lower altitude than to risk waking up severely ill and possibly in need of rescue.

Danger signs of worsening AMS include confusion, which may indicate the onset of progressive brain edema (swelling). Immediate descent is critical. It should not be delayed for any reason except extreme danger. Descent of as little as 1,000 feet may provide a seemingly miraculous cure, but it is recommended that the casualty descend at least 3,000 feet, and only reascend with caution, because of the risk of AMS reoccurring.

High Altitude Pulmonary Edema (HAPE)

HAPE is a form of lung edema (swelling) that occurs most commonly in persons who have ascended rapidly to altitudes above 8,000 feet and who then engage in heavy physical activity such as skiing, climbing, or trekking. HAPE is much less common than acute mountain sickness, but is more severe and may be fatal if not recognized and appropriately treated. Persons who develop HAPE may also have symptoms of acute mountain sickness.

How to Tell

Initial symptoms generally develop after 1 to 3 days and include:

- a progressive cough, producing white, pink, or bloody sputum, which is worse at night
- gurgling sounds in the chest
- increasing fatigue
- weakness
- marked shortness of breath after only modest exertion or even at rest
- rapid pulse, generally above 100 per minute at rest
- rapid breathing rate, over 15 per minute
- possible cyanosis (bluish discoloration of lips, finger nail-beds).

Note that cyanosis may not be detectable in a coloured tent, so the casualty should be observed in natural light.

What to Do

The most important factor in the treatment of HAPE is early recognition that the problem is developing. Death is related to delay in treatment. Persons trained in wilderness first aid should be alert to the possibility of HAPE because recognition and early descent can be life-saving.

- Keep the casualty warm.
- Arrange urgent descent or transport to a lower altitude.
- Administer oxygen, if available.

Immediate descent of 1,000 to 3,000 feet usually provides startling relief.

High Altitude Cerebral Edema (HACE)

High altitude cerebral edema (swelling) is a severe form of acute mountain sickness in which the early symptoms of AMS progress to increasing confusion, loss of coordination, difficulty walking, disorientation, irrational behaviour, and eventually coma. HACE is uncommon, but persons with acute mountain sickness who develop confusion or other signs of mental dysfunction or difficulty walking should be considered to have HACE.

HACE usually occurs above 13,000 feet, and is often associated with HAPE. It may be difficult to determine whether one or both are present, but as either can be rapidly fatal, immediate descent should be the overriding consideration.

How to Tell

Signs and symptoms include:

- headache that does not respond to medication or rest
- lack of coordination, staggering

- vomiting, which may lead to dehydration
- fatigue, weakness, apathy, confusion, visual problems (note that these are also symptoms of hypothermia).

What to Do

First aid is the same as for HAPE, but may only buy time, and is no substitute for rapid descent. Get the casualty *down*, regardless of his wishes, and carry him if necessary. As with AMS, recovery on descent may seem almost miraculous, but the casualty should exercise caution and not climb again until he has had authoritative medical advice.

Miscellaneous Altitude Problems

Fainting

New arrivals at a high altitude are more prone to fainting. Initial treatment is similar to that for faints at low altitude – elevate the feet and keep the individual lying down until he has fully recovered from the episode.

Retinal Haemorrhages

Small haemorrhages (bleeding) in the retina at the back of the eye are common at very high altitude but generally do not cause symptoms unless they involve the centre of vision. In such cases, the individual may notice a blind spot in his vision, and should descend from altitude and see an ophthalmologist (eye doctor).

Further detail on high altitude medical problems is beyond the scope of this book. Additional information can be found in texts specializing in this subject area.

Critical Incident Stress

The role of first-aiders is to rescue, treat, comfort, and support casualties with injuries or sudden illness. Often first aid must be provided under extremely stressful conditions. Rescuers are often required to make life and death decisions, and assume, rightly or wrongly, responsibility for the outcome of those decisions.

The stress to rescuers, in addition to their own personal stressors such as family or financial problems, often causes physical, emotional, and/or behavioural responses. The manifestation of responses in rescuer workers, as a result of their first-aid duties, is called *critical incident stress*.

A critical incident is a situation faced by rescuers that causes them to experience unusually strong emotional reactions that have the potential to interfere with their ability to function either at the scene or later. The severity of the incident and degree of response is determined by a number of factors. **People do not respond to the same event in the same way; what is traumatic for one may have little or no impact on another.**

A critical-incident-stress management program includes educational and preventative programming, organized intervention, and a resource and referral network. Components include identifying:

- rescuers at greater risk
- possible signs and symptoms of critical incident stress
- healthy lifestyle alternatives that may reduce the severity of a reaction
- on-scene critical-incident-stress management techniques
- ways of reducing delayed reactions to the stress of a rescue
- goals and principles of demobilization, defusing, and debriefing
- the need for referral to a health professional.

Further detail on the subject is beyond the scope of this book. Rescuers and those responsible for the management of rescue teams are encouraged to seek additional information from local emergency services.

Appendices

Improvising First-Aid Supplies

Improvising Bandages

It is easy to forget the difference between a *dressing* and a *bandage*. Remember that a *dressing* goes next to a wound and should be sterile or at least very clean, while a *bandage* is used to hold a dressing or a splint in place, or immobilize part of the body. Bandages need not be sterile, though they must be dry and should be reasonably clean.

Bandage Fabrics and Materials

Cotton or cotton-synthetic blends are the best materials for bandages, as they are easy to handle and tie, absorbent, and comfortable against the skin. Stretchy fabrics such as tee-shirts are good because they conform to body shapes well, and they are excellent substitutes for roller bandages. The more cotton the better; blends with a high synthetic content are harder to handle and less absorbent. Cotton or cotton-synthetic sweat-shirts are good. Denim fabrics, such as jeans, are a bit stiff and do not stretch to fit the body shape, but denim bandages can be used to put pressure on a dressing or tie on a splint.

Knit synthetics, such as polyester knits, are stretchy and strong and make good roller-type bandages.

Wool can be used, but is itchy against the skin.

Nylon or other pure **synthetics** are poor, as they are slippery and hard to tie, do not stretch to fit body shape, are cold and non-absorbent.

Plastics are poor. Bandages should not be waterproof, because moisture from the skin will condense (turn to water) within them. In cold weather, frost will form inside. If necessary, large plastic bags can be used to make open bandages such as those used for tying leg splints, or for a normal arm sling. And if bad weather makes it difficult to keep bandages dry over an injury, a plastic bag may be rigged loosely as a rain shield.

Making Bandages

Roller bandages can be cut from tee-shirts. A long one can be made by starting at the bottom of the shirt, and cutting upward in a spiral, being careful to keep the bandage the same width all the way. (**Fig. A-1**) Being stretchy, these are excellent for irregular body parts such as the head, knee, elbow, hand, and shoulder. They are also good for doing a final full wrap around a splint to stabilize it for travel.

Short bandages may be cut from a cross-section of a sleeve or pant leg. (**Fig. A-2**) These provide only a single thickness, but several layers may be used. If cut from a loose sleeve or pant leg, they are often long enough to fasten by tying. If not, they may be pinned with pins, wire, nails, or even wood splinters.

Fig. A-1: Long, stretchy roller bandages can be cut in a spiral from a clean cotton tee-shirt.

Fig. A-2: Short bandages can be cut from roomy trouser legs or shirt sleeves. Pin them if they are too short to tie.

Fig. A-3: A clean sock can be cut into a good four-tailed bandage, which holds well on knees or elbows. The heel should be at the outer, centre part so that it fits a joint naturally.

Four-tailed bandages that hold well can be made from (clean!) socks. (**Fig. A-3**) These are especially good for irregular surfaces like the elbow, knee, back of the hand, bulge of the calf, the heel, or even the chin. The longer the sock the better. Since they are not against the wound, synthetics can be used.

Arm slings can be quickly rigged from jacket sleeves by pinning or tying the sleeve into the desired position. (**See again Fig. 16-3, p. 171**) They may be further secured by using a wide bandage, or swathe, to hold the arm firmly against the body. They are superior in some ways to applied slings because they keep the casualty warm, will not slip off, and distribute the weight of the arm well on the shoulders. This is an excellent temporary sling if a casualty has to be moved to shelter before first aid is entirely finished.

They have some disadvantages. Unless the jacket is a very roomy one, a forearm splint may not fit inside it. The injury is not accessible for inspection without removing the jacket. These problems may be reduced by slitting the upper part of the sleeve just enough to alleviate the problems, and pinning the slit shut or wrapping it with roller bandage.

Head bandages of a temporary nature may be improvised by pinning a toque or other knit cap over a dressing to tighten it.

Pelvic bandages, for a fractured pelvis, may be improvised by pinning or tying the trousers to support the pelvis. Three pins – aligned with the upper edge of the pelvis and the hip bone, and with one midway between – will provide good support. If trousers are sturdy, you can cut slits into them for a lace system which will give good, even, and quickly adjustable support. (**Fig. A-4**)

Soakers, or thick absorbent bandages used over dressings to soak up large amounts of fluids, may be fashioned from disposable diapers, which are commonly carried by families on extended camp stays. Sanitary napkins are also excellent for this use. If necessary, thick pads of paper towel or toilet paper can be wrapped in cloth and used as soakers. Dry moss is also an excellent absorbent, and may be used if it can be wrapped in enough cloth to prevent any bits of moss or dirt getting onto the dressing.

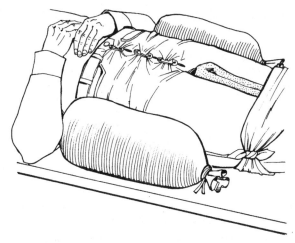

Fig. A-4: If good bandages are not available, the casualty's trousers may be pinned or laced snugly across the front to support a fractured pelvis.

Tapes

Tapes of various kinds can be substituted for the usual white first-aid adhesive tape; however, some tapes – even surgical tapes – may cause skin irritation. If they do, stop using them.

All tapes stick poorly when cold, and may not stick at all at subzero temperatures. It may be necessary to keep the roll inside clothing for a time before using it, or to hold strips of tape near a stove, sticky side toward the flame, to make it usable. Be careful not to let the sticky part bubble with the heat, or you may burn the casualty. Once applied, press a warm hand against the tape for a time to ensure it adheres. Body warmth will soon increase its stickiness.

Tapes also stick poorly or not at all if there is any moisture on the tape, the skin, the dressing, or the bandage. They can be extremely difficult to use in blowing snow or rain.

Duct tape, the well-known wide, silver tape that finds a host of uses in wilderness and camp situations, works well. It is stiffer than normal adhesive tape, does not stretch, and is quite strong. Cut or tear it into thinner strips as needed. Use it sparingly in thin strips on skin, as it is waterproof and does not breathe.

It is excellent when used to prevent blisters. Apply it directly to the heel at the first sign of soreness, starting on the underside of the foot and bringing it part way up the ankle. Be sure the skin is not wrinkled beneath it. It may also be applied to the ball of the foot, generously overlapping the potential blister. Remove it if irritation occurs, or as soon as the need for protection is over. (**Fig. A-5**)

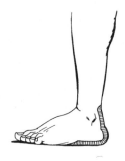

Fig. A-5: Prevent foot blisters by taping with first-aid tape or duct tape as soon as irritation is felt. Remove tape when it is no longer needed.

Electrical tape is a common repair item in camp. It can be used to hold dressings or bandages that do not require pressure, but it stretches easily when warm and is quite stiff when cold.

Filament packing tape is quite sticky and extremely strong, and does not stretch. It is best used to hold bandages or splints.

Improvising Dressings

Dressings go directly on injuries, and should be sterile or very clean. They must be absorbent, but should not have much "nap" or fuzz on the outside to stick to the wound. White fabrics are preferred, as some dyes may "run" into a wound if it is wet with blood.

Dressing Fabrics and Materials

Cotton is the best dressing fabric. Cotton-synthetic blends are passable if they are mostly cotton. Nylon, polyester, and other synthetics are very poor, as is wool. Paper should not be used, as it comes apart and sticks to the wound.

Cotton tee-shirts or bandannas (handkerchiefs) are very good, as are clean cotton socks. The type of cotton fabric used in dress shirts is also good, even with some synthetic content. Light flannels with very little fuzz are acceptable. Cotton or cotton-blend sweatshirts make good dressing material, provided you place the *outside* (smooth side) of the fabric against the wound. Soft, well-used cotton denim will do, provided it has been washed repeatedly so that the dye no longer runs. Many jeans are synthetic, and the fabric is not good for dressings.

Sanitary napkins are excellent dressings, especially for heavy bleeding or for oozing burns. If they are in their original package, they are clean enough to use without sterilization.

Making Dressings

When you are improvising a dressing to cover an existing wound, you have the opportunity to make the dressing the right size and shape, rather than using ready-made ones. Be sure to cut it so that it will cover the wound completely, with plenty of overlap at the edges.

For any wound that bleeds or oozes moderately, make the dressing up to a .6 cm (¼-inch) thick, or about six thicknesses of tee-shirt material. For heavy bleeding, use two or three times as much, or back up the dressing with a "soaker," as above.

Sterilizing Dressings with Flame

If a dressing must be improvised immediately to cover a wound, there will be no time to wash and dry it. You can, however, attempt to sterilize fabrics with flame. This is not perfect by any means, but may be used if no other method is available. Remember not to let anything touch the dressing after it is sterilized. Select the cleanest suitable fabric available, and follow these steps:

- **Light a camp stove or campfire.** Be sure the wound is ready to be dressed.

- **Cut the fabric to shape.** If the material is cut in a long band, such as a 10 cm (4-inch) strip from a tee-shirt, it may easily be folded onto the wound without touching the important part.

- **Wash your hands** well with soap and water (if possible) and let them air-dry. Do not touch anything.

- **Hold the dressing near the flame**, moving it constantly so that it singes to a uniform light tan colour. Singe both sides. Brown spots are okay as long as the cloth does not start to fall apart. You won't be able to singe it where you are holding it. The heat will kill most bacteria on the surface. If you are using a camp-fire, have someone hold a burning stick and hold the cloth *beside* the stick, *not above it*, so that you avoid getting soot and smoke on the dressing. You can even use a butane cigarette lighter or a torch made of twisted paper to sterilize. Any flame will do. You should experiment first with an extra piece of cloth, so that you do not make a mistake and ruin the dressing.

- **Lower the centre of the dressing onto the wound**, and allow one side to fold into several thicknesses before lowering the corner you are holding. Do the same with the other side. If you are using a square piece, such as a bandanna, fold it on using the same method, so that several thicknesses of steril-ized cloth are in place before the part you touched is folded on. You are now ready to apply the bandage.

If you are in a permanent camp, you can wrap your pre-cut dressings in clean paper or another cloth and place them in a hot camp oven for about 20 minutes. Place a pan of water just below the rack to keep the material from charring, and watch it closely. If you know you will have to change dressings later, you can make several individually wrapped dressings and sterilize them all at once, unwrapping them later as needed. If you are going to use just a single dressing right away, you can simply put the cloth on the rack above the water, bake it for 20 minutes, and pick it up by the corners when it is ready to apply.

You will have to take great care singeing fabrics with any syn-thetic content, as they may partially melt, shrink, and harden if you get them too hot.

Cleaning Dressings with Soap and Water

If time allows, you can get dressing material very clean simply by scrubbing it well with dish detergent or soap and water and hanging it to air-dry. For better cleanliness, leave the fabric to soak in the detergent and clean water solution for half an hour. Rinse in clean water, preferably boiled. Hang it away from dust and flies, in the sunlight, if possible, as the ultraviolet rays kill some organisms. When it is dry, handle it only by the corners and do not let it touch anything until it is folded onto the wound as described above.

If bleach (e.g., Javex) is available, add a little to the water before washing for 10 minutes, and also use a few drops in the water used to wash your hands before dressing wounds.

NOTE: do *not* use gasoline, gas line anti-freeze, or other chemicals to try to sterilize cloth for dressings.

If time allows, dressings may be cut to size, boiled for 20 minutes, and hung to dry in sun and air. Touch only the corners when handling, and keep these away from the wound.

Improvising Splints

Although many rigid objects can be used to immobilize limbs, too much size, thickness, or weight will make an uncomfortable, clumsy, and impractical splint. Do not use metal (except for commercial aluminum splints), as it is often too heavy and usually too cold. Avoid heavy boards such as two-by-fours.

Pillow splints for the ankle or foot may be improvised from pillows, cushions, 7.5- or 10-cm (3- or 4-inch) foam sleeping pads, loosely rolled sleeping bags (mummy type), blankets, or even bulky, heavy insulated jackets. They may be secured with tape, bandages, or cord.

All will soak up water, so if the casualty is to be transported in the rain, the splint should be protected with a plastic garbage bag or some other waterproof material.

Rigid splints for the arm or lower leg may be made from any flat board. Ideally, the splint should be about the same width as the limb and long enough to immobilize the joints on either side of the break. (See the illustrations in Chapter 16.) Some good possibilities are pieces of boat floorboards, grub boxes, sled crosspieces, or a dry tree branch split to shape or flattened

PAD IN HOLLOWS

Fig. A-6a: A sheet of birchbark or cardboard can be folded into an excellent splint. Cut it into this shape, and (1) place it flat under the limb, (2) pad well under and around the limb, (3) fold A up against the sole of the foot, (4) fold the splint around the limb, (5) fold B and C across the foot bottom, and (6) secure the splint with tape or bandages and the foot with a figure-8.

Fig. A-6b: Birchbark or cardboard folded into a splint.

with knife or axe. Excellent smooth, dry, flat pieces can often be found in driftwood.

Hides of big game animals make good splints after they are dry and stiff. They can be rolled around a well-padded limb and tied in position to form a rigid tube. Raw caribou skins, such as are often used for winter bedding in northern camping, are good if not too old and soft. They can be rolled once or twice around the padded limb with the fur inside for extra padding and cold protection. A "window" may be cut to allow for observation of the injury site. Be sure any open wounds are very well dressed and bandaged before applying hide splints, as the hides carry many bacteria.

Sleeping pads of closed-cell foam make good forearm or lower leg splints. They require little extra padding and are warm and comfortable. At least one layer of cloth should be used between the skin and the splint, as the pad does not breathe. These may be cut to shape and rolled around the limb in one or two thicknesses and secured with ties or tape. If desirable, a "window" may be cut out over the injury to allow observation.

Birchbark and cardboard may be cut to fold around the well-padded limb. If cardboard is used, cut with the lines in the cardboard running parallel to the limb. Fill in the hollows with pieces of padding. (**Figs. A-6a,b**) Cardboard splints are light, and are warm if well padded, but must be protected from moisture. Birchbark splints are less vulnerable to water, but require better padding.

Canoe paddles can be used for long femur splints if a suitable flat board cannot be found. The paddle end can be trimmed down to body width, padded, and placed under the arm. The paddle should be long enough so that the grip end sticks out 10 cm (4 inches) or more past the foot. Inner splints should be as wide as the leg, or the legs may be tied together with suitable padding between them. (**Fig. A-7**)

Sandbags for stabilizing fractures may be improvised from plastic bags, food bags, or stuff bags filled with sand or dirt. Bags of beans, rice, or flour work very well when taped in place. Mounds or bags of snow may be used temporarily while applying splints, provided they are padded to prevent cold injury or hypothermia.

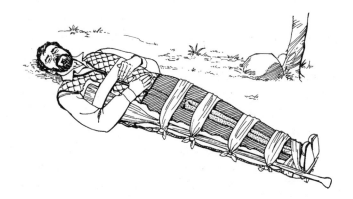

Fig. A-7: A canoe paddle can be used in place of a long board for the outer femur splint.

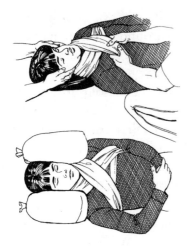

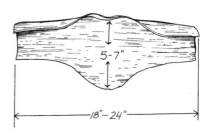

Fig. A-8: Use a rolled blanket, sleeping bag, or other fabric to stabilize a neck injury.

Fig. A-9: Bark or stiff cardboard cut in this shape and well padded with cloth wraps makes a good cervical collar. Be sure to try it on an uninjured person of about the same size as the casualty before placing it on him.

Cervical (Neck) Collars

SAFETY NOTE: improvised collars will require careful fitting to the casualty. To avoid any unnecessary movement, *fit the collar to an uninjured person* of about the same size before applying it to the casualty. **The collar alone does not prevent further neck injury; the head should be supported on either side with sandbags and taped or bandaged securely to a rigid backboard.**

Rolled blanket collars provide excellent stability, but are bulky and difficult to apply to a casualty who is lying down. Roll the blanket to a thickness that holds the neck well extended and prevents movement. Place it around the back of the neck and cross it under the jaw while a second first-aider holds the head stable. Tape or tie the ends so that they cannot sag and loosen the blanket roll. **(Fig. A-8)** Some sleeping bags may be tightly rolled and used in the same way.

Birchbark or cardboard and cloth can be made into a good, rigid collar. Cut it so that the part between the jaw and the clavicle (collarbone) supports the chin. Fit it to another rescuer about the same size. Wrap it with several layers of soft cloth, which may be taped in place. Only when it is fitted and completed should it be placed on the casualty and tied or taped in position.

If cardboard is used, cut it so that the ridges in the cardboard run from clavicle to chin, and use several thicknesses to assure stiffness. (**Fig. A-9**)

Sleeping pads of closed-cell foam make excellent collars when cut to the above pattern. Two thicknesses, taped together, work best. **Open-cell pads** ("foamies") of 7.5- to 10-cm (3- to 4-inch) thickness, cut to size in the above pattern, are not quite as rigid, but much more comfortable than most. They will need to be wrapped well with bandages or tape.

Backboards

Full-length backboards, to immobilize a fractured spine, are often difficult to improvise in the wilderness, unless long boards, boat floorboards, cabin doors, etc., are available.

A stretcher that is rigid from head to foot may be made from boards or poles, either woven together with rope or lashed to crosspieces. Head-to-foot stiffness is important, but the board may flex side-to-side. If it does, "cup" the padded, woven "board" around the casualty and tie firmly so that the casualty and board move as a unit.

If no long boards are available, you can nail, screw, tie, or tape boards together with a good overlap.

Backboards must be rigid. They should not sag in the middle under body weight, nor bounce when carried. If an improvised board (e.g., a piece of plywood) is too flexible, make it stiffer by attaching stronger poles or boards beneath. Because of the danger of further injury to a casualty, you should first try out an improvised board with an uninjured subject.

Neither a western dogsled nor a komatik is rigid enough by itself to protect a spinal injury. Both are made with tied joints so that they will flex over uneven snow, and this action will certainly cause pain and could easily worsen the injury. Place the casualty on a rigid board *before* transporting him on a sled.

The ideal backboard will be about the same length and width as the casualty. If the board is much wider, it will be difficult to handle and transport and very difficult to secure the casualty with ties around the board. Boards about the same width as the hips are adequate, and easy to secure.

A backboard must be padded if the casualty is to be on it for more than a few hours.

Other Improvised First-Aid Supplies

Incontinence pads (diapers) for long transport may be made from almost anything absorbent. Infants' disposable diapers are of course excellent, but may not be large enough to absorb adult volume. Use two thicknesses, being sure to strip off the waterproof outside layer on the inside unit.

A piece cut from an open-cell foam sleeping pad and wrapped in cloth will work well. A cloth bag loosely filled with dry moss is excellent. Miscellaneous extra clothing may be used, held loosely in place by the casualty's own underclothes. However, it should be primarily of soft cotton or cotton blends for absorbency and comfort.

A piece of plastic or plastic tarp may be used under the casualty to keep leaked fluids from getting into the sleeping bag. It should be covered with a thick pad of cloth, otherwise it will condense perspiration from the casualty and become uncomfortable.

A man's urinal may be improvised from any bottle or other *tightly* sealable container with a wide-enough mouth to accommodate the penis. Plastic wide-mouth bottles are best. If such a bottle is to be placed inside the casualty's sleeping bag so that he can use it when needed, be sure to warm it first.

You may place a container filled with warm drinking fluids inside the bag at the start of transport, and get several different uses from it. It starts out as a hot-water bottle, its contents may be drunk later, and when empty it can serve as a urinal. *Do not* give a casualty a very cold glass container for a urinal, as the warm urine may cause the cold glass to shatter, making a mess inside the bag.

It is always best to have an incontinence pad under the casualty's hips when using an improvised urinal, in case of spills.

A woman's urinal or bedpan may be improvised from any shallow pan. Tape two flat bits of wood across the top to serve as a seat or support. Always use it over an absorbent pad as spills are likely because of its shallow depth.

Spilling or splashing of urine may be reduced if the pan is first partly filled with absorbent material, such as soft cotton material, dry moss, toilet paper, etc.

Women may prefer to be helped into a normal position to relieve themselves if their injuries or illness permit. In a real emergency, modesty is more easily put aside. Ask the casualty what her wishes are in this regard.

If the casualty is unconscious or unable to move and must undergo long transport, put in "soakers" or diapers before starting. Be sure to check their condition frequently and change them as necessary, so that the sleeping bag does not become damp and cold.

"Body heaters," hot pads, and hot-water bottles are discussed in Chapter 7.

Cold Packs

Cold packs may greatly reduce swelling in fractures and sprains, but must be used with caution in cold climates.

If the casualty starts to shiver, remove the ice pack.

In all cases, you should keep at least one layer of fabric between the cold pack and bare flesh; more if you are using snow or ice. Check frequently to be sure that there is no cold injury or exposure developing. When plastic bags are used, check them for leaks before filling by blowing them up, sealing and squeezing them. Leave enough extra space in the bags so that the contents can flow and fit the contour of the injured limb.

Some possible cold packs follow.

A plastic bag of cold water will work very well, and should be doubled if possible. This is one of the safest types, as it is unlikely to cause cold injury.

Before using it, wrap it in a piece of cloth or put it in a food bag, to reduce the chance of breakage.

A plastic bag of snow makes an excellent cold pack, but there must be several layers of fabric between it and the skin to prevent frostbite.

A plastic bag of water with ice or snow is also excellent and will conform better than just snow, but it must be used with the same caution as the snow-only ice pack.

A plastic bag of soil or sand, dug from near permafrost level, works extremely well. These materials are more likely to tear the plastic bag, but easier to clean up if they do.

A bottle or jar of any of the above can be used, but is not as good, as it will not conform to the shape of the injured limb. Its surface is also colder and harder, and may produce a small localized cold injury at point of contact.

A cold, damp cloth folded over the injury works only if wrung out often in cold water.

Improvising Large Basins

Large containers may sometimes be needed to thaw a frozen foot or to soak an infected foot or forearm. Most camp pots and pans are too small for this use. Even a full-size bucket is too small to do a good job.

A 5-gallon plastic jerry can (fuel can) with the top cut off makes an excellent basin, but must be well scrubbed with soap and water to remove any fuel or oil.

Plastic garbage bags, waterproof tarps, or large sheets of plastic can be used to line a box or a frame made of boards.

If necessary, a hole may be dug in firm snow, well insulated with several layers of closed-cell foam sleeping pads or sleeping bags, and then lined with a waterproof tarp. If well enough insulated, the hole will maintain water temperature long enough to serve its purpose.

Improvising Irrigating Equipment

Clean or sterile water is used to irrigate contaminated or infected wounds, as described in Chapter 11. Any clean, fresh water is probably all right, and it need not be drinkable, as the germs which cause sickness in your intestines are generally not the same ones which cause wound infections. Avoid water which is silty. Water that has been standing for a long time, or has lots of plant or animal material in it (such as from tundra or beaver ponds), should if possible be boiled first.

A stream or jet of water under slight pressure is most effective, much more so than water poured from a container. Syringes are not usually available in a wilderness setting. A large, cubical, 5- to 10-litre (2½- to 5-gallon) folding plastic water container with an on/off spout serves very well for irrigation. The bag may be squeezed or held well above the wound to increase the pressure of the water jet.

If water quality is questionable and is to be boiled, try the following:

- ·fill several plastic bags (1 litre, or quart, size is convenient) with clean water and tie them shut
- cover them with water in a cook pot and boil them for 15 minutes
- allow them to cool to body temperature
- puncture a bag near the bottom with a very thin, sharp nail or splinter to start the stream
- hold it well above the wound to get more impact
- squeeze the bag gently to get better pressure.

You can also boil water and pour it into a plastic cube carrier that has been washed well with soap and water.

First-Aid Kits

Improvising first-aid supplies is sometimes necessary but takes time and is rarely as satisfactory as simply opening a good kit and going to work immediately with well-designed, sterile supplies.

Many different kits are available commercially, but few have been designed with wilderness first aid in mind. Many of the compact, inexpensive kits found in drug or outdoor stores are good only for small nicks and cuts, and are too small and incomplete to be of much use in a serious emergency. More complete first-aid kits are often fairly expensive, and even these are rarely designed with wilderness first aid in mind.

Many first-aid kits come without latex gloves. You should add one or two pairs to every kit to protect yourself and the casualty. They are obtainable at drugstores and nursing outposts, and are quite inexpensive.

Commercial Kits

Unless you are an experienced medical technician and know how to make up a custom kit, it is best to buy a complete first-aid kit and add a few items to it. One excellent kit for wilderness groups is the St. John Ambulance Family First-Aid Kit, which comes in a water resistant nylon pouch, is compact, and contains most of what is needed.

Wilderness Supplements to Commercial Kits

For extended wilderness trips, you should add to the Family Kit:

- *The Official Wilderness First-Aid Guide*
- 30 mL (6 teaspoonsful) table salt, sealed in strong plastic bag
- 30 mL (6 teaspoonsful) baking soda (*not* baking powder), sealed as above
- 60 mL (12 teaspoonsful) sugar, sealed in plastic bag
- several plastic bags, 1-litre (or 1 quart) size
- 2 large plastic garbage bags
- medicines as recommended by your local doctor or nursing station
- written instructions for the use of all medicines carried
- 2 or 3 Assessment Checklists (Appendix D)
- a Consciousness Record (Appendix D)
- an oral temperature thermometer in an unbreakable case
- razor and new blades
- ground-air signal card (Appendix F)

You will find that certain items such as Band-aids, Aspirin, or Tylenol (acetaminophen), antacids, etc., are used often by a group of any size, so they will quickly disappear from your kit, and the kit is often messed up as people go through it. Carry extras of these items where you can get at them easily without having to open your main kit.

Custom Kits

If you decide to make up your own wilderness kit, the following checklist may help. Use more items if you are equipping a large party or will be out for a long time.

- *The Official Wilderness First-Aid Guide*
- 2 to 6 sterile gauze pads, 10 cm (4 in.) square
- 1 to 3 pressure dressings, 17 cm (6 in.) square
- 1 to 3 non-adherent dressings, 25 × 40 cm (10 in. × 16 in.)
- 2 to 4 adhesive pads, 7.5 × 5 cm (4 in. × 2 in.)

- 12 to 24 plastic strips (Band-aid type)
- assorted knuckle, fingertip, and elastic adhesive pads
- 1 to 3 sanitary napkins, sealed
- 1 roll adhesive tape, 2.5 cm (1 in.) wide
- 3 to 7 cloth triangular bandages
- 1 to 2 elastic bandages, 8 cm (3 in.) wide
- 10 to 20 cleansing wipes (antiseptic)
- 10 to 20 cotton-tip applicators
- About 30 mL (6 teaspoonsful) table salt (sealed in strong plastic bag)
- About 30 mL (6 teaspoonsful) baking soda (not baking powder, sealed as above)
- About 60 mL (12 teaspoonsful) sugar (sealed in plastic bag)
- several small plastic bags (1-litre or 1-quart size)
- 2 large plastic garbage bags
- scissors
- tweezers
- razor and new blades
- antiseptic solution (Povidone-iodine, Hibitane, etc.) in a *plastic* bottle
- rescue blanket (aluminized lightweight plastic)
- latex gloves
- medicines as recommended by your local doctor or nursing station
- written instructions for the use of all medicines carried
- 2 or 3 Assessment Checklists (Appendix D)
- 2 or 3 Consciousness Records (Appendix D)
- an oral temperature thermometer in an unbreakable case
- ground-air signal card (Appendix F)

St. John Ambulance offers a range of comprehensive first-aid kits designed for Canadians at home, at work, and at play.

Family First-Aid Kit

Our largest kit contains everything the first-aider needs to treat small, medium, and large wounds, and burns. The lightweight nylon bag tucks neatly in your bathroom cupboard or car. **$41.95**

Personal First-Aid Kit

Designed for people on the move, this kit fits easily in your backpack or on your belt. It contains materials needed for the treatment of small and medium wounds.

$21.95

Compact First-Aid Kit

Packed with everything you need to treat small and medium wounds, this tiny kit goes anywhere you go. Its bright red design makes it a practical and attractive gift.

$10.95

First-Aid Fanny Pack

The newest kit in the St. John Ambulance line is this handy belt pack, filled with everything the first-aider needs to treat small and medium wounds. There are extra pockets for personal items.

$24.95

Use the order form below, or simply stop in at your local St. John Ambulance training centre. (Prices subject to change.)

Please send my   Qty: ☐   Family   @ **$41.95** each*
First-Aid Kit(s)   ☐   Personal   @ **$21.95** each*
                             ☐   Compact   @ **$10.95** each*
                             ☐   Fanny Pack @ **$24.95** each*

Name _____

Address _____

_____ Prov. _____ PC _____ Tel. (____)_____

☐ Cheque   ☐ Money order (M.O.)   ☐ Mastercard   ☐ Visa

Card No. _____ Exp. ____ Signature _____

Add $4.00 per kit shipping and handling, plus GST, plus applicable PST. Make cheque or M.O. payable to St. John Ambulance and mail to: 312 Laurier Ave. East, Ottawa, Ontario K1N 6P6. Please allow four weeks for delivery.

Sample Outpost Medical Kit

The following kit is similar to one issued by Public Health Service nurses in Iqaluit, N.W.T., to families living in remote outpost camps. Such camps are often a day's travel or more from town, and are frequently cut off by bad weather or ice conditions. In some cases, Rescue Coordination Centre aircraft from hundreds of miles away have parachuted in medical technicians to prepare people for evacuation by helicopter. These operations cost many thousand dollars, so if these kits prevent even one such rescue, they have paid for themselves.

Outpost camps are normally in radio contact with medical authorities, so the family can ask for advice before giving any medication. Senior family members are coached when the kit is issued.

This list may assist you in planning with your local health authorities for possible medical emergencies in remote camps.

Family Pack:

- Band-aids – 24 to 30
- 2 Tensor bandages
- 2 triangular bandages
- 12 gauze pads – 10 cm × 10 cm (4 in. × 4 in.)
- 2 butterfly dressings
- 2 rolled gauze bandages – 5 cm (2 in.) wide
- adhesive tape – 2.5 cm × 2.5 cm (1 in. × 1 in.) roll
- 2 field dressings (waterproof pkg.)
- disinfectant (Savlon 1.100 or Zephiran Chloride)
- Tylenol Regular 325 mg tablets
- Tylenol 80 mg chewable tablets for children

- 2 Bacitracin or Polysporin Topical Ointment – 15 g
- 2 Bacitracin or Polysporin Ophthalmic Ointment – 3.5 g
- Gamophen soap – 1 bar
- 2 Kwellada Cream – 60 g
- 100 Erythromycin tablets – 1 bottle
- *The Official Wilderness First-Aid Guide*

Optional Items:

- Acetaminophen (Tylenol) drops – 2 bottles
- Gastrolyte.
- Proper instructions in the native language of the area should be included for the medications.

The "pack" should be signed out by the user and returned to the nurse upon return from the land.

Checklists to Include in First-Aid Kit

This section contains checklists which are designed to guide you through a complete examination of a casualty so that you do not miss anything important, as an aid to help you determine what is wrong, and as a record of what you have discovered and what you have done.

When you make radio contact with medical authorities, have your completed checklists with you so that you can give a complete picture of the situation.

Remember – always check the ABCDEF'S before you do anything else.

You should use these for any serious injury or illness, and should send them with the casualty when he is evacuated to medical care. They will be of great help to the doctors or nurses who treat him.

Two or three copies of each should be carried in a wilderness first-aid kit. Keep at least one copy of each in the manual so that you may make photocopies when you run out.

Injury Checklist

Use this when a casualty has been seriously injured, especially if you think there is a chance of more than one injury.

If the casualty is unconscious, you will not be able to ask him questions but will be able to observe and feel many signs of injury. When he recovers consciousness, you can go back and fill in his answers to the questions.

Illness Checklist

Use this when a casualty falls ill and you do not know or are not sure what is wrong.

Again, if the casualty is unconscious, you will not be able to ask questions. Fill the answers in later when he recovers. Go ahead and get all the information you can from observation and examination.

If it is an illness that the casualty has had before, he may know exactly what is wrong and what to do about it, but if you are not absolutely certain of this, try to get radioed medical advice.

Consciousness Record

Use this record whenever a casualty remains unconscious for more than a few minutes, or does not regain his normal alertness. Use the checklist every 15 minutes for a casualty in critical condition, reducing this from every 30 minutes to once every few hours when all signs are nearly normal, until the casualty is in medical care. Be sure to take or send the checklist to the hospital with the casualty.

The changes you see indicate what is happening to the brain. Your records will be extremely important to the physician.

You should also use either the Injury or Illness Checklist to record the other information on the casualty.

INJURY CHECKLIST

CASUALTY'S FULL NAME _____

ADDRESS _____

FAMILY PHYSICIAN _____ CLOSEST RELATIVE _____ AGE _____

MEDICAL # _____

AIRWAY OK? _____ BREATHING OK? _____ PULSE PRESENT? _____

NECK SPINE OK? _____ EXCESSIVE BLEEDING STOPPED? _____

WHAT HAPPENED? _____

WHAT SIGNS DO YOU SEE? _____

WHAT DOES THE CASUALTY FEEL? _____

HEAD-TO-TOE EXAM

Watch his face as you examine him. Note all tenderness, bruising, deformity, bleeding, swelling, loss of use (ANYTHING UNUSUAL). Work down the list.

HEAD _____	PELVIS _____
EYES _____	MESSED PANTS _____
EARS _____	LEGS _____
NOSE _____	JOINTS NORMAL _____
MOUTH _____	FOOT COLOUR _____
FACE _____	FOOT TEMPERATURE (COMPARE) _____
FACE COLOUR _____	FEELING IN FEET _____
BREATH ODOUR _____	EQUAL STRENGTH IN FEET _____
SWEATING _____	ARMS / HANDS _____
NECK _____	JOINTS NORMAL _____
NECK VEINS _____	HAND COLOUR _____
COLLARBONES _____	HAND TEMPERATURE (COMPARE) _____
RIBS _____	FEELING IN HANDS _____
CHEST RISE – BOTH SIDES _____	EQUAL GRIP _____
BELLY _____	MEDIC ALERT _____

TIGHTNESS (WHERE?)

BLOATING

NOTES ON ABOVE

VITAL SIGNS

TIME									
PULSE									
BREATH RATE									
CONSCIOUSNESS									
PUPILS									
SKIN									
TEMPERATURE									

CURRENT MEDICAL CONDITIONS

SIGNIFICANT PAST HISTORY

WHAT DO YOU THINK IS WRONG?

CURRENT MEDICATIONS

ALLERGIES

TREATMENT GIVEN – CASUALTY CONDITION RECORD
Describe exact treatment and the casualty's condition at the time. Keep a complete record.

TIME/DATE:

ILLNESS CHECKLIST

CASUALTY'S FULL NAME _____

ADDRESS _____ AGE _____

FAMILY PHYSICIAN _____ CLOSEST RELATIVE _____ MEDICAL # _____

WHAT IS THE MAIN COMPLAINT? _____

DESCRIBE PAIN (E.G. SHARP, DULL, CRUSHING, ETC.) _____

WHEN DID IT START? _____ DID IT START GRADUALLY/SUDDENLY? _____

TIMING OF PAIN (E.G. CONTINUOUS, COMES & GOES, HOW OFTEN, HOW LONG BETWEEN) _____

DOES IT MOVE OUTWARD? _____ (WHERE TO WHERE?) _____

WHEN DID IT START? _____ (SUDDEN OR GRADUAL?) _____

HAS THIS HAPPENED BEFORE? _____

WHAT MAKES IT FEEL BETTER/WORSE? _____

OTHER COMPLAINTS? _____

IS A DOCTOR BEING SEEN NOW? _____ FOR WHAT? _____

TAKING ANY MEDICINES? _____ WHAT KIND? _____

HOW MUCH, HOW OFTEN? _____

ALLERGIES? _____ TO WHAT? _____

HEAD-TO-TOE EXAM

HEAD _____ LUNGS FILL EQUALLY _____

EYES _____ MESSED PANTS _____

EARS _____ UNUSUAL DISCHARGE _____

NOSE _____ HANDS/ARMS _____

MOUTH _____ COLOUR/TEMP. _____

FACE COLOUR _____ EQUAL STRENGTH _____

BREATH ODOUR

SWEATING

NECK

NECK VEINS

BELLY – TENDERNESS

BELLY – TIGHTNESS

BLOATING

NOTES ON ABOVE

OTHER THINGS OBSERVED

FEELING IN HANDS/ARMS

LEGS/FEET

COLOUR/TEMP.

EQUAL STRENGTH

FEELING IN LEGS/FEET

MEDIC ALERT

VITAL SIGNS

TIME									
PULSE									
BREATH RATE									
CONSCIOUSNESS									
PUPILS									
SKIN									
TEMPERATURE									

WHAT DO YOU THINK IS WRONG?

TREATMENT GIVEN – CASUALTY CONDITION RECORD

Describe exact treatment and the casualty's condition at the time. Keep a complete record.

TIME/DATE:

CONSCIOUSNESS RECORD

CASUALTY'S FULL NAME _____ AGE _____

ADDRESS _____

FAMILY PHYSICIAN _____ CLOSEST RELATIVE _____ MEDICAL # _____

CHECK THE CASUALTY'S CONDITION AT LEAST ONCE EVERY HOUR. RECORD SUDDEN CHANGES IMMEDIATELY. SEND OR TAKE THIS RECORD AND THE INJURY OR ILLNESS CHECKLIST WITH THE CASUALTY TO MEDICAL HELP.

TIME														
GLASGOW COMA SCALE														
EYES OPENING	SPONTANEOUS	4												
	TO VOICE	3												
	TO PAIN	2												
	NONE	1												
MOTOR RESPONSE	OBEYS COMMAND	6												
	LOCALIZED PAIN	5												
	WITHDRAW PAIN	4												
	FLEXION (PAIN)	3												
	EXTENSION (PAIN)	2												
	NONE	1												
VERBAL RESPONSE	ORIENTED	5												
	CONFUSED	4												
	INAPPROPRIATE WORDS	3												
	INCOMPREHENSIBLE SOUNDS	2												
	NONE	1												
GLASGOW COMA SCALE TOTAL														

Time										
Pulse rate (per minute)										
Breathing Rate (per minute)										
Skin Colour										
Nausea, vomiting										
Sees clearly (yes/no)										
Personality change										
Unequal pupil size or reaction										
Twitching or seizures										

Medications

Prescription drugs may be obtained only through a doctor. They can be extremely dangerous if incorrectly used.

Your doctor or nurse may be held responsible if he prescribes a drug that you use incorrectly or that falls into the wrong hands; therefore, he is absolutely right to refuse to prescribe them unless he has first-hand knowledge of your understanding and ability, and assurance that no one is likely to steal and abuse them. You should not expect to receive prescription medicines simply because you are going to an isolated area, nor as a personal favour.

If you do receive them, you accept responsibility for their careful control and correct use.

Also note that the possession of controlled drugs can result in legal problems if you try to carry them across an international border, or if police find you carrying them without the correct prescription.

If you plan to carry medications into the field, you must *always*:

- Discuss the use of each medicine carefully with your doctor or nurse, and carry with it written directions for its use. You must be sure that you understand these instructions perfectly *before* you depart on the trip. Even then, whenever possible, you must obtain medical advice by radio before giving any medicine.

- Check with the patient before giving a medicine to be sure he is not allergic to it, and stop giving it immediately if he shows any sign of allergy.

- Keep careful records of their use; how much was given, when they were given, when they were stopped.

- Watch expiration dates carefully, and destroy all medicines when they are expired. Old medicines may change chemically and become ineffective or dangerous.

You should *never* make up your own medicine kit using left-over prescription drugs. The possibility of incorrect doses, wrong labels, or overaged medicines is great.

Non-Prescription Medicines

Non-prescription medications are occasionally useful in wilderness first aid. Remember that even though they are easily purchased, they may still be dangerous. If given at the wrong time or for the wrong reason, they can harm rather than help. *Never give any medicine unless you know exactly why you are giving it and what effect it will have.*

Some people mistakenly believe that doses larger than recommended on the instructions will work better or more rapidly. This is usually not true and can be very dangerous.

Aspirin (acetylsalicylic acid or ASA) comes in 325 mg and 500 mg tablets for adults, and in 80 mg fruit-flavoured tablets for children. It is a mild pain reliever, reduces fever, and works against inflammation. Some authorities feel it improves circulation in frostbitten tissues after thawing.

Aspirin slows blood clotting and may increase or prolong bleeding. It may be irritating to the stomach and sometimes causes bleeding within the stomach. Do not give Aspirin to anyone who is bleeding badly or who has "heartburn," history of an ulcer, or other stomach irritation. It is also the most common medicine causing overdose poisoning in toddlers and infants, and must be carefully controlled. Do not administer Aspirin to children without medical advice because of its association with Reye's Syndrome.

Dosage – Adults: 325 to 650 mg every 4 hours, with lots of water. A little food in the stomach will reduce stomach upset. **Children**: It is best to see your doctor or nurse for children's dosages before going into the field. Otherwise, follow instructions on the package. A basic rule for children under 12 is 10 to 15 mg for each kilogram (approx. 2 lb) of body weight, every 6 hours.

Tylenol (acetaminophen) comes in 325 mg and 500 mg tablets, and as a syrup for children. It is a mild pain reliever and reduces fever. It is not as irritating to the stomach as Aspirin, and does not prolong bleeding.

Dosage – Adults: 325 to 1,000 mg every 4 to 6 hours, with water. Do not take more than 4,000 mg in 24 hours. **Children**: Follow instructions on bottle. Do not give a full tablet to small children. A basic rule is that children may have 10 to 15 mg for each kilogram (approx. 2 lb) they weigh, every 4 to 6 hours.

Antacid tablets of many kinds are available. Liquids are also available, but are heavier, harder to transport, and may freeze in cold weather. They reduce burning ("heartburn") in the stomach and esophagus. Take along as many as you think you may need. **Dosage**: One or two will usually relieve burning. *People who often need antacids should get medical advice.*

Laxatives are used for constipation. Constipation is common after use of medicines containing codeine. Follow the instructions. People who often require laxatives should see a physician.

Disinfectants such as Povidone-iodine, Hibitane, Savlon, and benzalkonium chloride solutions are good for cleaning hands before first aid, and for cleaning around wounds. Ask your local nursing station what is recommended. It is best not to place any disinfectant within a wound; if it must be cleaned out, ordinary water or saline solution will do the job.

How to Signal for Help

In today's wilderness, help often comes from the air. Frequently, there will be no radio contact between the ground party and the aircraft and an immediate landing may not be feasible, so it is important that those on the ground be able to make themselves understood. Certain internationally recognized signals are used to communicate the most common ground-air messages.

Body Signals

When a party on the ground is being observed directly, it may transmit messages by using the signals below. In order to be seen and understood clearly, you should:

- signal from a clear, open space so that your body is easily seen and separated from the background
- if possible wear clothes that contrast with the background or are bright colours
- have only one person signal while the rest stand well aside, motionless.

You should notice that the typical "friendly wave" with one hand means that all is well, while *both* hands raised means "pick me (us) up." If you do not have a signal card with you, remember this difference!

Symbol Signals

Large signals built from contrasting materials are most effective in attracting the attention of aircraft. These are composed of straight lines, because straight lines are extremely rare in the wilderness and attract immediate attention.

It is important that the material used to make the signal is a contrasting colour to the background, or that shadows be used to make the signals stand out.

On bare ground, successful signals have been made of toilet paper, strips of plastic tarp, strips of tent material, fragments of aircraft, tree boughs, light-coloured rocks, flagging tape, torn-up magazines with pages weighted with rocks, and a variety of other materials.

On snow or light sand, dark materials such as tree boughs or logs are most effective, as are shadows.

In snow or on a beach or mudflat, signals may be tramped or dug into the surface. If any digging is done, pile the extra material along the edge of the trench to cast a longer shadow.

Because shadows are what make this sort of signal effective, they will be *least visible* in flat light or at noon when the sun is high. They will be *most visible* early and late when the sun is low.

If time allows, use a stamped-in trench with boughs or other dark material laid within. If the light is flat, the dark contrasting material will be seen; if sunny, both the material and the shadows will be visible.

Symbol signals should be as large as you can make them, with 6 metres (20 feet) as an absolute minimum. Fifteen metres (50 feet) would be better, 30 metres (100 feet) better yet.

The most commonly used attention-getter is the giant "V", used to signal "unable to proceed" or "here I am." This is commonly made by downed pilots if their planes are not clearly visible. It is easily seen from a long distance if properly made.

If you are in a forested area, place the signal in the centre of a *large* clearing. If you place it in a small clearing, it will be shielded by trees until the aircraft is directly overhead – and the observers will be looking ahead and to the sides, not directly down.

If smoke can be used near the signal, it will increase the possibility of attraction.

Notice that the "require doctor" signal is an "X". Until

recently the "**X**" meant the same as the "**V**" does now, and is still used in this way by some.

If you are travelling on snow and expect aircraft to be looking for your trail, place an arrow beside the trail every kilometre or so. This will help the pilot determine which way to follow your trail in case direction is not clear from the air.

If you use these signals while aircraft are watching, they can be made much smaller.

Other Signals

A series of three of almost anything indicates "Help!" or trouble of some sort, while a series of two indicates "All well."

People have died simply because they did not know this simple code and signalled with a whole series of flashlight blinks, which were thought to be of no importance.

Three smoky fires have been used successfully (by the author, among others) to summon help. If fires are used, build them about 45 metres (50 yards) apart, so that the three smokes are distinct.

Three shots, three flashes from a light, three shouts, even three blows on a pot or pan indicate trouble.

Fires are often used to attract attention, but smoke is some-times not easily seen. Typical campfire smoke is light gray or white. If it hangs low, it tends to blend into a snowy back-ground. It is more effective in a dark-coloured summer forest, and during forest-fire season tends to attract fire scouts rapidly.

Several fires are far more effective than a single one. The larger the fire and the more smoke, the more easily it will be seen.

If you are tending a fire while waiting for help, keep a pile of spruce or pine boughs at hand. Throw them on the fire the moment an aircraft is heard. Do not wait. It takes time for the smoke to form and rise or spread, and if you wait this may not happen until the aircraft is past.

If you have access to gasoline, kerosene, or oil, these can be used to make a sudden puff of black smoke, which contrasts well with a snowy background. However, throwing gasoline or naphtha on a fire is extremely dangerous. Throw gasoline or naphtha out of a small can from a distance, *upwind and uphill* from the fire.

If you have survived a plane crash, materials such as seat cushions may be used to make black smoke. **Tires** burn long and hot, with black smoke, *but should not be set afire until the tire is punctured*, otherwise they may explode violently.

Some aircraft wheels, such as those of the de Havilland Twin Otter, commonly used in the north, are made of magnesium. This looks like aluminum, but is lighter and will burn with tremendous heat and brilliant light. It is necessary to build a smaller fire on it to ignite the metal.

Mirror signals are extremely effective in bright sunlight. Even the small mirror of a compass is enough to attract an aircraft from several miles distant.

To signal with a mirror, hold it next to your eye, hold one hand out with a finger or thumb following the aircraft, and repeatedly flick the spot of light from the mirror across the thumb and the aircraft. Do not bother with a series of three; hit the plane repeatedly with the flash.

You can also use the tops of trees as guides to see where your flash is going in relation to the aircraft.

Other bright metal may be used instead of a mirror, but is not likely to be as effective.

Ground–Air Emergency Signals

V NEED HELP	**X** NEED MEDICAL HELP	**N** NO	**Y** YES
→ GOING THIS WAY	**LL** ALL WELL	**F** NEED FOOD AND WATER	**L** NEED FUEL AND OIL

The first five are international signals; LL, F, and L are Canadian only. Stamp symbols deep in snow or use material which contrasts with the background. The symbols should be 6 to 15 metres (20 to 50 feet) long, and in a large clearing.

G

Glossary

abdomen – the part of the body between the chest and the pelvis

abrasion – a scrape of the skin

abscess – a localized collection of pus surrounded by inflamed tissue

acetaminophen – a medication used for relieving pain and reducing fever

acute – sudden in onset; severe

Adam's apple – the bump or protrusion on the front of the throat, usually larger in men

adrenaline – blood pressure-raising hormone used medicinally as a heart stimulant, and as a muscle relaxant in bronchial asthma

air medevac – medical evacuation by air

airway – the complete passageway for air into the lungs

akio – a boat-shaped sled pulled by man or machine; a skimmer

allergy – exaggerated reaction (sneezing, runny nose, itching, skin rash, difficulty in breathing) to substances that do not affect other individuals

amputate – to cut from the body

anaesthesia – loss of sensation

angina pectoris – temporary chest pain caused by insufficient oxygen supply to the heart

antacid – a material that will neutralize acidity, especially in the stomach

antibiotic – drug used to kill bacteria

antihistamine – drug used to inactivate histamine

anti-inflammatory – drug used to prevent or reduce inflammation

antiseptic – substance that limits or stops the growth of bacteria

antivenin – drug used to neutralize or reduce the effects of a venom

anus – final opening from the intestine

aorta – the large artery that carries oxygenated blood from the heart to the body

appendicitis – inflammation of the appendix

appendix – worm-like protrusion of the lower intestine, located in the right lower quadrant of the abdomen

arrest – sudden stop

arterial – pertaining to an artery

artery – blood vessel that carries oxygenated blood from the heart to the body

arthritis – inflammation of the joints

asphyxia – loss of consciousness due to too little oxygen and too much carbon dioxide in the blood; suffocation causes asphyxia

aspirate – to draw in by suction; to inhale into the lungs

asthma – laboured breathing caused by narrowing of the smaller air passages in the lungs, associated with shortness of breath, wheezing, coughing, and cyanosis

ATV – all terrain vehicle

bacteria – microscopic organisms which may cause disease

bandage – fabric wrapping which holds a dressing or a splint in place

bannock – a frying-pan bread

belay – to protect a climber with a rope; the protection provided by the belay; the use of rope around a climber or rescuer or around a fixed point higher up (tree, rock, or person), used to lower a casualty or climber safely

bile – green fluid produced by the liver and stored in the gallbladder, where it is released into the intestine to aid in digestion and absorption of fats

blister – fluid-filled swelling of the skin surface
bowel – intestine
brain compression – blood or fluid collections within the
    skull pressing on the brain
bronchitis – inflammation of the bronchi
bronchus – main passageway from the trachea to the smaller
    air passages in the lungs (plural: bronchi)
bruise – injury which ruptures blood vessels causing blue or
    purplish discoloration, but does not break the skin
buttocks – the seat; the rump
calorie – the amount of energy necessary to raise the
    temperature of one gram of water 1°C; one food calorie
    (or kilocalorie) is equal to 1,000 energy calories
cancer – malignant tumour; uncontrolled growth of cells that
    invade normal body tissues but serve no purpose
carbon dioxide – poisonous, colourless, odourless gas found
    in exhaled air
carbon monoxide – colourless, odourless gas produced by
    incomplete combustion
cardiac – pertaining to the heart
carotid artery – main artery which passes up the neck and
    carries blood to the head and brain
carotid pulse – pulse felt in the neck at the carotid artery
cartilage – elastic tissue that is transformed into bone or
    found in joints
casualty – the victim of an injury or illness
caustic – corrosive; capable of destroying by chemical action
cell – the smallest unit of structure of animals and plants
    (a group of cells forms a tissue, a group of tissues forms an
    organ, a group of organs forms a system)
central nervous system – the brain and spinal cord
cerebral – pertaining to the brain
cervical – pertaining to the neck
chilblain – inflammation and swelling of the toes, feet, and
    fingers caused by long exposure to cold
chronic – long lasting
chronic obstructive pulmonary disease – a progressive condi-
    tion causing inability of the lungs to perform their function

closed-cell foam – any of the thin, firm waterproof plastic or rubber foams often used for sleeping pads by backpackers and campers

colic – acute pain caused by spasm, obstruction, or twisting of a hollow organ

colon – the large intestine

coma – a state of profound unconsciousness

compound fracture – an open fracture; broken bone accompanied by torn skin

concussion – a condition of widespread but temporary disturbance of brain function following an injury to the head

conduction – transmission through or by means of a conductor

conscious – aware; able to respond

contagious – spread by direct or indirect contact; communicable

contaminate – to soil, stain, or pollute; to introduce bacteria to

convulsion – seizure; abnormal involuntary contractions of the muscles

COPD – chronic obstructive pulmonary disease

core – centre; involving the abdomen and chest organs

core temperature – temperature in the core of the body

cornea – the transparent covering of the eyeball that allows light to enter the eye

CPR – cardiopulmonary resuscitation, with rescue breathing and chest compressions

crepitus – a crackling sound or feeling

cyanosis – blue or purple colour of the skin due to inadequate oxygen in the blood

cyst – an abnormal sac containing gas, fluid, or solid material

debridement – the surgical removal of dirt and dead or damaged tissue from a wound

defecate – to empty or evacuate the bowels

dehydration – loss of water from the body or tissues

diabetes – a chronic disease characterized by inability to metabolize sugar properly

diagnose – to identify a disease or injury

diaphragm – muscular wall which aids in breathing and separates the chest from the abdomen

diarrhea – frequent passage of watery bowel movements

discharge – fluid released from an organ or tissue surface

dislocation – continuing separation of bones at a joint

diuretic – medicine/substance that promotes urination

dressing – covering for a wound; goes directly against the wound

edema – swelling caused by the accumulation of fluid

emphysema – a chronic lung disease caused by distention of the alveoli (the tiny sacs in the lungs where the exchange of oxygen and other gases takes place) and/or destruction of their walls

epidural haematoma – a collection of blood between the skull and the dura, the lining of the brain

epilepsy – disorder causing convulsions, associated with abnormal electrical discharge in the central nervous system

esophagitis – inflammation of the esophagus

esophagus – muscular tube from the pharynx to the stomach; the "food pipe"

eugenol – a soothing, pungent liquid antiseptic from oil of cloves; used in dentistry

evacuate – to move a casualty from the site of injury to a place of treatment; to empty, especially the bowels

evaporate – to convert into vapour; to expel moisture from

exhale – to breathe out

exposure (cold exposure) – common term for hypothermia

extremity – arm and hand (upper extremity) or leg and foot (lower extremity)

facial – pertaining to the face

feces – solid waste discharged through the anus

femoral artery – large artery that carries blood to the leg

femur – large bone of the thigh

fibrillation – irregular quivering

flail chest – segment of broken ribs that cannot move properly to assist with breathing

foamie – any of the thick (usually 3" to 4") lightweight plastic foam pads used for mattresses – they are made of open-cell foam and are absorbent

forceps – pincers or "tweezers"

fracture – to break; a break in a bone

frostbite – freezing of the tissues; formation of ice crystals within the tissues

gallbladder – muscular, hollow organ that stores bile produced by the liver

gangrene – tissue death due to loss of blood supply which may be caused by injury or infection

gastritis – inflammation of the stomach

gastroenteritis – inflammation or irritation of the stomach and/or intestine

Gatorade – a commercially produced rehydration formula

genitals – external sex organs

gland – any organ or group of cells that produces secretions

gonorrhea – a sexually transmitted disease

graft (skin) – piece of skin taken from one area of the body to cover an injury in another area

grand mal seizure – convulsion involving violent general muscle contractions, loss of consciousness, and a period of confusion after the event; a major or generalized seizure

groin – the hollow or fold where the abdomen joins either thigh

grub box – a wooden box used to carry food and a stove and used for a work surface

hallucinate – to see visions

heartburn – burning discomfort high in the chest, usually caused by irritation or spasm of the lower esophagus

Heimlich manoeuvre – technique for ejecting an object caught in the upper airway

haemoglobin – red pigment in blood cells, high in iron, which carries oxygen

haemorrhage – bleeding; usually referring to very heavy bleeding

hepatitis – inflammation of the liver

hernia – protrusion of part of an organ through a wall of the space in which it is normally contained, usually the lower abdominal wall

histamine – chemical compound which plays a major role in allergic reactions

hives – itching, burning, reddened skin bumps or wheals associated with allergic reactions

hydrate – to cause to take up water

hyper- (prefix) – excessive; over

hyperglycemia – high blood sugar

hypertension – elevated blood pressure

hyperthermia – elevated core body temperature

hyperventilation – overbreathing

hypo- (prefix) – insufficient; underneath; below

hypodermic – under the skin

hypoglycemia – low blood sugar

hypothermia – low core body temperature

immobilize – to prevent freedom of movement; splint

immune – not susceptible to

immunity – condition of being able to resist a specific disease

inflammation – a response to injury that involves redness, pain, warmth, and development of pus

inhale – to breathe in

inspiration – the act of breathing in

intercranial pressure – the pressure within the skull

intestine – the series of digestive tubes that pass from the stomach to the anus; the major divisions are the small and the large intestine

intoxication – state of poisoning; drunkenness

intravenous – into a vein

Inuit – the native people of the far north; "Eskimo"

irrigate – to rinse, wash out

-itis (suffix) – inflammation of

kamiks – high skin or fabric moccasins designed for cold weather

kg (abbreviation) – kilogram

kilocalorie – the energy necessary to raise the temperature of 1 kilogram of water by 1°C; one food calorie or 1,000 calories

kilogram – 1000 grams; 2.2 pounds

komatik – a long, flat Inuit sled up to 5½ metres (18 feet) long pulled by dog team or snowmobile

laceration – rough tear or cut of the skin

lateral – away from the midline; outer

larynx – the voice box; the portion of the trachea that contains the vocal cords

lb. (abbreviation) – pound; .45 kg

lethargy – drowsiness or unwillingness to be active, caused by disease

ligament – the connective tissue that attaches bone to bone at a joint

litre – the volume of water that weighs 1 kilogram; 1,000 mL or 1,000 cc; approx. 1 quart

litter – stretcher

LOC – level of consciousness

localized – confined to a specific area

lumbar – pertaining to the lower back

lymph – yellowish fluid that contains white blood cells and circulates in the lymphatic system

lymphatic – related to lymph glands, cells, or fluid, or the system of vessels that transports them

lymph node – group of lymph cells that function as a gland

mandible – lower jaw bone

manipulate – to move with the hands

meatus – opening for urine

medevac – abbreviation of medical evacuation

meningitis – a disease involving inflammation of the covering of the brain and upper spinal cord

mental status – condition of alertness and comprehension

metabolism – the energy-producing and energy-utilizing processes of living things

mg (abbreviation) – milligram

microorganism – small life-form that requires a microscope to be seen

migraine – severe headache usually accompanied by dizziness, nausea, and vomiting

milligram – 1/1000 of a gram

millilitre – 1/1000 of a litre

mL (abbreviation) – millilitre

molar – one of the large rear teeth used for chewing

mucus – slippery secretion created by mucous membranes (such as those that line the nose, mouth, and throat), which provide lubrication and some protection against bacteria

mucous membrane – tissues that secrete mucus

mukluks – western term for kamiks

nausea – feeling a need to vomit

neurological – pertaining to the nervous system

oil of cloves – an oil derived from cloves, used as a soothing antiseptic in dentistry

organ – group of tissues with a specific function

ounce – measure of weight equal to 28.35 grams or $\frac{1}{16}$ pound; (a fluid ounce is 29.6 mL)

oxygen – colourless, odourless gas necessary for life and for combustion

oxygenate – to supply with oxygen

oz (abbreviation) – ounce

pallor – pale skin colour

palpate – feel with the hands

palpitation – abnormal heartbeat felt by the subject

pancreas – gland that secretes digestive juices and insulin

paediatric – pertaining to children

pelvic – pertaining to the pelvis

pelvis – the strong, irregular, basin-shaped bony structure which lies between the hips

periapical – occurring at the tip or apex of a tooth

pericoronitis – an infection of the gum around the crown of a tooth

periodontal – occurring around a tooth

periosteum – thin covering of the bone

peritoneum – lining of the abdominal cavity

peritonitis – inflammation of the peritoneum

petit mal seizure – type of epilepsy characterized by a brief period of confusion without major convulsions; a partial or minor seizure

pharynx – the throat

PLB – personal locator beacon; a transmitter that sends a signal through a satellite to a rescue centre

pleura – the covering of the lungs and lining of the chest cavity

pleuritis – inflammation of the pleura; pleurisy

pneumonia – inflammation of the lungs

pneumothorax – collapsed lung with air in the pleural space

prognosis – projected outcome

prone – lying flat, face down

psychiatry – dealing with disorders of the mind

psychiatric – pertaining to psychiatry

pubic – pertaining to the area of the pubis

pubis – the bone of the pelvis which lies just above the genitals

pulmonary – pertaining to the lungs

pulp chamber – the cavity in the centre of a tooth which contains blood vessels, nerves, and tissues which produce tooth material; commonly called the "nerve"

pupil – the dark, variable opening in the centre of the eye, through which light passes to the lens

pus – white, yellow-green, or cream-coloured fluid produced by decomposing tissue, white blood cells, and tissue fluids

quadrant – one of the four quarters into which a region, such as the abdomen, can be divided

rabid – having rabies

rabies – an acute viral disease of the nervous system of warm-blooded animals

radial artery – the main artery that passes through the wrist to carry blood to the hand

radial pulse – pulse felt at the radial artery

radiation – the emission of energy in the form of waves or particles

radiation of pain – pain that travels from one region to another, such as from the chest to the shoulder

rebound tenderness – pain which flares in the abdomen upon the sudden release of compression

rehydration – restoration of normal fluid levels

renal – pertaining to the kidney

respiratory – pertaining to the organs or the act of breathing

resuscitate – to bring back to life

rigor mortis – stiffening of the body after death

root canal – the narrow passage from the pulp chamber of a tooth to the tip of the root, which carries blood vessels and nerves

saline solution – a solution of salt in water; "normal saline," a liquid compatible with most human tissues, is 0.9% sodium chloride in water

saliva – lubricating and digestive fluid produced by glands around the mouth; the moisture of the mouth

salivate – to produce saliva

scrotum – the sac that contains the testicles

seizure – an epileptic convulsion; a sudden attack of pain, disease, or symptoms

serum – the fluid portion of the blood after the cells are removed

shock – a state caused by the disturbance of oxygen supply to the tissues

sign – an observable indication of an illness or injury

sinus – a cavity within a bone; a cavity, canal, or passage; most commonly the cavities within facial bones

skimmer – a boat-shaped sled which is pulled behind a snow-mobile; an akio

SOB – abbreviation for shortness of breath

soft tissue – body tissue other than bone or cartilage; usually muscle, skin, and fat, but not including internal organs

sorrel – a perennial plant with kidney-shaped leaves and an acid taste; "sour grass"

spasm – involuntary muscular contraction

sphincter – circular muscle constricting an opening or between segments of a tube

sprain – stretching or tearing of ligaments

sputum – "spit"; fluid expelled from the throat and respiratory passages

stabilize – to make stable or firm; to keep from changing
status – state or condition
sterile – not contaminated by bacteria or infectious agents
sternum – breastbone
strain – partial stretching or tearing of tendon or muscle
sub- (prefix) – underneath
subcutaneous – under the skin
subdural haematoma – a collection of blood under the dura, the lining covering the brain
sublingual – under the tongue
supine – lying flat, face up
suture – to unite by stitching; the material used to stitch a wound closed; a "stitch"
symptom – an indication of illness or injury which is felt by the subject, and not visually observable
syndrome – a group of signs and symptoms that indicates a particular disease or abnormality
syringe – device used to inject or suction fluids
system – a set of things which are related to form a whole; a number of bodily organs working together to perform a specific function
systemic – affecting the entire system
tendon – fibrous tissue which joins muscle to bone
tetanus – an acute infectious disease caused by a specific toxin, which is usually introduced through a wound
thwart – a brace extending across a canoe or boat
tissue – group of body cells which serves a specific function
TK – abbreviation for tourniquet, usually seen on a tag on the casualty
tourniquet – a device used to control bleeding by compressing blood vessels
toxin – a poisonous substance
trachea – main passageway for air from the pharynx to the bronchi (throat to the lungs)
tract – a pathway or passageway
trauma – mechanical injury

traumatic – related to mechanical injury

travois – a hauling device of two poles and a platform, pulled by a human or animal

tumour – abnormal growth of tissue in the body without purpose; may be cancerous or noncancerous (benign)

ulcer – open sore

ultraviolet – light beyond the violet end of the visible spectrum with a wavelength shorter than that of visible light; the portion of light which causes sunburn and snowblindness

unconscious – without consciousness; unaware; unable to respond

ureter – muscular tube that carries urine from the kidney to the bladder

urethra – tube that carries urine from the bladder to the external opening in the genital area

urinary – pertaining to urine

UTM – universal transverse mercator

vaccinate – to inoculate; to inject a material into the body to cause it to become resistant to disease

vagina – the birth passage

vaginitis – irritation of the vagina

vascular – pertaining to the blood vessels

vein – blood vessel that carries blood from the body back to the heart

venom – poison from animals and insects; usually injected into the casualty with a bite or sting

venous – pertaining to the veins

ventricle – one of two large chambers of the heart

vertebra – one of the bones which form the spinal column (backbone) (pl. vertebrae)

vessel – a tube or container; a blood vessel may be a vein, artery, or capillary

Following are some terms which may not be used in this text, but which may be found on the labels of medications carried by individuals:

antiemetic – medication to control vomiting
complications – added health problems which may develop in the course of disease
contraindication – circumstance under which a medicine should not be taken
decongestant – medicine which helps relieve stuffiness of nose or sinuses
dermal – pertaining to the skin
eclampsia – sudden convulsions caused by toxemia of pregnancy
emetic – medicine which causes vomiting
expectorant – medicine which helps a person cough up mucus
hypertension – high blood pressure
insomnia – inability to sleep
laxative – medicine which encourages bowel movements
lingual – pertaining to the tongue
nasal – pertaining to the nose
ophthalmic – pertaining to the eyes
oral – by mouth
otic – pertaining to the ears
parenteral – by injection
prophylactic – preventive
suppressant – medicine that helps to reduce or stop something, such as a cough
topical – to be placed on the surface of the skin

Index

St. John Ambulance offers a variety of comprehensive training courses in first aid, CPR, and health promotion, designed for all ages and interests, and taught by nationally certified instructors.

Training centres can be found in communities across Canada. In Ontario, call 1-800-268-7581 for the location nearest you; in other parts of the country check your local directory.